D1243686

HYMNS AND HUMAN LIFE

HYMNS AND
HUMAN LIFE

ERIK ROUTLEY
B.D., D.Phil.

★

WM. B. EERDMANS PUBLISHING COMPANY
GRAND RAPIDS, MICHIGAN

FIRST EDITION 1952
SECOND EDITION 1959

Printed in Great Britain by Butler & Tanner Ltd., Frome and London
and published by John Murray (Publishers) Ltd.

TO

MARGARET

MY WIFE

Contents

Preface

JUST fifty years ago, in 1902, there appeared from the hand of R. E. Prothero, who became Lord Ernle, a book called *The Psalms in Human Life*. There must be many thousands of readers who can bear witness to the learning and devotion of its author and the felicity with which his material was deployed. *The Psalms in Human Life* has taken its place alongside *A Chain of Prayer* as one of the devotional classics for which we must be grateful to the publishing house of John Murray.

In 1948 Sir John Murray suggested to the late Canon C. S. Phillips, D.D., of St. Augustine's, Canterbury, the preparation of a book on *Hymns and Human Life*. Dr. Phillips thereupon began on a task which his untimely death in 1949 prevented him from finishing. He left only a few chapters in note form, and when he knew that he would never be able to bring the work to a conclusion, he suggested to Sir John Murray that the task should be handed on to me. This is therefore the place for me to pay tribute to the work of one who did so much, especially in his book, *Hymnody Past and Present*, to remove hymnology from the region of casual pastime to that of serious study. Dr. Phillips was an excellent historian and a man of refined taste and skilful craftsmanship, as his work in the revised *Hymns Ancient and Modern* shows.

I thought it best not to try to carry on from the point at which Dr. Phillips laid down his pen, but to make a fresh start; and I feel it necessary to share with the reader some of the problems with which I was confronted. I cannot hope to justify the obvious shortcomings of the following pages; but I can perhaps give my reasons for casting this book in a form so different from that taken by Lord Ernle's.

Here, then, is the great difference between my subject and his. He has two thousand years of history and a hundred and fifty psalms. I have two thousand years, yes, but only three centuries of what we now know as hymnody ; and I have, I suppose, half a million hymns to cope with. Nobody except the most advanced scholars pays any attention to the authors of the psalms ; they are timeless and integral to Christian worship, and everybody loves them. The most illiterate Christian knows one or two closely. But hymns are part of history ; they can rarely be assessed or appreciated without some knowledge of their authors ; and not everybody likes hymns. Some people positively dislike them, this dislike being only less than what they feel for the people who sing them.

I have therefore thought it best to approach the subject from the point of view of a person who vaguely knows a few hymns and whose interest in them is not of a special kind. I shall try in my introductory chapter to put the challenge that hymn-singing presents. Then I shall try to show how hymns have come out of human history. Then, in Part II, I shall say something about the people in the story. My third Part will be devoted to some indication of how hymns are used and thought of in this country, and of the part they play in the spiritual life of our nation. My final chapter will be an attempt to meet the challenge of the first, to discuss the shortcoming of some kinds of hymn, and to demonstrate how the masters have achieved their mastery.

My reader's favourite hymn may go without mention in these pages. While I apologize in advance for this, I hope the reader will not miss my intention, which is not so much that he may be edified or instructed or moved to admiration as that he may enjoy himself. I have tried to quote hymns that illuminate the Gospel, and I have done my best to avoid that partisanship which would provide good entertainment but a distorted picture. We shall travel quickly over the ground that has already been better covered in better books, and we shall loiter in those regions less thoroughly charted.

Except in giving references for quotations, so that a reader may quickly look up the complete hymn if he wishes, I have virtually abjured footnotes. An appendix of notes, however, may make it possible for a reader to check his information and use this as a source-book if he wants to do so. As for the quotation references, I have always referred to the *English Hymnal* when the hymn in question is in that book. Where it is not, I make my second choice *Congregational Praise*, which happens to supplement the *English Hymnal* for my purpose better than any other book. These two books will furnish the reader with four-fifths of the required references. Sometimes, of course, I have had to go further afield. When I refer to *Hymns Ancient and Modern*, I give the number in this form—180/198—if the hymn is in both the standard and the revised editions ; otherwise I specify the edition to which I am referring. The only abbreviations I use in the footnotes are *E.H.* for the *English Hymnal* (1933) and *C.P.* for *Congregational Praise*.

I have done my best to keep the text as free as possible from dates. All authors' dates will be found in the Index.

It remains for me to express, as any writer of such a book as this must express, my indebtedness to that monumental work, Julian's *Dictionary of Hymnology*, published by the house of John Murray. I wish further to record my personal gratitude to Sir John Murray, the publisher of this book, for much valuable advice and criticism, to the Librarian and Keeper of the Muniments at Westminster Abbey, by whose courtesy I was made free of the material embodied in Chapter 19, and to my friends in the Hymn Society, from whom I have learnt so much of what I have been able to set down here.

ERIK ROUTLEY.

Oxford.

11 June, 1951.

Acknowledgments

I HAVE to record my gratitude to the owners of certain copyright hymns who have given me permission to quote them in the following pages. In those cases which I have noted with an asterisk permission was granted on payment of a fee.

I am grateful to the proprietors of *Hymns Ancient and Modern* for Julian's " Father of all, to Thee " (p. 202) ; to Messrs. Burns, Oates and Washbourne, Ltd., for Mgr. Ronald Knox's translation of " O quanta qualia " * (p. 30) ; to the Reverend R. T. Brooks of the B.B.C. for " O Christ our Lord " (p. 103) ; to the Carey Kingsgate Press, Ltd., for W. Y. Fullerton's " I cannot tell why he whom angels worship " (p. 155) ; to the Reverend P. B. Clayton for his hymn " Come, kindred, upstand " (p. 200) ; to the Congregational Union of England and Wales, by Mr. Honess of the Independent Press, for " Give me, O Christ, the strength " by H. C. Carter and " Spirit of flame " by A. H. Driver, both from *Congregational Praise* (pp. 98 101,) ; to Canon J. M. C. Crum for his hymn, " O once in a while " (p. 257) ; to the Trustees of the *Fellowship Hymn Book* for F. J. Gillman's " God send us men " (p. 163) ; to Miss Doris Gill for her hymn, " Come, let us sing of the joys of the town " (p. 259) ; to Messrs. Hodder and Stoughton for " Close by the heedless worker's side ",* from *The Unutterable Beauty*, by G. A. Studdert-Kennedy (p. 199) ; to Miss C. Morley Horder for Benjamin Waugh's " Now let us see Thy beauty " * (p. 197) ; to the Reverend Dr. Howell Elvet Lewis for his hymn, " The light of the morning is breaking " (p. 156) ; to Lt.-Col. Maurice MacDonald for George MacDonald's " They

all were looking for a king " (p. 177) ; to Messrs. Methuen
& Co., Ltd., and Mrs. George Bambridge for Rudyard
Kipling's *Recessional*, from *The Five Nations* (p. 94) ; to
the Oxford University Press, the Clarendon Press, and
the English Hymnal Company Ltd., for Charles Bigg's
translations, " Creator of the earth " (p. 21) and " High
Word of God " (p. 26) from the *English Hymnal* ; for
F. C. Burkitt's translation, " Wake, O Wake " (p. 42),
from the *English Hymnal*, for Laurence Housman's " Father
eternal " (p. 103), from *Enlarged Songs of Praise*, for Lesbia
Scott's " I sing a song of the Saints of God " (p. 260), from
the *B.B.C. Hymn Book*, for Jan Struther's " God, whose
eternal mind " (p. 181) and " When a knight won his
spurs " (p. 257), both from *Enlarged Songs of Praise*, for
G. K. Chesterton's " O God of earth and altar " (pp. 6 and
94), William Canton's " Hold Thou my hands " (p. 179),
and L. B. C. L. Muirhead's " The Church of God a Kingdom is " (p. 116), all from the *English Hymnal*, for G.
W. Briggs's " I love God's tiny creatures " from *Enlarged
Songs of Praise* (p. 259) and " Son of the Lord most high "
from *Songs of Faith* (p. 311) ; for Percy Dearmer's " Remember all the people " from *Enlarged Songs of Praise*
(p. 259), and for three hymns from the *Yattendon Hymnal*,
edited by Robert Bridges and H. E. Wooldridge, " Ah,
holy Jesu, how hast thou offended ? " (p. 45), " O splendour
of God's glory " (p. 25), and " The duteous day now
closeth " * (p. 309).

I further acknowledge the courtesy of Mrs. Rawnsley
for the late Canon Rawnsley's " Lord God, our praise we
give " (p. 197) ; of Messrs. Schott & Co. for G. R. Woodward's " Morning star, in midnight gloom ",* from
Songs of Syon (p. 48) ; of the Bishop of Sheffield for John
Hunter's " Dear Master, in whose life I see " (p. 154);
of the Reverend Thomas Tiplady for his hymn, " All ye
who know that on the Cross " (p. 159) ; of the Bishop of
Truro for his hymn, " Thee, living Christ, our eyes behold "
(p. 137) ; of Mr. C. G. Thomas for Dr. Arnold Thomas's

" Brother, who on thy heart didst bear " (p. 312), and of the Reverend W. A. Whitehouse of Durham University for his translation, " O faithless, fearful army " (p. 121).

I thank the following owners of American copyrights for giving me free permission to include hymns under their charge : the Reverend F. Bland Tucker and the Church Hymnal Corporation, for " All praise to Thee " (p. 236) ; the Reverend H. C. Robbins and the Morehouse-Gorham Company for " And have the bright immensities " (p. 235) ; Dr. Fosdick and the Fleming Revell Company, for " God of grace and God of glory " (p. 236), and Dr. Merrill and the *Presbyterian Tribune*, New York, for " Rise up, O men of God " (p. 229)

A few hymns that I have quoted may still be under copyright but lacking acknowledgment here. I have done my best to trace their owners. I trust that I may be forgiven for any infraction of rights that I may thus accidentally have committed, and undertake, should this book reach a further edition, to rectify any omissions that may be pointed out to me.

E. R.

Preface to the Second Edition

MANY correspondents have been good enough to write to me pointing out certain errors of detail in the first edition of this book. A second edition gives me the opportunity of having these corrected, and of expressing to all these people my sincere thanks for their help. A little new material, chiefly by way of bringing Chapter 19 up to date, will be found in the additional notes on pp. 327–8.

E. R.

H.H.L.   B

CHAPTER I

Hymns and Human Life

'Ere 'e comes, the 'oly 'umbug, 'umming 'is 'ymn.
'Ow I 'ate 'im !

Overheard in the Law Courts, about a learned
judge, c. 1880.

(Songs of Praise Discussed, p. 123.)

UPON this apparently harmless study of hymnology many books have been written during the past fifty years or so. What object is there in adding this one ? Let me answer that question by referring the reader to the erudite quotation with which this chapter is headed. My point is that, although we have had many books—good books, learned books, devotional books—on the history of hymnody, I believe we have not yet had a book which at its beginning came to terms with these words of the eminent lawyer. I mean, in fact, that hymnody is not by any means a harmless subject.

What pictures come to the reader's mind when the word "hymn" is mentioned ? Let me say what picture comes first to mine. We were at a Youth Conference at a delectable place which shall remain nameless. There was a handful of parsons and a gang of a hundred or so young people between the ages of sixteen and thirty. I forget what we were conferring about, but I am sure it was important. Here and there in the course of our conference we turned frivolous and danced ; at other points we turned pious and sang hymns. Now this place where we were staying was staffed by a too small company of overworked young ladies who had nothing to do with us or with the Christian subjects which were occupying us ; the usual sort of cheerful, amiable heathen, I suppose. They did their

work well and made us comfortable. What I heard after
the conference was over was that they wouldn't have minded
our leaving our bedrooms in a mess and bringing the dirt
into the nice clean lounges ; they wouldn't have minded
our noise and clamour and all the work we made for them ;
but what they couldn't stand was hearing us sing hymns.
Only after we had sung our hymns did the complaint
become articulate.

I love to think of the church where I was brought up,
and the hymns my mother and father taught me before
I went even there. I love to hear over again " Ye holy
angels bright " as it was sung by the shrill, unbroken voices
of the boys in the chapel of my preparatory-school, or
" Come, O thou Traveller ", which I associate with the
more august setting of the school chapel of Lancing (to a
tune * by the organist, the late Alexander Brent Smith).
I even take pleasure in the hymns as we sing them in the
college chapel which I now have the honour to attend in
term time. But I can't get the other picture out of my
mind. So I must set it down here in black and white, and
we must face it together : is this Holy Humbug or is it a
sacrifice of praise ? Behind that question there lies a great
truth. Hymn singing is the articulation of Christian worship. It is not the only such articulation, of course. Christian worship becomes articulate in ways which appeal to
all our senses. Musically, there is the wider activity of
church music, the sung Evensong, the *Mass in B minor*.
For the eye there are architecture and drama. Another
sense is strongly appealed to by incense. For the rest—

> We taste of thee, the living Bread,
> And long to feast upon thee still.

But hymn-singing is, as a matter of fact, the most insistent
and clamorous of all the ways in which Christian faith and
worship makes impact on the world around it. The reason
is very simple. You can close your eyes ; you can stay

* *Congregational Praise*, 496.

away from the church and so neither taste nor see that the Lord is good. But you cannot close your ears, and if a group of Christian people chose to sing a hymn under your windows you are defenceless. You will probably not hear *Stanford in B flat* outside a cathedral even when the choir within is singing at its lustiest; but if a good congregation is singing " How firm a foundation " in some rickety non-conformist chapel in industrial Yorkshire the neighbours hear about it; indeed, their only defence is to turn on the radio.

Hymns are the folk-song of the church militant. They are, essentially, the people's music. If a hymn cannot be sung by the congregation present, it has become for that occasion not a hymn but a choir-anthem or even an organ solo. (I was present in one of our most celebrated parish churches when the acting-organist was playing from a book different from that which the congregation held in their hands; the first hymn turned out to be " Breathe on me, breath of God " to the tune of " Who are these, like stars appearing ? " ; the second, " O God of Truth " to the tune of the National Anthem.) A hymn, more-over, must be sung by people whose minds are directed not primarily to poetic or musical but to religious values ; which means that the poetry and the music have to be the kind of poetry and music which do not fight against religious values ; they have to fit into the ancient scheme that prevailed in the Middle Ages when there was no difference between goodness and piety in art. This is a discipline, but not a limitation. Again, and by the same token, unless the words and the tune say in an effective way what the people singing them are prepared to say, they will not " take ", and the hymn will not do its work. This means that a religious company who want to say the right things will have one sort of hymnody while one that wants to say the wrong things, the irrelevant or romantic or false or misleading things, will have another. But if a hymn " takes ", so to put it, it becomes more integral a part not only of the people's worship but also of their ordinary speech and thought than anything else except the Bible and the Book of Common Prayer.

Hymns have in this sense become an integral part not only of English church worship but of English thought and speech. To prove this, consider the fact that over two hundred hymns are cited in the *Oxford Dictionary of Quotations*, in some cases many citations being taken from a single hymn. " God moves in a mysterious way "—that first line is itself a commonplace of English colloquial speech— is given six quotations embodying the whole hymn except for two lines. This happens to be an outstanding example of terse, epigrammatic, memorable writing, and, by the judgment of the editor of that beguiling work of reference, it has many lines that have " stuck "—

> God moves in a mysterious way
> His wonders to perform . . .

> Ye fearful saints, fresh courage take ;
> The clouds ye so much dread
> Are big with mercy, and shall break
> In blessings on your head.

> Behind a frowning providence
> He hides a smiling face.

> The bud may have a bitter taste,
> But sweet will be the flower.

> God is his own interpreter
> And he will make it plain.

Without at present judging the religious value of this hymn to those who are familiar with it, consider how much of its text and thought-form has found its way into our common speech. Of course, the eighteenth century, from which that hymn comes, was a great period for literary neatness, for the brief and witty saying, the epigram and the satirical poem, the resounding stamp of the heroic couplet (often the

resonance of emptiness, of course) and the balanced prose of
Swift and Johnson and Burke. Eighteenth-century hymns
are therefore among the most popular, and we shall have
much to do with them. But we shall find, if we think for a
moment on the matter, that it is this felicitous phrase, this
lyrical forcefulness, this holy wit that really makes a successful hymn. Here is Cowper again :

> Mine is an unchanging love,
> Higher than the heights above,
> Deeper than the depths beneath,
> Free and faithful, strong as death.

Here is Charles Wesley :

> Mild he lays his glory by,
> Born that man no more may die,
> Born to raise the sons of earth,
> Born to give them second birth.

Here is Isaac Watts (the *Oxford Dictionary of Quotations*
doesn't like Watts ; it thinks he is merely funny) :

> Were the whole realm of nature mine,
> That were a present far too small ;
> Love so amazing, so divine
> Demands my soul, my life, my all.

Other centuries could do it : here is H. F. Lyte in 1847 :

> Hold thou thy cross before my closing eyes ;
> Shine through the gloom and point me to the skies ;
> Heaven's morning breaks, and earth's vain shadows flee ;
> In life, in death, O Lord, abide with me.

Lyte again—

> Praise him for his grace and favour
> To our fathers in distress,
> Praise him, still the same for ever,
> Slow to chide and swift to bless.

And, not to multiply examples just yet, here is a twentieth-century author, G. K. Chesterton—

> Tie in a living tether
> The prince and priest and thrall ;
> Bind all our lives together,
> Smite us and save us all.

I do not want to show more here than that the hymns of our language have found their way into our consciousness by straight speaking, economy of words, and clear thinking. All those I have so far quoted, except perhaps the last, are well known to hundreds of thousands of people who have no use for the church and hate and fear what it stands for. " Abide with me " brings God down into the milling crowds at Wembley. " Hark, the herald " proclaims the everlasting mercy through the lips of an urchin singing for coppers outside a suburban front door as surely barred to formal Christianity as to the hawkers and circulars who are more explicitly, and indeed less relevantly, warned off at the gate.

Perhaps Christmas hymns and carols are a rather special case ; for at Christmas even the cold scorn of the general public for religious things thaws a trifle over the turkey and plum-pudding. But consider what " Our God, our help in ages past " * means to us when we pause in remembrance of the sacrifices and heroisms which flower on the muck-heap of war. Consider what that hymn, and " Eternal Father, strong to save ", and " Onward, Christian soldiers " meant to the harassed and heroic statesmen, the dumb and determined troops, who sang them on the battleship when the Atlantic Charter was signed. Consider what " O perfect Love " and " Love divine, all loves excelling " and " Gracious Spirit, Holy Ghost " mean to a couple at their wedding ; hallowed, indeed, by their use

---

* My readers will, I hope, forgive me for quoting this venerable hymn as Isaac Watts wrote it. Isaac Watts meant something by " *Our God* ".

by Royalty, but speaking as plainly to, and through, the factory-girl as the princess. Think of the hearts that have been warmed by Blake's words, which he would have been vastly surprised to hear set to Parry's music—

> I will not cease from mental fight
>   Nor shall my sword sleep in my hand
> Till we have built Jerusalem
>   In England's green and pleasant land,

whether " Jerusalem " is the women's suffrage, the abolition of war, or the triumph of the Public School Ideal.

I used to speak disparagingly of the musical merits of a hymn tune called HURSLEY,* which is often associated with " Sun of my soul, thou Saviour dear ". I still cannot think it a very good tune : but after recently speaking with a German teacher of theology I think of it not without awe : it appears that Hitler sent one of his henchmen to exhort the German people of Berlin at a time when it was thought proper to build up the slightly shaky morale of Nazidom ; this emissary of perversity found it impossible to make himself heard forasmuch as, over the space of three hours, a body of German Catholics sang the hymn " Grosser Gott, wir loben dich " to the original of this tune, over and over again. I do not know what happened to their choirmaster, but I cannot speak of the hymn now with contempt.

Some of us have poked fun at the trite jingles of the Sankey revival. But trapped miners have sung " Hold the fort ! " and who knows how many people have calmed elemental fears of death with " Shall we gather at the river ? " and beaten off the gnawing fear of hunger and insecurity and dispossession with " Will your anchor hold ? " †

There will, of course, be something to be said a little later on about the other side of this picture, the hateful sentimentality and ponderous moralism of some people who were not trapped miners or persecuted Catholics or Atlas-

---

* *English Hymnal,* 274.   † See further, page 239.

loaded statesmen, and who have complacently sung of the saving blood of the Lamb slain from the foundation of the world. But if we allow for all that, we still have the fact that the hymns of the church have dug themselves into our national life and consciousness. I want later on to show that it is neither the greatest nor the worst of the hymns that have done this ; I shall have to say that some hymns may, on balance, do more harm than good. I shall have to introduce my reader to some hymns which may take him further along the road of devotion than he has yet gone. But let us treat it as settled, at this point, that our hymns are a great national heritage, and that at times of stress or exaltation, when the most casual of us reach out towards the merciful, delivering, ennobling power of God, we turn to our hymns and find in them what we were looking for. Even the most commonplace of them all, the most trite, one of the worst-written, the most worn-out, came to life one chilly evening in December, 1936, when His Majesty, King Edward VIII, closing his broadcast to his people and with it, his brief and troubled reign, said in a voice harsh with sorrow, " God save the King ! "

*　　*　　*

But I promised to deal with the eminent lawyer. These opening pages have shown, I take it, that hymns have made their way into our minds whether we let them or have tried to prevent them. But there are people who don't like hymns, and they are of two kinds.

First, there are the people who dislike them from what we might call professionally religious motives. Just three hundred years passed between the publication of Luther's first hymns (1524) and the authorization of hymns in worship by the Church of England (1821). The Puritans, who are the fathers of English hymnody, for a long time followed Calvin in thinking that hymns, being man-made, are therefore pernicious instruments for public devotion, and they sang nothing but metrical psalms (with a few

negligible exceptions) until Benjamin Keach and Isaac
Watts came to the rescue. More of this later. In modern
times there are many thoughtful Christians who find hymns
irrelevant to public worship ; hymns have, of course, no
place in the Catholic Mass, and they are still, with the
sole exception of Cosin's " Come, Holy Ghost " and another
version of the same hymn, absent from the rubrics of the
Book of Common Prayer. I have heard a distinguished
Christian teacher say that hymns are " dead wood " so far
as he is concerned.

These objections are mainly liturgical or technical,
although there is in them sometimes a trace of the quality
of the other kind of objection. For there are certainly
many people, like my friends at the Conference centre or
the eminent lawyer, who see in hymns a symbol of everything that was ineffective, pompous and Pecksniffian in
the church of the nineteenth century. They are the folk-
song not of the army advancing with the royal banners
but of a gang of hypocrites and time-servers. They are
the smeary carols of that dreadful superiority and spiritual
snobbery which has distinguished some of the frequenters
of parish churches and working-class Gospel halls, a dis-
order graphically described, for example, in the novels of
Mr. Howard Spring, where many quotations are to be
found from the hymns of the Sankey tradition and of
Charles Wesley. Those who hate the superiority of the
religious hate hymns as its expression ; those who identify
the church with a political party at variance with their
own hear hymns as the expression of political reaction, or of
cynical and pious oppressiveness. Those whose consciences
are quickened by the church's existence but who have
rejected its message are frightened, irritated, scandalized,
and angered by its hymns. And those who have, in their
own view, out-thought the church find its hymns the classical
expressions of its stupidity, obscurantism and futility.

This is all quite natural. If hymns have the power
over people's imaginations and emotions that we have

described, then that power will not always be a comforting
or a sustaining power. Sometimes it will be deadening,
sometimes it will be provocative. But it remains that in
its hymns the church comes nearer to the man of the world
than in any other part of its ministry. They do not always
do him good, but where sermons and even sacraments pass
him by, hymns still hit him. The B.B.C. will tell you
that the fashion of broadcasting programmes of hymns has
brought more listeners to the programmes of the Religious
Broadcasting Department than the services and the talks,
however excellent, which that Department has provided.
It is, we are told, " The Chapel in the Valley " and " Sunday Half-Hour " and " Think on these things " that really
catch the people's ear.

We have, then, certain obvious tasks before us. We
ought to give some account of how people have used and
invented and reacted to hymns in the past. We ought to
say something about how they are used now. And we
ought to say something about the manner in which some of
them are written and the purposes which their authors have
in mind. On the way we shall come across some odd
scraps of information and even entertainment.

PART ONE

THE STORY OF HYMNS

CHAPTER 2

How it Began

THE FIRST CENTURIES

CHRISTIANS have been singing hymns ever since our Lord walked the earth. The first hymns they sang were, of course, the Psalms, and Christians have never tried to do without the hymn-book of the Jews. Lord Ernle's great book, *The Psalms in Human Life*, shows how every kind of Christian devotion and the consciousness of people in every Christian land and age are pervaded by the Psalms. So complete is the possession that the Psalms have taken of our public praise, indeed, that not only have metrical psalms been the sole diet of public praise for whole sections of the church over long periods, but hymn-writers have come back again and again to the Psalms for the inspiration of their hymns. " Our God, our help " is a careful paraphrase of the first part of Psalm 90 ; " Jesus shall reign " and " Hail to the Lord's Anointed " are Psalm 72 ; " O worship the King " is Psalm 104 ; " Praise to the Lord, the Almighty ", and " Praise, my soul " neither go far from their original, Psalm 103 ; " Far from my heavenly home " begins from Psalm 137, and Milton's " Let us with a gladsome mind " keeps puritanically close to Psalm 136.

There are, of course, important distinctions to be made between four kinds of hymn. First, there are the Psalms in the original Hebrew or literally translated in the ancient rhythm in the authorized Latin or vernacular versions of the Bible. Only the Hebrews, the Latin-speaking Catholics, and English-speaking Protestants have made any attempt to sing the psalms in this form. Protestants of tongues other

13

than the English have never done so. The Hebrews did
it in the process technically called " cantillation ", which is
not a congregational act at all. The Latin-speaking
Catholics sang them to that derivative of Eastern music
which is known as plainsong ; English-speaking congregations have sung them either to plainsong or to its modern
derivative, the Anglican Chant.

Second, there are metrical versions of the Psalms, distinguished by the fact that although they are arranged for
singing to measured hymn tunes they are as near the original
as they can be ; to this literal accuracy they sacrifice
poetic imagery and lyrical phrasing in the sternest fashion,
and any Scottish Kirk, in using the Scottish Psalter as
revised in 1650, will provide an example of true metrical
psalmody. This form of psalmody is to be found in Protestant congregations of all tongues, but not at all in Catholic
circles.

Thirdly, there are those free paraphrases of the Psalms of
which we have just given a few examples. The invention
of this technique is the work of Isaac Watts, who, becoming
impatient of the confinement of public praise to the literal
rehearsing of the Old Testament, with its local references
to David, Solomon, and Israel, and its picturesque allusions
to harps and cherubs, sought to re-interpret the Psalms
through the New Covenant. Where the 72nd Psalm, no
doubt referring to King David, says

He shall have dominion also from sea to sea, and from the
river unto the ends of the earth,

Watts, fortified by Christian theology and an improved
knowledge of geography, writes

Jesus shall reign where'er the sun
Doth his successive journeys run ;
His kingdom stretch from shore to shore
Till moons shall wax and wane no more.

Taking the same technique a little further, where the
135th Psalm says, in its last verses,

Bless the Lord, O house of Israel; bless the Lord, O house of Aaron :

Bless the Lord, O house of Levi ; ye that fear the Lord, bless the Lord ;

Blessed be the Lord out of Zion, which dwelleth at Jerusalem. Hallelujah !

he brings all this up to date in the following fashion :

> O Britain, know thy living God,
>   Serve him with faith and fear ;
> He makes thy churches his abode,
>   And claims thine honours there.

Watts's zeal for reformation and impatience of the outdated carried him to points well beyond the bounds of absurdity ; but he opened the way for the magnificent psalm-hymns of Montgomery and Lyte. One of the most beautiful of all is Montgomery's short hymn, taken from a few verses of Psalm 27 :

> God is my strong salvation,
>   What foe have I to fear ?
> In darkness and temptation,
>   My light, my help is near.
>
> Though hosts encamp around me,
>   Firm to the fight I stand ;
> What terror can confound me,
>   With God at my right hand ?
>
> Place on the Lord reliance ;
>   My soul, with patience wait ;
> His truth be thine affiance,
>   When faint and desolate.
>
> His might thine heart shall strengthen,
>   His love thy joy increase ;
> Mercy thy days shall lengthen,
>   The Lord shall give thee peace.*

There is a great difference between a hymn of this kind,

* *C.P.*, 501.

H.H.L.

C

which takes a few thoughts from the Psalmist and weaves them into a hymn of congregational length and devotional shape, and a metrical version in which the omission of verses and the interpretation of the original thought by later experience are strictly forbidden.

Finally, of course, there are the hymns that are original compositions, and they will form the greater part of our material. Most of these we shall find to contain a great deal of scriptural thought and expression, but they are original works and carry their author's impress on them. Hymns of this sort we shall find in all ages.

Now you might think that the story of hymns in Christian worship will follow the shape which these four categories suggest. It is obvious that the four classes, in proceeding from " The Lord is my Shepherd ; I shall not want " through " The Lord's my Shepherd, I'll not want " (1650) and " The King of love my Shepherd is " (1861) to " Father, hear the prayer we offer," * (1864) (which both uses the words of the Psalm and roundly contradicts its aspirations), are proceeding from the severely " canonical " or technically " inspired " to the clearly invented and original. You might be disposed to expect that the church, beginning with an iron discipline that accepted nothing for public worship that was not canonical, proceeded to relax its disciplines as changing times called for such a course, until it admitted first the metrical version, then the paraphrase, and finally the new hymn. But church history is not like that, and hymns are not like that, and altogether it is a very different story.

It does seem that hymns of a kind, quite distinct from the Psalms, were not unknown in the very early church. It is natural that the early Christians should, without doing anything so formally organized as composing hymns of full length, express their new and overwhelming experience in phrases which in a brief and homely fashion summarized what they all felt and knew. Some of these, it is thought,

* These will all be found in *C.P.*, 807, 729, 61 and 523.

are embedded in St. Paul's letters—and it is as likely that the Apostle in his exalted moments should turn to some well-known phrase as that a modern preacher or leader should crown his exhortation with some familiar quotation from hymn or scripture. Look at some of these phrases :

Awake, thou that sleepest, and arise from the dead ; and Christ shall give thee light (*Ephesians* v. 14).

He who was manifest in the flesh, justified in the spirit, seen of angels, preached among the nations, believed on in the world, received up in glory (*I Timothy* iii. 16).

Who is the blessed and only Potentate, the King of kings, and Lord of lords ; who only hath immortality, dwelling in light unapproachable ; whom no man hath seen, nor can see : to whom be honour and power eternal, Amen (*I Timothy* vi. 15–16).

If we died with him, we shall also live with him ; if we shall deny him, he also will deny us ; if we are faithless, he abideth faithful ; for he cannot deny himself (*II Timothy* ii. 11–13).

The Spirit and the Bride say, Come. And he that heareth, let him say, Come. And he that is athirst, let him come : whosoever will, let him take of the water of life freely (*Revelation* xxii. 17).

Great and marvellous are thy works,
O Lord God Almighty ;
Righteous and true are thy ways,
Thou King of the ages.
Who shall not fear, O Lord, and glorify thy name ?
for thou only art holy ;
For all the nations shall come and worship before thee ;
For thy righteous acts have been made manifest.

(*Revelation* xv. 3–4.)

We cannot say positively that this is the first Christian hymnody ; but we can see in these phrases or slogans some of the characteristics of hymnody. They have a memorable terseness ; they say mighty things in homely language and tell a great story in half a dozen words.

What was it that the early Church wanted hymns for ? Why should we assume that these are hymns at all ? They

wanted to express their experience ; they naturally coined
phrases that would do this and passed them from one to
another ; and they wanted to go forth and meet their
Lord, to invoke the living Christ into the precarious and
even desperate situations in which they found themselves.
They wanted hymns, that is, as a record of their experience,
as a means of binding them one to another, and as a vehicle
of worship.   They were, if we can believe the younger
Pliny, an interested but not sympathetic observer of the
activities of Christians in Bithynia about A.D. 110, singing
to Christ " as God "—a dangerous enough thing to do when
a Roman Emperor not long dead (Domitian) had insisted
on being called " Lord and God " by all his subjects.
Possibly in the same century, certainly in the third, they
were singing the original of " O gladsome light " * at a
ceremony of candlelighting in the catacombs.   What else
they were singing we do not know ; they put nothing in
writing and hymnology was not studied in the universities
of Athens or Alexandria.   But that they did sing words
which summed up their faith and that they had some sort of
thin stream of traditional hymnody which was distinctively
Christian is as hard to disbelieve as would be the idea that
the children of Israel did not sing in the wilderness after
the deliverance from the Red Sea or that the Eighth Army
never sang on the beaches of Italy.   Every movement has
its songs, and always for the same reason—to place its
experience and vision outside itself and make it public ; to
bind itself together against adversaries ; and to urge itself
on in its daily task towards the goal for which the movement
was founded.   Whether it is *Lilliburlero* or " God save the
Queen " or " Tipperary ", you can depend on vision, pur-
posefulness, prophecy and heroism to bring forth music as
surely as you can depend on a good fruit-tree to bring forth
blossom in spring.

As times change, of course, one aspect of hymnody will
be emphasized at the expense of another.   When the

* *E.H.*, 269.

church is not fighting it will be less concerned to express its unity than to develop the aesthetic of its devotion, and the result will be perhaps an increased complexity and even extravagance in its music ; as it was in the later Middle Ages when plainsong came to glorious fruit and then ran to seed in a remarkable effusion of tropes and flourishes [1] (see *English Hymnal*,* 738, for example), or as it was in Victorian England, when hymnody multiplied itself and cheapened itself almost beyond recall. Again, when the church is defective in culture but sound in devotion, we may find theology of the soundest sort crudely expressed, as in the Scottish Psalms and some of the hymnody of eighteenth-century Calvinism. But these three functions of codifying doctrine, unifying the body, and glorifying God are the functions of hymnody, and if any of them disappears completely from the mind of the composer of hymns, his work will have the short life of all rootless things.

As soon as Christianity became a lawful religion in the Empire of Rome, we find ourselves on firmer ground. In that great and tragic fourth century we have two manifestations of hymnody which are of the greatest importance.

The first is the hymns of the church at war, of which no direct records survive, but of which we hear in the writings of the Fathers. The church was divided over what is often dismissed as an academic and inessential point, but what is in fact the vital point of all its doctrine —the question whether, and in what sense, Jesus Christ is the Son of God and the Son of Man. Upon the one side was Arius, with those who followed him, who held that Christ was a " creature "—more like God than we are but not truly and fully God ; on the other were those who followed Athanasius, and through him the Gospel of St. John, and who were content to say that " He who hath seen him hath seen the Father ", to believe that " before Abraham was, I am ". Tragedies and cruelties and atrocities can

---

[1] See page 317.　　　　　　　* *1906 edition.*

come from high or from low beginnings ; of the horrors of the time we need be in no doubt : read Kingsley's *Hypatia*, for example. But the issue at stake was not the ownership of a tract of land or a trade-route ; it was not even a controversy on the scale of that between Communism and Private Enterprise. It was on the question whether Jesus Christ was or was not the one real thing in the world : was he real, and was he in the world ? Those who believed in the fullness of the Incarnation had to vindicate their belief at every possible level, to stand by it, to suffer privation, separation, estrangement, despair and death for it. The two main parties at the Council of Nicaea (A.D. 325), where the question was first put to the test, increased and subdivided and cross-divided into an immense confusion ; " such confusion of men against themselves " * did the church endure, even as the writer to the Hebrews had proclaimed. It was war, and war on the grand scale, hideous and protracted. The " orthodox " Christians defended their beliefs in the barber's shop and at the stake, in reasoned discussion and in martyrdom, in ink and in blood. Athanasius was exiled five times for it. Some enthusiasts died for it. It was fifty-six years before, at the Council of Constantinople, men declared, in effect, that they were now surer than they had ever been of two things —that Christ was in very truth God made man, and that they would never prove it by force or by philosophy. The result of it all was (except for two alterations made subsequently) what we now call the Nicene Creed.

It seems that when the battle was at its highest both sides burst into song, and that the Arians, the unorthodox, began it. When the Arians were forbidden by the orthodox Emperor Theodosius (378–96) to hold public worship in Constantinople (the political capital), the Arians retorted by parading through the streets singing hymns. John Chrysostom organized rival processions of hymn-singers, and since these things took place at sunset, the custom of

* *Hebrews* xii. 3 (revisers' reading).

evening hymn-singing became either established or at least immeasurably strengthened in the Christian church.

The war was not over, of course, when the Creed of Constantinople was published. It went on, and the first half of the fifth century is marked by its continuation on slightly different territory but with little less heat. But in all this confusion and distraction there stood firm the great pillars of the church's culture and learning, of whom one was Augustine, from whom we learn a good deal that enables us to piece this story together, and another was Ambrose (*c.* 340–97), Bishop of Milan.

Ambrose it was who first introduced the second manifestation of this century in hymnody—the " office hymn ". Hymns born of such confusion as had reigned were, of course, likely to be more rhetorical than edifying ; who knows how much popular, not to say personal, abuse may have been interlarded in these dogmatic war-cries ? But when it looked as if hymn-singing had come to stay as an inseparable part of Christian public worship, it was necessary to subject it to the kind of discipline that would make it appropriate to the church in the days of contemplation and peace which it was hoped would follow these days of strife. Ambrose, therefore, composed and caused to be composed the first of what we now call the " office hymns "—hymns prescribed to be sung at certain stages of the church's worship. These hymns are extremely simple, entirely objective and non-controversial, and of the homely sort that wear well in constant use. Here are a few verses of his most famous hymn, in which we can see the emphasis on the evening-time, the note of personal discipline so characteristic of the early church, and the Trinitarian doxology which became, of course, after the great controversy an essential part of Christian hymnody.

> Creator of the earth and sky,
> Ruling the firmament on high,
> Clothing the day with robes of light,
> Blessing with gracious sleep the night.

Day sinks ; we thank thee for thy gift ;
Night comes ; and once again we lift
Our prayer and vows and hymns that we
Against all ills may shielded be.

Thee let the secret heart acclaim,
Thee let our tuneful voices name,
Round thee our chaste affections cling,
Thee sober reason own as King.

Pray we the Father and the Son,
And Holy Ghost : O Three in One,
Blest Trinity, whom all obey,
Guard thou thy sheep by night and day.*

Only three hymns are certainly identifiable as by Ambrose [2]
(this because Augustine says they were his) ; but several
others may be his, and there is a considerable system of
office hymns running through the first two centuries of the
Middle Ages which are clearly modelled on his pattern.
Of these the best known are " O Christ, who art the light
and day ", " O Trinity of blessed light " and " Now that
the daylight fills the sky." †
    The history of hymnody is excellently set out in various
books already available, and it is not my purpose to rehearse
it here in any detail. I have dwelt on this early period
in order to show the necessity of hymnody, the emergence
of hymnody from the clash of controversy, and the beginnings
of the more recollected hymnody of the monastic Middle
Ages. I may fittingly add here, however, a celebrated
quotation from St. Augustine.

It was only a little while before that the church of Milan
had begun to practise this kind of consolation and exultation,
to the great joy of the brethren singing together with heart and
voice. For it was only about a year, or not much more, since
Justina, the mother of the boy emperor Valentinian, was perse-

* A translation of *Deus creator omnium* by Charles Bigg, see *E.H.*, 49,
verses 1, 3, 4, 8.
† *E.H.*, 81, 164, 254.

cuting Ambrose in the interests of her own heresy : for she had been seduced by the Arians. The devoted people had stayed day and night in the church, ready to die with the bishop, Your servant. And my mother, Your handmaid, bearing a great part of the trouble and vigil, had lived in prayer. I also, though still not warmed by Your Spirit, was stirred to excitement by the disturbed and wrought-up state of the city. It was at this time that the practice was instituted of singing hymns and psalms after the manner of the Eastern churches, to keep the people from being altogether worn out with anxiety and want of sleep. The custom has been retained from that day to this, and has been imitated by many, indeed in almost all congregations throughout the world.*

* *Confessions*, IX, 7, *ad init.* Quoted in my book, *The Church and Music* (Duckworth, 1950), pp. 234 f. Translation of F. J. Sheed. In my book, should the reader care to consult it, some account is given of Christian opinion concerning the use of music for religious purposes.

CHAPTER 3

How it Came to Stay

THE MIDDLE AGES

AMBROSE, then, laid the foundations of systematic hymnody : and we can indeed trace a continuous line of development from Ambrosian hymnody to certain uses of the present day. During the Middle Ages the church in western Europe was the centre of culture and, for long periods, the arbiter of the political destinies of nations. The power and security which it achieved in those thousand years may be measured by the great weight of corruption which it was able to sustain in its later centuries without being overturned altogether. For these thousand years the unit of the church's life was, substantially, the monastery, and the system of public devotion was based on the monastery. The great act of public worship was the Mass, in the celebration of which the people took only a passive part. But subsidiary to the Mass, and performed only by the " religious ", that is, the members of monastic orders, were the " offices " of the church, short acts of worship during which the Scriptures were read and the psalms recited and prayers offered. The offices were the machinery by which the religious performed intercession on behalf of the world, and it was considered proper for the peasant and the landlord of the feudal society to look to the local monastic community at office-time and recall that on their behalf the prayers were being offered by those who were set aside to do so. The layman was not expected to do more than participate passively in the Mass and receive instruction and absolution from his parish priest. Hymn singing, therefore, was not the layman's business at all. The offices (of which the most familiar to English readers will be the office of Compline, an Anglican form of which is broadcast monthly) contained their proper office hymns, but the Mass did not properly use hymns at all.

There is one notable exception to this, however, although it still does not bring the Catholic Mass within the realm of congregational hymnody of the primitive or modern kind. This was the *Prose* or *Sequence*. Scriptural passages were chanted at certain stated times in the Mass, and some of these were variable. Some of the variable ones ended with the word " Alleluia ", the last syllable of which was, on festive occasions, extended over a long musical phrase. The difficulty of memorizing the phrase led to words being set to it, and the generic name for these words was " Sequence " (that which followed the Alleluia). Later the practice arose of composing independent hymns to take the same place in the Mass ; these also were called Sequences, and the earlier prose forms were distinguished by being called Proses. A well-known modern version of a prose sequence is " The strain upraise of joy and praise ", and a later metrical one is " Come, thou Holy Paraclete ". But these sequences were still a professional affair confined to the monks and the choir, and were no business of the layman.

The subject-matter of these office hymns and sequences was always objective and doctrinal. Although we constantly find this sort of sentiment in the office hymns—

> Our mind be in his keeping placed,
> Our body true to him and chaste,
> Where only faith for fire shall feed,
> To burn the tares of Satan's seed,*

the chief end of the office hymn is adoration and declaration of the divine truth. The only personal element that ever

* From the Ambrosian *Splendor paternae gloriae,* translated by Robert Bridges, *E.H.,* 52, verse 5.

appears is the prayer for deliverance from temptations and
from the devices of the devil, against which monastic
communities had need to be well armed. The Sequences,
similarly, are declarations of doctrine and adoration.

This objectivity, often expressing itself through verse
turned with extreme care and artistry (like Stephen Lang-
ton's *Veni Sancte Spiritus* *), is characteristic of the atmosphere of serenity and security that pervades the church of
the Middle Ages at its best. The hymnody of the Greek
Church of the earlier Middle Ages, mediated to us in the
great work of John Mason Neale (translator of " The day
of Resurrection ", for example) is even more strictly
objective, being confined in its classical age (the seventh and
eighth centuries) to close commentary on certain specified
Biblical lyrics. In the Greek church of today, therefore,
and in the Western Catholic church and those communities
of the Church of England which have revived the Catholic
offices, we see this essentially monastic hymnody still in
being. The *English Hymnal* is the most accessible source of
the Anglican system of office hymns, and in it you will find
office hymns for the times of the day, the seasons of the
church's year, and the saints' days. Alongside the office
hymns are given hymns of the modern kind for these occasions, and you can see at a glance the difference between
the almost threadbare sobriety of the office hymn and the
more lyrical and rhetorical technique of the modern hymn.
Compare, for example, two short extracts from hymns for
advent. Here is the medieval hymn :

> High Word of God, who once didst come,
> Leaving thy Father and thy home,
> To succour by thy birth our kind,
> When, towards thine advent, time declined,
>
> Pour light upon us from above,
> And fire our hearts with thy strong love,

* Translated at *E.H.*, 155, " Come, thou holy Paraclete ".

That as we hear thy Gospel read,
All fond desires may flee in dread.*

This contrasts notably with the divine discontent and
sacred rhetoric of Philip Doddridge :

Hark, the glad sound, the Saviour comes,
    The Saviour promised long !
Let every heart prepare a throne,
    And every voice a song.

He comes the prisoners to release,
    In Satan's bondage held ;
The gates of brass before him burst,
    The iron fetters yield.†

But there are two important exceptions to the generalization that medieval hymnody was professional and serene.
One of these is not a real exception at all, inasmuch as it
concerns literature that is not in its origin hymnody—the
sacred poems of medieval poets like Bernard of Cluny.
This Bernard of Cluny is a typical example of the inspired
monk-poet.   It was not unusual for sensitive spirits in the
monasteries to put their religious thoughts into verse, rather
than expressing them in massive disputations and voluminous treatises.   Bernard of Cluny, afterwards Abbot of
Morlaix, committed to writing an astonishing poem of
nearly three thousand lines, in which he unburdened his
soul concerning the hideous abuses of his time (he died in
1153).   It is not my intention generally to quote Latin in
the text of this book—but listen to the remarkable *noise*
that these opening lines make :

Hora novissima tempora pessima sunt, vigilemus !
Ecce minaciter imminet Arbiter ille supremus.
Imminet, imminet, ut mala terminet, aequa coronet,
Recta remuneret, anxia liberet, aethera donet.

* *Verbum supernum prodiens*, ? tenth century, translated by Charles
Bigg, *E.H.*, 2, verses 1–2.
† *E.H.*, 6, verses 1–2.

So it continues for a length equal to about 75 pages of a book of this sort, triple rhyme and all. The literal translation of these four lines would be something like this :

> The last hours, the worst hours are here : let us keep watch !
> Behold that most mighty Judge threatens loweringly.
> He threatens, he threatens that he may end the evil and
>   crown the right,
> To reward the just, to set free the anxious, to grant us heaven.

John Mason Neale's translation of 1851 tones it down, but it is still stern enough :

> The world is very evil,
>   The times are waxing late ;
> Be sober and keep vigil,
>   The Judge is at the gate.
> The Judge that comes in mercy,
>   The Judge that comes with might,
> To terminate the evil,
>   To diadem the right.*

" The Judge that comes in mercy " is a very polite rendering of " Imminet, imminet ". But later on Neale has beautifully rendered the passages where Bernard speaks of the glory of heaven as compared with the squalor of earth—

> O one, O only mansion !
>   O Paradise of joy !
> Where tears are ever banished
>   And smiles have no alloy ;
> The Cross is all thy splendour,
>   The Crucified thy praise :
> His laud and benediction
>   His ransomed people raise.†

> They stand, those halls of Sion,
>   Conjubilant with song,
> And bright with many an angel,
>   And all the martyr-throng . . .

---

* *E.H.*, 495, verse 1.   † *E.H.*, 392, verses 5–6.

> Exult, O dust and ashes !
> The Lord shall be thy part :
> His, only his for ever,
> Thou shalt be and thou art.*

There is also a celebrated poem beginning *Dulcis Jesu Memoria*, variously translated in English, but best known perhaps in Caswall's version, beginning :

> Jesu, the very thought of thee
> With sweetness fills my breast ;
> But sweeter far thy face to see,
> And in thy presence rest.†

Nobody knows who wrote the original of that ; it is the work of some more or less obscure but immortal Christian poet, and we have to leave it there.‡ It is a poem of intense personal devotion, rich in the luxuriant detail of medieval symbolism.

These and similar poems, I say, were not designed for singing, and it is only nineteenth-century English translators who have made them into congregational hymns. But we must pause just long enough to note that we have here the beginnings of that kind of modern hymnody which is essentially personal in its conception. Bernard is giving us what arises in his soul on contemplating the hypocrisy and dirt of medieval civilization as he saw it. The other author is giving us his vision of the Saviour. It happens that the personal thoughts of both can, through the translators, be sufficiently universalized to become proper material for congregational use. Similarly personal and universal are " When I survey the wondrous Cross " and " Abide with me " and the 23rd Psalm. But we have noted that such personal devotion had no place whatever in the public praise of the medieval church. Possibly the nearest thing to original hymnody outside the office hymns which we have in the Middle Ages is the hymn book which

* *E.H.*, 412, verses 2 and 4.

† *E.H.*, 419.   ‡ See below, page 204.

Peter Abélard (1079–1142) wrote for Heloïse to use in her convent of the Paraclete after they had separated in the circumstances so movingly recounted by Miss Helen Waddell in her *Peter Abélard*. This was a book of 93 hymns, all written by Abélard with some original tunes supplied also, of which one has become famous and is thus translated by Monsignor Ronald Knox almost in its original metre :

> O what high holiday, past our declaring,
> Safe in his palace God's courtiers are sharing,
> Rest after pilgrimage, spoil after fighting !
> God, all in all, is their crown and requiting.
>
> Truly Jerusalem's townsmen we call them—
> Peace everlasting doth fold and enthral them ;
> Never they crave, but the boon hath been granted,
> Never that boon leaves their hope disenchanted.*

On the preoccupation of these medievals with heaven we crave the reader's indulgence, and the forbearance of his impatience, until we get to a later chapter.†

But the other great exception to the office hymns in the Middle Ages is indeed congregational hymnody ; it is true congregational hymnody, even if its subject matter is here and there very odd indeed. This is the popular hymnody associated with some of the " enthusiastic " sects of the late Middle Ages. The activities of troubadours and trouvères, minnesinger and meistersinger and the rest of the travelling musicians served to keep secular life well supplied with music of a popular sort. It was inevitable, however, that here and there this ballad-technique of lengthy musical narration should spill over into the church in an unofficial way. There is, for example, that queer business of the " Prose of the Ass ", which survives in a manuscript confidently dated by the experts from the early thirteenth century. The context of this is a procession commemorating

---

* *O quanta qualia sunt illa sabbata. Westminster Hymnal* (1940), 205, verses 1–2.

† Chapter XXI.

the flight of Jesus and his Mother into Egypt, in which a young woman was seated on a donkey and proceeded in the procession for the occasion. The tune which was used in the popular hymn associated with this festival has survived as ORIENTIS PARTIBUS.* ³ Then there are the *Laudi Spirituali*, long hymns of ecstasy uttered by the " flagellants " during the outbreak of that curious enthusiasm about 1259 ; once again a tune has survived from this movement—ALTA TRINITA BEATA †—though as Dr. Burney has arranged it in the eighteenth century it would scarcely be recognizable by a revenant from the company of flagellants. Similar popular hymns are to be found among the Waldenses and the Albigenses and other sects of the days immediately before the Reformation. All this need not detain us here except that we have to admit that here we have enthusiastic or ecstatic hymnody at its rawest. We shall have to deal with some objections on psychological grounds to the practice of hymn-singing ; but we cannot possibly get away with the statement that hymn-singing has never been associated with disorderliness of mind. We shall have to face that truth and turn it to the service of Christian apologetic before we have done. Here we merely mention the advent of it as a resuscitation in some kind of the ancient ecstasies distinguished by St. Paul as " speaking with tongues ".

This hymnody of ecstasy or eccentricity has, of course, much in common with the hymnody of controversy and spiritual war which we noticed in the last chapter. Theologically disciplined, we shall see it again as soon as we turn the page of history to the chapter headed " Reformation ".

But we may summarize our findings so far by saying that in the Middle Ages we have examples of every sort of hymnody that we shall find in later times. We have liturgical hymnody, ecstatic hymnody, controversial hymnody and devotional hymnody, the last three over against the first and firmly excluded from the offices of the church.

* *E.H.*, 129.   † *E.H.*, 184.

What the Reformation did was to harness the forces which produced the hymnody of devotion and controversy and ecstasy and develop a new kind of congregational hymnody, sternly disciplined and immensely powerful. It was the medievals who showed us what hymns could do ; it was the Reformers who showed us how to use them.

CHAPTER 4

How it Came to Life

THE REFORMERS

WE might say that the Reformers taught Christendom how to sing hymns ; but there were Reformers and Reformers, and they disagreed rather strongly among themselves about the use of hymns.

Martin Luther,[4] that versatile and vivid genius, loved hymns. He was full of what people often call the " artistic temperament " ; which means in this context that he was the kind of person whom half the world execrates for a perverse and loud-mouthed meddler while the other half venerates him as a kind of saint. Luther was a witty, full-blooded, shrewd person with a dash of the mystic and a very keen intellect indeed. He was capable of sustained and careful reasoning, as you can see in his Commentaries ; he was incapable of expressing himself otherwise than forcefully, as you can see in his polemics ; and when he went wrong, as he did, we must feel, over the Peasants' Revolt, he went wrong spectacularly and resoundingly. A stern critic of what he judged, in the light of his experience of the grace of God, to be ugliness and perversity in the organization of the church, he was not one of those theologians to whom system and discipline, personal or intellectual, is the foundation of all things. Less than any of his reforming brethren was he concerned to prune, to restrict, to canalize ; more than any of them he desired richness and fullness of religious life, and his charge against the peddlers of indulgences and sellers of benefices was that they withheld it from the common man. Luther was a

33

musician and a poet, and he would not exclude music and
poetry from the church. He was enough a son of the
Renaissance to respect the creations of men, provided the
creators themselves were obedient to and forgiven by their
own Creator. It was with reluctance, indeed, that he
abandoned any ceremony of the Roman Mass, so sensitive
was he to what drama and art could do for religion.

From this fountain-head came Lutheran hymnody, and
from the first Lutheran hymns were respectful but not literal
paraphrases of the Scriptures.

> A safe stronghold our God is still
> A trusty shield and weapon ;
> He'll help us clear from all the ill
> That hath us now o'ertaken.
> The ancient prince of hell
> Hath risen with purpose fell ;
> Strong mail of craft and power
> He weareth in this hour ;
> On earth is not his fellow.*

They have called that the " Marseillaise of the Reformation ", and it was first printed in 1529. But it had been on
the last day of October, 1517, that Luther threw down the
gauntlet. When an academic disputation was announced,
you nailed to the parish-church notice-board a summary of
your arguments, and your opponent did the same. It was
the most ordinary thing in the world to happen in a university city. But this was different. The arguments of the
proposer were not nailed to the notice-board ; they were
walking the streets of the German towns and villages selling
the forgiveness of God for so many pieces of silver ; so, at
least, Luther saw it. And when he saw that he had started
a landslide, Luther began to sing, and the people sang with
him. Luther wrote a few dozen hymns and possibly tunes
also with his own hand ; others followed him, and so was
begun the great stream of Lutheran hymnody which flowed
in spate for two centuries.

* *Ein' feste Burg*, translated by Thomas Carlyle, *E.H.*, 362, verse 1.

But look again at this battle-hymn—a hymn of war as surely as the Arian and orthodox hymns of the fourth century, but this time immeasurably richer and saner. It is founded on the 46th Psalm : but the psalm has passed through Luther's great heart and on his lips it is embellished with all the topical rhetoric that would send people to the stake for their faith. " The Lord of hosts is with us : the God of Jacob is our Refuge " sang the Psalmist. To which Luther had added on his way to the Diet of Worms, " Were the houses of Wittenburg tiled with devils, I would on ! "

What was it all about ? Was this war anything but a mask for political intrigue and ecclesiastical wrangling of the baser sort ? We cannot paint one side white and the other black and say that there is an end of the matter ; but let this question be asked : if you firmly believe that your next-door neighbour is living a shapeless life and missing the forgiveness and the promises of God which alone make a human life worth more than the bucketful of chemicals that compose a human body ; and that he is thus floundering because the institution whose business it is to make free the progress of this forgiveness and promise is deliberately blocking up the channels and turning it into a mockery—what do you do ?

If you are Martin Luther, you march. And Luther marched to some purpose. He was not, as a matter of fact, a saint ; not a supernaturally good or well-tempered or charitable or brave person. He did lose his temper with his friends and fall out with his best supporters ; he was capable of misunderstanding and impatience. But he saw his duty and did it. Now and then it was too much for him, and there is a well-attested story that one day, in the Castle at Coburg, during the Diet of Augsburg (1530), which was perhaps the most critical point the Reformation cause ever reached, he fainted from loss of sleep and overwork. When he regained consciousness the first thing he said to his anxious servant was " Come, let us defy the

devil, and praise God by singing a hymn ", and they sang
together the original of this :

> Out of the depths I cry to thee,
>   Lord hear me, I implore thee !
> Bend down thy gracious ear to me,
>   Regard my prayer before thee !
> If thou rememberest each misdeed,
> If each should have his rightful meed,
>   Who may abide thy presence ? *

I suppose they sang it to that unforgettable tune which
surges up out of the depths and combines as no tune has
ever done before or since courage and self-abasement.†
It is, of course, a paraphrase of Psalm 130, " Out of the
deep have I called unto thee, O Lord " ; and if you think
with Luther that the devil's work is to cut you off from the
power and forgiveness of God and leave you self-made,
self-supporting, self-sufficient and lonely, then to sing
Psalm 130 like that is indeed to defy the devil.   There is no
self-pity here ; only a longing to bring men back to communion with God in Christ.   To that end Luther published
this and many others of the same sort in 1524.

But lest any should think that Luther could only march
and strut and set his face in firm and commanding lines,
let it be recalled that he was very much a family man, and
that Christmas Eve was a special day of celebration in that
family.   On one of these occasions (on others, for all we
know, as well) Luther wrote a carol for his little son, Hans.
It ran to fifteen verses, of which the first few were sung by
an angel announcing the birth of Jesus, and the rest by the

---

* *Aus tiefer Not schrei ich zu Dir*, translated by Catherine Winkworth,
as it appears in *C.P.*, 381, verse 1.

† *Aus tiefer Not*, first published with the hymn in 1524 ; English
hymn-books are shy of it, but a modern version will be found with
the words in *Congregational Praise*.   The G (the second of the scale)
was flattened throughout in the original version.   Its first phrase is a
startlingly early example of instinctive " pictorial " music.

children in response.   A translation of two of the responding
verses reads thus :

> Ah, Lord eternal, heavenly King,
> Hast thou become so mean a thing ?
> And hast thou left thy blissful seat
> To rest where colts and oxen eat ?
>
> Were this wide world much wider made,
> With gold and costly gems arrayed,
> E'en then, by far too mean 't would be
> To make a little crib for thee.*

Luther was often a man of wrath, but always a man of
compassion.

The other focal point of the Continental Reformation
was, of course, Geneva.   John Calvin,[5] who died in the year
in which Shakespeare was born, aged only 55, was as different
from Luther as one Christian man could be from another.
Calvin was a systematic theologian of the most rigorous
temper, and he had to spend his best years (the last twenty-
three of his life) doing a duty which came strangely to him.
The figure of Calvin is generally represented to us as of a
man whose preoccupation was with the predestination of
guilty souls to hell and the enforcement of the Scottish
Sabbath.   Only Luther has been more persistently vilified
than Calvin by those who are clear in their minds that the
Reformation was a mistake.   Those who call Luther a
sottish and foul-mouthed bully call Calvin a morose and
fanatical despot.   And indeed the most faithful Calvinist
has to admit that Calvin did burn Servetus at the stake,
that he did write harshly and feverishly about predestination
in the third edition of the *Institutes*, and that he did turn
Geneva into something like a strict Presbyterian church of
seventeen thousand members without consulting the people
very closely.   But Calvin had one great thing to say, and
it can be put not too misleadingly in this way : " You

* *Vom Himmel hoch*, translated by John Hunt.   *C.P.*, 78, verses 4 and 5.

call yourself a Christian. Then remember three things. God's promises cannot fail : He has said this and He means it. Do your duty and rely on Him to see you through. Don't congratulate yourself on being a member of His church ; keep the rules and give Him the glory."

Calvin was a man of grace, but he was more alive to the necessity of having a few traffic-regulations in the City of God than Luther ever was. At bottom, he was saying what Luther said—" Leave a man the right to be humble before his God " ; but he gave certain directions about the putting into practice of this ideal, and among them was the axiom that nothing man does is free from the blurring and confusion that is technically called sin. He said in effect that a man is never himself in this world ; that whenever he stretches out his hand to point towards the Eternal, the devil gives his arm a nudge and turns it, perhaps only a little, perhaps a long way out of true. He also said that God had a remedy for this which men could get hold of by coming to church. Modern psychology has raised horrified clamour against the doctrine of total depravity, and its practitioners (especially the more amateurish ones) have substituted the theory that every man in the street is a psychological " case ". That is, in a sense, just what Calvin was saying, except that Calvin places the remedy in God's hands and the pseudo-Calvinist deterministic psychologist puts it behind some brass plate in the West End of London.

Not to labour this point, we have to say that one of the results of this was that such human compositions as hymns were, for the Calvinist tradition, ruled out of public worship as being quite unsuitable and misleading. Calvin was a high churchman and a purist, and if there was any difference between the inspired literature of the Bible and the compositions of Martin Luther and Michael Weisse, then the Bible must have priority. Nothing but the best was good enough for public worship. This view was so logical, and the literature of the book of Psalms so rich, that for two hundred years the official view of English Protestantism was the same (as we saw further back).

Calvin's hymnody therefore lies entirely outside our province and in that of Lord Ernle, for it is all psalmody of the strictest kind—metrical psalms not deviating from the original nor interpreting it nor adding to it, but reproducing it in such a way that a congregation could sing it to something that had not the associations of plainsong, namely, a metrical hymn tune.

But one thing we must say. It is one of the most glorious examples of the way in which God can turn confusions and trivialities to noble ends that out of this sternness and turmoil and distraction that was Presbyterian Geneva came the most gracious and serene hymn-music that the world ever saw. Perhaps no generalization is quite safe, and it is true that I did once hear a man describe the OLD HUNDREDTH as a dreary and dismal tune. But the reader will probably not quarrel with me if I say that this was an eccentric judgment. In Calvin's Psalters, from the first (1539) to the last (1562), we have the cream of hymn-music, the archetypal hymn-tunes, the tunes which inspired the great English and Scottish psalm-tunes, and which are therefore the foundation of English hymnody. We owe the passion of words to Luther, but we owe the poise and simplicity of our best hymn-tunes to John Calvin ; and of the Genevan psalm-tunes the finest and the most universally known is the OLD HUNDREDTH (All people that on earth do dwell) ; not far behind it is the OLD 124TH (Now Israel may say).

But we must not pursue this subject because this is not a book about hymn-music. We must turn a few more pages of history and see how these two great traditions developed in later years.

CHAPTER 5

War and Peace

GERMAN HYMNODY

I HOPE it was made clear in the first part of the preceding chapter that in Lutheran circles it was thought more important that the people should sing than that a distinction should be carefully made between sacred and secular songs. If you are concerned to see that the devil shall not have all the good tunes, you can do one of two things ; you can compose a complete new set yourself and make sure that they are better than the devil's ; or you can march on the devil and recapture what he has taken from you. On the whole, Genevan Presbyterianism took the former line, and Lutheranism took the latter. The hymnody of evangelism is thus distinguished from that of the settled and organized church. It was the revivalists —the medieval enthusiasts, Luther, the Moravians, the Wesleys, Sankey—who went and grabbed their music and words from the devil ; it was the high churchmen—the orthodox medievals, the Calvinists, the English Puritans, the editors of *Hymns Ancient and Modern*—who developed the distinctively " church " idiom, and kept it apart and unspotted by the world.

But of course there is no denying that the churches that begin with revival usually settle down into the stable equilibrium of orthodoxy and organized churchmanship after a generation or two. This was certainly what happened to the Lutheran or Confessional Church. So remarkable was the change in its temper in two centuries that very respectable Christian thinkers have often fallen into the error of attributing to Luther [6] the doctrines of later

Lutherans and have as a result found themselves involved in controversy.

Within a century after Luther threw down his challenge, the primitive fire of reforming Lutheranism had been largely replaced by a cooler and more recollected piety. But three things prevented Lutheran religion from subsiding too soon into respectability. The first was an inseparable property of Lutheranism—the essentially domestic and local nature of its piety. This piety has always been one which sprang from the individual's experience of forgiveness and rippled out through the family, the local church, and the city to the church universal. The outermost ripples have always been as mild as the central impulse has been fervent ; the Lutherans have not, on the whole, been at their strongest in missionary and ecumenical work. They have sung of the church only when the church was drawn together against an enemy. Their hymnody, if we look at three centuries of it, has been largely the hymnody of the family circle and the locality. Every community in the classic days of Lutheranism had its own hymn-book. Now this primitive and robust sense of the family and the local circle produced some great pastors and some immortal hymns. The local Lutheran pastor, confronted by some crisis in his village, would be as likely to compose a hymn for the occasion as to look for a suitable one in the existing hymn-book.

This is how one of the greatest of Lutheran hymns was made. One winter's day in 1597 Pastor Philip Nicolai was looking out of his window at a sad little town where every other house was a house of mourning. The plague had come, and in six months he had buried 1,400 people. He went back to his desk and wrote the noble hymn, *Wachet auf*,* with its tune which has come to be known as the " King of chorales ". It is a hymn, richly embroidered with Scriptural reference, about heaven and the promises of God.

* *Wachet auf*, translated by F. C. Burkitt. *E.H.*, 12.

> Wake, O wake, with tidings thrilling
> The watchmen all the air are filling,
>   Arise, Jerusalem, arise !
> Midnight strikes ! no more delaying,
> " The hour has come," we hear them saying,
>   Where are ye all, ye virgins wise ?

To his bereaved flock, Nicolai tells the good news that death is meeting with Christ, the Bridegroom. The village cowers in fear and gloom, the people's faith burns low as neighbours, friends, and loved ones are carried out to the churchyard, but—

> Sion hears the watchmen shouting,
> Her heart leaps up with joy undoubting,
>   She stands and waits with eager eyes . . .

Not content with this, Nicolai wrote another hymn : they say he missed his lunch to finish it [7]—

> O morning star, how fair and bright
> Thou beamest forth in truth and light !
>   O Sovereign meek and lowly.*

This, a gracious and restrained hymn of praise, to which again Nicolai supplied a tune, is known as the " Queen of chorales ".

This pastoral aspect will be found all through German hymnody. A chance for its exercise was provided by the second thing that brought Lutheranism to its feet as a fighting force—the Thirty Years War.

From 1517 to 1618 the battle between Catholic and Protestant was rather a matter of high-level intrigue punctuated by local (and often bloody) skirmish than of open and continuous warfare. But from 1618 the war was on in the fullest sense, and through the generation following the land of western Germany was desolated by grief, starvation, plague, and destruction. Revival of religion does not find its immediate cause in war : we have been often

---

* *Wie schön leuchtet der Morgenstern*, translated by Catherine Winkworth. *Songs of Praise*, 90.

enough disappointed in the effectiveness of war for bringing people back to God to have given up before this our
trust in misery as a vehicle of evangelism. But from the
Thirty Years War came heroism. Two great hymns of
this time have been good friends to Protestants ever since
—Löwenstern's *Christe du Beistand* and Rinkart's *Nun danket*.
The first was freely paraphrased, in circumstances which
we recount below,* by Philip Pusey as " Lord of our life
and God of our salvation " ; † the second, in Catherine
Winkworth's translation beginning " Now thank we all our
God ",‡ has become one of our national anthems.

" Nun danket " is probably the elder, since it is thought
to go back to 1636. Its author was a pastor in the small
town of Eilenburg in Saxony, in the middle of the great
battlefield. War had brought pestilence and hunger to
the town, and part of Rinkart's duties had been the con-
ducting of 4,480 funerals. On top of this came the demand
from the Swedish army of occupation for a tribute of
30,000 thalers. Rinkart spoke with the invaders to such
purpose, supported on the prayers of his people, that the
tribute was reduced to 2,000 florins. He had said to his
parishioners, " Come, my children ; we can find no mercy
with men ; let us take refuge with God," and like a good
pastor he had not only prayed but acted, at the risk of his life.[8]

When you think of a situation like that, taking place
during a war at a time when there were men and women
of twenty who had never known a time without war, *Nun
danket* reads like a page out of Isaiah of Jerusalem.

> Now thank we all our God
> With heart and hands and voices,
> Who wondrous things hath done,
> In whom his world rejoices ;
> Who from our mothers' arms
> Hath bless'd us on our way
> With countless gifts of love,
> And still is ours to-day.

* Page 111.   † *E.H.*, 435.   ‡ *E.H.*, 533.

Rinkart, like Isaiah, could look over the heads of the exiles and see on the far horizon the coming deliverance. He knew, because the Gospel said so, that God in Christ had delivered his people and defeated the devil's army of suffering and hunger ; and so, though he knew not the times and seasons when this deliverance would come, he lifted up his voice and prophesied, " Comfort ye ".

Löwenstern's hymn is less prophecy than exhortation.

> Christ, thou the champion of that war-worn host
> Who bear thy cross, haste, help, or we are lost ;
> The schemes of those who long our blood have sought
> Bring thou to nought.[9]

That literal translation, made by Catherine Winkworth in 1855, shows that where Rinkart carried his people high above the conflict, Löwenstern, another pastor, went down with them into the thick of it, and urged them to fight the real battle and strive for the real peace, beyond the earthly and political struggle in which they were then only half-comprehendingly engaged.

A third pastor of the Thirty Years War was Johann Heermann. He lived at Köben, another little town over which the tide of war ebbed and flowed. Out of his collection of pastoral hymns come two which we partly know in England. One is the earliest of missionary hymns :

> O Christ, our true and only Light,
> Illumine those who sit in night ;
> Let those afar now hear thy voice,
> And in thy fold with us rejoice.
>
> Fill with the radiance of thy grace
> The souls now lost in error's maze,
> And all whom in their secret minds
> Some dark delusion hurts and blinds.*

The other is even more moving. It was a great thing, when most of his people must have been saying, " What have I

* *Herr Jesu Christ, meins Lebens Licht* (1625), translated by Catherine Winkworth, 1863. *C.P.*, 316, verses 1 and 2.

done to deserve all this suffering ? " for the pastor to be
able to write this :

> Ah, holy Jesus, how hast thou offended,
> That man to judge thee hath in hate pretended ?
> By foes derided, by thine own rejected,
> O most afflicted !

> Who was the guilty ? Who brought this upon thee ?
> Alas, my treason, Jesus, hath undone thee.
> 'Twas I, Lord Jesus, I it was denied thee,
> I crucified thee.*

But another movement of revival was on the way. This
was the rich development of personal devotion which,
during the few halcyon decades before it degenerated into
a fugitive pietism, gave German hymnody its crowning
glory in the hymns of Paul Gerhardt (1607–76). Here he is
at his best, well translated and interpreted (though not
in his own metre) by John Wesley :

> Commit thou all thy griefs
> And ways into his hands,
> To his sure truth and tender care
> Who heaven and earth commands.

> Give to the winds thy fears,
> Hope and be undismayed :
> God hears thy sighs, and counts thy tears,
> God shall lift up thy head.

> Through waves and clouds and storms
> He gently clears thy way ;
> Wait thou his time ; so shall this night
> Soon end in joyous day.†[10]

That first appeared two years before the end of the
Thirty Years War, in 1646 ; it represents yet another way
of dealing with the distresses of this life : Rinkart praises,

---

* *Herzliebster Jesu*, translated by Robert Bridges, 1899, *E.H.*, 70,
verses 1 and 2.

† *Befiehl du deine Wege*, translated by John Wesley. *C.P.*, 487,
verses 1 and 4.

Löwenstern calls to battle, Heermann calls to prayer and penitence, Gerhardt quite simply comforts. Among his other hymns, published between 1646 and 1656, are the originals of the Christmas hymn, " All my heart this night rejoices " * and the Passiontide hymn, " O sacred head, sore wounded ".†

One of the signs of the religious enthusiasm of the time was the great length at which Gerhardt wrote : " Commit thou all thy griefs " was in fifteen verses, which was normal for him.   This was a quality which the Wesleys inherited. Gerhardt and the Wesleys shared this also, that they could write a hymn a hundred lines long without wasting a word.

This devotional revival finds expression in certain other great authors of the same period.   Here is Georg Neumark, writing in 1657 :

> If thou but suffer God to guide thee,
>   And hope in him through all thy ways,
> He'll give thee strength whate'er betide thee,
>   And bear thee through the evil days.
> Who trusts in God's unchanging love
> Builds on the rock that nought can move.‡

And here is Johann Scheffler, a Breslau physician who became a Roman Catholic, and wrote at the time of his conversion to Catholicism a series of devotional songs of an almost medieval richness, of which the following is the simplest and most famous :

> O Love, who formedst me to wear
>   The image of thy godhead here ;
> Who soughtest me with tender care
>   Through all my wanderings wild and drear ;
> O Love, I give myself to thee,
> Thine ever, only thine to be.§

* C.P., 81.   † E.H., 102.   See also *Songs of Praise*, 478.
‡ *Wer nur den lieben Gott lässt walten*, translated by Catherine Winkworth, 1863.   C.P., 389, verse 1.
§ *Liebe, die du mich zum Bilde* (1657), translated by Catherine Winkworth, 1858.   E.H., 460.

The distinguishing mark of true mysticism, of which these hymns are examples, is its teaching that a man can approach God the Father directly. Its varieties are, many scholars have pointed out, legion, and the whole system has been attacked on the ground that it implies a contradiction of the dominical injunction, " No man cometh to the Father but by me." The German mystics of the 1650's, however, express as we find it nowhere else expressed the Christian's yearning for a personal trust in God. There is in them nothing unhealthy and everything creaturely.

But when the devotion is to God the Son exclusively, producing a passionate and even amatory address to the earthly figure of our Lord, then you have not mysticism but pietism, which was the next development in Lutheran song. Pietism was originally a derisive nickname given to the movement which one Jakob Spener initiated in 1670 by founding in Berlin the *Collegium Pietatis* : this was to be the home of a religious revival which should have as its aim the extension of practical and philanthropic Christianity, the encouragement of pure and strict Christian living, and the cultivation of personal devotion. The hymnody of this movement had its greatest influence in this country through the Wesleys, whose ideals in the Oxford " Holy Club " had so much in common with the best in Pietism.

Two names among the Pietists are worth quoting here. The first is that of Joachim Neander (1651–81), who became at 24 head master of the Berlin " Gymnasium " (High School). His fervent and insistent introduction of religious exercises into all parts of the curriculum got him into the kind of trouble that a head master of revivalist tendencies whether in religion or politics might expect in a modern State school, and he was hounded out of the town. After a few months' exile, during which he lived in a cave, he returned to be assistant preacher at the Reformed Church in Bremen, and attracted much attention, largely unfavourable, by his preaching. It is probable that his early

death, at 30, cut short a life that would have seen much
persecution, but during those few years he found time to
write a number of hymns and tunes. He is the author of
the original of one of our great modern hymns of praise,
" Praise to the Lord, the Almighty ",* and composer of
the tune we usually sing to " Come, ye people, raise the
anthem ".†

The other great name in Pietism is that of the pastor,
poet and hymn-writer, Benjamin Schmolck (1672–1737).
We do not now sing many of his hymns, but the following
lines will show the essence of a pietism which, in its second
generation, had added to its qualities a certain humanistic
and literary air.

> Morning star, in midnight gloom
> Thou who dost the world illume,
> Jesu mine, come and shine,
> In my bosom make thy shrine.
>
> Come, then, golden Light, from far
> Speed the axles of thy car ;
> Jesu mine, come and shine,
> In my bosom make thy shrine.‡

The personal fervour and literary preciousness of this make
little appeal to a modern congregation to whom a " car "
is not a mysterious and supernatural chariot but a stinking
projectile. But the classicism of this sort of diction is a
quality which the Wesleys picked up and used in such
lines as

> Those amarynthine bowers,
> Inalienably ours.

We must not go further here into pietism, but those
who wish to drink more deeply of it may turn to the arias
and choruses of the Passions and Cantatas of J. S. Bach.[11]

---

* *E.H.*, 536.   † *E.H.*, 380.
   ‡ *Morgenstern der finstern nacht* (1704), translated by G. R. Woodward,
1910. *Songs of Syon*, 354, verses 1 and 6.

Next, and we are now nearing the end of the great days
of German hymnody, there came the spectacular revival
known as Moravianism.   This movement had come down
from the evangelical fervour of John Hus, who was burnt
for heresy in 1415, through the Bohemian Brethren of
Luther's days.   The Hussites or Bohemian Brethren had
always been a small company, noted and frequently persecuted for enthusiastic tendencies, suspected by Luther,
harried by sixteenth-century potentates, and spending much
of their time virtually " under ground ".   What the squire
of Berthelsdorf, Count Nicolaus von Zinzendorf (1700–61),
did for this movement in the eighteenth century can be well
read in Mgr. Ronald Knox's *Enthusiasm*.   Zinzendorf combined a generous inheritance of this world's goods with a
passionate religious zeal to set this movement on its feet ;
and it became under his influence a going concern which
still survives as a small but flourishing denomination, called
Moravian, in Germany, England, and America.   He built
on his estate the model village of Herrnhut—and we shall
have more to say about Herrnhut.

Zinzendorf, whose zeal owed much to Pietism, wrote
about two thousand hymns.   John Wesley has given us this
translation of one of his finest :

> Jesus, thy blood and righteousness
> My beauty are, my glorious dress ;
> 'Midst flaming worlds, in these arrayed
> With joy shall I lift up my head.
>
> Thou God of power, thou God of love,
> Let the whole world thy mercy prove !
> Now let thy word o'er all prevail ;
> Now take the spoils of death and hell.*

The important thing for us about these hymns of Zinzendorf
is not their literary merit, which is never very high, but
the fact that they were the songs in which the congregation

---

* *Christi Blut und Gerechtigkeit* (1739), translated by John Wesley.
Methodist Hymn Book (1933), 370, verses 1 and 9.

of Herrnhut sang themselves hoarse for the love of Christ ; and we must further imagine a young Englishman of 35 walking up the path to the church door and stopping to listen. What came of that we shall tell in a later chapter.

This was, however, the beginning of the end in Lutheran hymnody. Zinzendorf's two thousand marked the high water-mark of Lutheran productivity in hymnody, and by now, what with the enormous output of the earlier Lutherans, of Löwenstern, Gerhardt, Schmolck, Tersteegen and the rest, Germany was pretty well sated with hymnody. Further, " Enlightenment " had now broken out, and reason, science, humanism and naturalism were beginning their assault on the foundations of the faith. In 1761, when Zinzendorf died, Voltaire was 47 and Rousseau 49. Hymnody and preaching had to turn at last from private devotion to primitive teaching. One brave name stands out in the early days of stirring, that of Christian Fürchtegott Gellert,[12] another prolific hymn-writer who is properly celebrated in England by a hymn that is indeed primitively apologetical :

> Jesus lives ! thy terrors now
> Can no longer, death, appal us.*

And after the storm has broken and the day of the common man has dawned ; after the Bastille has fallen and French secularism has set itself up in open opposition to Catholic and Protestant churches alike ; while Karl Marx is writing *Das Kapital* and Hegel is lucubrating on Dialectic ; when the Duke of Wellington has had his windows broken over the Reform Bill and the Chartists are parading the streets of London, and a rising young scientist is laying out his foolscap in the preparation of a work to be called *The Origin of Species*—while the church is coping in a blundering and resentful way with all this, there is in Germany at any rate one commonplace hero who can see the hand of God

* *Jesus lebt,* translated by Frances E. Cox. *E.H.,* 134.

in it. Karl Johann Philipp Spitta (1801–59) wrote this in the " hungry forties " :

> We praise and bless thee, gracious Lord,
>   Our Saviour kind and true,
> For all the old things passed away,
>   For all thou hast made new.
>
> The old security is gone,
>   In which so long we lay ;
> The sleep of death thou hast dispelled,
>   The darkness rolled away.
>
> New hopes, new purposes, desires
>   And joys thy grace has given :
> Old ties are broken from the earth,
>   New ties attach to heaven.* [13]

And so, in this swan-song (so far as English hymnody is concerned) of Lutheran hymnody we come back full circle to the primitive pioneering strength, adventurousness, and courage of the early Reformation.

* *O treuer Heiland*, 1843, translated by Jane Borthwick, 1855. *C.P.*, 404, verses 1–3.

CHAPTER 6

Muscular Christianity

THE ENGLISH PURITANS

IT may surprise one or two readers to be told that one of the great benefactors of English hymnody was Queen Mary Tudor. Her spirited attempt, in sympathy with the Catholic cause, to put the religious clock back behind Henry VIII (and who would not react with some violence against such a father ?) led to the wholesale persecution of English Protestants, many of whom left the country. Had they not been persecuted they might have stayed at home, and so, perhaps, they might never have found their way to France and Geneva, and might therefore never have seen Geneva in the great and turbulent days of John Calvin. But they did find their way there, and we may suppose that some of them walked into the great new church in Geneva one Sunday and heard the 134th Psalm being sung (in French, of course) to a new tune that seemed to crystallize all their ideas of hymnody. We must suppose that they said to themselves, " England, if we ever get back there, must hear this ". And when they returned to England in 1558, much sooner than they expected, two things were firmly established ; the first was the confirmation of their conviction that public singing in church ought to be confined to the Psalms, and the second was that their music could not do better than follow the Genevan pattern. How they brought over the 134th Psalm tune and set it to the English 100th Psalm, how they took lessons in composing hymn tunes from Louis Bourgeois, and how they expanded their repertory of tunes up to and well beyond the limit of the common

man's memory in a few years it is not my business here
to recount.[14] But we must say something very briefly
about Psalmody.

English Puritanism died hard in its faithfulness to the
Psalter. In Lord Ernle's book you may read how Sternhold began the English metrical version, and how it was
completed during and after the Genevan exile by Kethe,
Norton, Hopkins, and Whittingham. Sternhold, in the
pre-Genevan days (he died in 1549), had written his psalms
in ballad-metre, presumably that they might be sung to
some of the great old ballad-tunes that are beginning to
turn up again in our hymn-books under the general ascription " English Traditional Melody ". After their experience
of Geneva the later writers varied the metres in order to
bring into use some of the Genevan tunes. The whole
work was completed by 1562, in which year the *Whole
Booke of Psalmes* was published, and this version, commonly
known now as the " Old Version ", reigned supreme in
English worship until two Irishmen, Nicholas Brady and
Nahum Tate, produced an official " New Version " in 1696.

There were, of course, competitors. The Scottish Psalter,
almost entirely independent of the Old Version, was published for Scotland in 1564 and remained in use until its
revision in 1650. King James I produced a version.
There was Ainsworth's Psalter of 1612 which the Pilgrim
Fathers took to America. There was William Barton's of
1644, which was unsuccessfully canvassed as a possible new
Presbyterian Psalter in 1646. There was an eccentric
volume compiled by one William Slatyer in 1643 presenting
the Old Version translated in parallel columns into Latin,
Greek, and Hebrew—which monumental frivolity he understandably gave up at Psalm 22. There were the versions
of Sandys (1637), famous because of the tunes of Henry
Lawes which first appeared in it, and there were, of course,
the few psalms of John Milton which he wrote as a youthful
exercise. And there were others with which we will not
trouble ourselves here.

Let us then see what it was that the English and Scottish Puritans used for their hymnody.   Here are a few lines of Psalm 42 in the Old Version :

Like as the hart doth pant and bray the well-springs to obtain ;
So doth my soul desire alway with thee, Lord, to remain.
My soul doth thirst, and would draw near the living God of
    might ;
O when shall I come and appear in presence of his sight ?

For I did march in good array with joyful company ;
Unto the temple was our way to praise the Lord most high ;
My soul, why art thou sad always and fretst thus in my breast ?
Trust still in God, for him to praise I hold it ever best.*

Here is the same psalm in the Scottish Psalter of 1650 :

Like as the hart for waterbrooks in thirst doth pant and bray ;
So pants my longing soul, O God, that come to thee I may.
My soul for God, the living God, doth thirst ; when shall I
    near
Unto thy countenance approach, and in God's sight appear ?

With them into God's house I went, with voice of joy and
    praise ;
Yea with the multitude that kept the solemn holy days.
O why art thou cast down, my soul ? why in me so dismay'd ?
Trust God, for I shall praise him yet, his count'nance is mine
    aid.†

Here, again, is the New Version :

As pants the hart for cooling streams
When heated in the chase,
So longs my soul, O God, for thee
And thy refreshing grace.

* Psalm 42, versified by John Hopkins, lines 1–4 and 9–12. Note that the Old Version was printed in fourteen-syllable verses with a caesura marked at the eighth syllable of each line. The rhyme at the eighth syllable was the exception, not the rule.

† Psalm 42, verses 1, 2, 5 and 6.

> For thee, my God, the living God,
>   My thirsty soul doth pine ;
> O when shall I behold thy face,
>   Thou majesty divine ?
>
> Why restless, why cast down, my soul ?
>   Hope still, and thou shalt sing
> The praise of him who is thy God
>   Thy health's eternal spring.*

Here is Sandys on Psalm 100 : †

> Man drew from man his birth ;
>   But God his noble frame
> Built of the ruddy earth,
>   Filled with celestial flame.
>   His sons we are,
>   Sheep by him led,
>   Preserved and fed
>   With tender care.

And here is the author of *Paradise Lost* on Psalm 84 :

> How lovely are thy dwellings fair !
>   O Lord of hosts, how dear
> The *pleasant* tabernacles are
>   *Where thou dost dwell so near.*
>
> There ev'n the Sparrow *freed from wrong*
>   Hath found a house of *rest,*
> The Swallow there, to lay her young
>   Hath built her *brooding* nest,

Elegance of style was not, as will be seen from these examples, a notable quality in the psalm-versions. Here and there they were rugged and even felicitous, but in the main it was sternly utility material. Puritanism revered the words of scripture and the versifiers had to keep as close as they could to the original. Sandys' " ruddy earth " was not the sort of thing the Puritan congregation wanted at

---

* Psalm 42 in *Tate and Brady. E.H.,* 367.
† *Worship Song* (1905), 190, verse 2.

all.   Milton wrote his 84th Psalm in 1648, when the struggle between Cromwell and the King was coming to its climax, and when Milton himself was as deeply involved in political controversy as he ever became ; his fighting Puritanism shows itself in the pedantry which makes him, following the lead of the Authorized Version, write in italics every word to which there is nothing to correspond in the original. Universal hymnody has gathered in from all these versions the following—

From the Scottish Psalter (1650) :

The Lord's my Shepherd (Psalm 23) *

From Tate and Brady (1696) :

As pants the hart (Psalm 42) †
Through all the changing scenes of life (Psalm 34) ‡

From Milton :

Let us with a gladsome mind (Psalm 136, 1623) §
How lovely are thy dwellings (Psalm 84, 1648) ‖
The Lord will come and not be slow (Psalms 82, 85, 86,
      1648) ¶ [15]

the Milton versions being in the first case edited, in the second abridged, and in the third selected from several psalms.

Psalmody is, we have said, Lord Ernle's province, and there is nothing to be gained by going over his ground again. Officially all the church's hymns were psalms during the sixteenth and seventeenth centuries, and during those great days of the Puritan struggles there were many occasions when the psalms had their place on the most august pages of history.   But the story of all this, as Lord Ernle tells it, is fascinating enough, and we must refer our readers to his book for the details.

The exceptions to the rule of Psalmody were very few,

* *C.P.*, 729.   † *C.P.*, 390.   ‡ *C.P.*, 46.
§ *C.P.*, 44.   ‖ *C.P.*, 257.   ¶ *C.P.*, 156.

and they fall into three groups. First there is the small
handful of non-scriptural hymns officially added to the
metrical Psalter. They are profoundly dull and of interest
only to the historical student. Second, there are the hymns
composed for private and domestic devotion. These were
either the cultured exercise of a musical circle, or the free
compositions of a devout mind for reading or singing by
such as might care to use them. Of the former kind was
a little book under the cheerful title, *Seven Sobs of a Sorrowfull
Soule for Sinne* (1583), by William Hunnys ; this consisted
of free paraphrases of the seven penitential psalms with
appropriate music. Of the other kind was Cosin's *Book
of Devotions* (1627), containing the celebrated translation
of *Veni Creator* beginning " Come, Holy Ghost, our souls
inspire ", which was one of the two hymns to find a place
in the 1662 *Book of Common Prayer*. George Wither's [16]
Hymns and Songs of the Church (1623), with music by Orlando
Gibbons, was a real attempt to enlarge on the Old Version
by adding to it a number of hymns on Scriptural and credal
subjects ; this book looked like being so much of a success
that the Company of Stationers, who had the monopoly of
printing the psalters, tried to proceed against Wither and
compel him to withdraw the book ; they saw to it, indeed,
that he received no profit from it, and the controversy
that followed was the occasion of much bitter humour from
the side of the defendant. Wither had a real gift, and
there are one or two gems in this book. His Ascension
hymn is quite admirable. This is its last verse :

> Then follow, follow on apace
> And let us not forgo
> Our Captain, till we win the place
> That he hath scaled unto ;
> And for his honour, let our voice
> A shout so hearty make,
> The heavens may at our mirth rejoice,
> And earth and hell may shake.*

* Song 57 in Wither's *Hymns and Songs*, verse 5. *C.P.*, 151, verse 3.

This merry, vigorous style is characteristic of the man, and
we find it again in " Come, O come, in pious lays " * and
" The Lord of heaven confess ",† both of which were
published in his *Hallelujah, Britain's Second Remembrancer*
(1641).

The third group of early hymns consists of sacred poetry
written without any intention of its being sung, and re-
discovered in later ages.   The most famous of such poems
is " Jerusalem, my happy home ",‡ which can be found in
full in several modern hymn books.   John Wesley was the
first to discover the possibilities of George Herbert's lyrics,
though he usually edited them rather severely ; [17] but now
we are well acquainted with four of them, " Let all the
world ", " The God of love my Shepherd is ", " King of
glory " and " Teach me, my God and King ", while some
hymn-books have experimented with one or two others.
Another discovery of Wesley's was John Austin, whose
hymn " Hark, my soul, how everything " has enjoyed considerable popularity since Wesley's day.   Modern editors
like Garrett Horder and Percy Dearmer have found hymns
in Donne, Traherne, and Henry Vaughan, and Richard
Crashaw has found a place in the latest *Westminster
Hymnal*.

Samuel Crossman and Richard Baxter are border-line
cases.   Crossman's beautiful lyrics " Jerusalem on high "
and " My song is love unknown " were written in a psalm-
metre and may have been sung in his day ; they have been
in vogue in this country for nearly a century now.   Baxter
wrote some sorry stuff when he versified the psalms—dual-
purpose verses that would go to a tune in Common or in
Long Metre, like this :

> The Lord himself my Shepherd is
>   Who doth me feed and [safely] keep.
> What can I want that's truly good,
>   While I am [one of] his own sheep ?

* *C.P.*, 4.   † *C.P.*, 744.   ‡ *E.H.*, 638.

> He makes me to lie down and rest
> In [pleasant] pastures, tender grass,
> He keeps and gently leadeth me
> Near [the sweet] streams of quietness.*

But when he was writing with no thought of being sung he made some hymns that no Christian cares to be without, notably " Lord, it belongs not to my care " † and " He wants not friends, who hath thy love ",‡ the first a priceless hymn of Christian faith, the second one of the most beautiful expressions of the doctrine of the communion of saints composed in any language.

These men wrote of the intimacies of the faith, and the seventeenth century, in its public worship, was not an age of intimacy. It was an age of loyalty, of controversy, of ferocity and bloodshed, but not of recollection. There was no thought yet of singing reflective or highly-wrought hymns in church.

The ascendancy of Puritanism, which, as any student of the matter will know, lasted long after its political over-throw at the Restoration, saw to it that there was no serious competition against the Psalter as a vehicle of public praise before 1700. Independent hymnody was a small and furtive trickle, no more. The reasons behind this were two.

In the first place, for the Puritans, and for that public opinion which Puritanism has so thoroughly informed, the words of Scripture carried an authority which they could concede to no other words. What the Bible says you may sing (they said), that you may sing, and nothing else.

In the second place, there was the more primitive and human fact that the Puritanism of seventeenth-century England found in the Psalter just what it wanted. For this force called Puritanism, in the sixteenth century a body of

---

* Psalm 23. Quoted in *Richard Baxter, Hymn Writer*, by the late Rev. W. T. Cairns, D.D., in the *Bulletin* of the Hymn Society, vol. **I**, no. 24, pages 1 ff.

† *E.H.*, 433.   ‡ *E.H.*, 401.

opinion to be found both within and outside the Established Church, had become in the seventeenth a clearly separated party, in 1612 oppressed and exiled, in 1640 openly rebellious, in 1649 victorious, and in 1662 punished ; but always fighting. What had begun as a movement to purify the English Church of Romish corruptions reinforced by a patriotism that sought to keep England secure from the molestations of foreign (and also, as it happened, Catholic) powers became in the next century a movement associated principally with opposition to the doctrine of the divine right of kings and with the abolition of tyranny.

As the fight developed into open civil war, the Puritans found the Old Testament thought-forms coming to new life. They were the children of Israel over again. Not Charles the First, but Christ the Son of David was King, and they were his army. More perhaps than any Christian body they took to themselves the covenant-faith of Abraham, the exalted monotheism of Moses, the fighting intensity of Joshua, the social purism of Nehemiah ; they revived a Levitical care about the details of conduct and a scrupulousness of a " called people " in keeping themselves uncontaminated by the surrounding society, which they found it their duty to denounce as godless. Some of the fighting was dirty, many of the fighters were men of singularly unexalted aims. We cannot altogether whitewash Cromwell and the Ironsides ; but whether the aims were high or low and the motives pure or corrupt, the Psalter, the hymnbook of the called people, with its sturdy faith and its indomitable courage and its vituperative genius met their needs exactly.

Thou, Lord, ev'n thou art he that should be fear'd ; and who is he
That may stand up before thy sight if once thou angry be ?

Surely the very wrath of man unto thy praise redounds :
Thou to the remnant of his wrath hast set restraining bounds.*

* From Psalm 76 in the *Scottish Psalter*, 1650.

When the Covenanters stood ready to join battle with Claverhouse at Drumclog and sang that 76th Psalm,[18] they may have been singing Scriptural words, but not a man there was in any doubt who was meant, on that occasion, by the kings and princes.

We must not think, of course, that the metrical psalms were sung only in the grey meeting-houses of the grey-coated Roundheads. You could hear Sternhold and Hopkins in any parish church or cathedral. But there was all the difference in the world between a worship in which a metrical psalm takes its place beside the anthem and the polyphonic canticle-setting and a worship in which no music but the unaccompanied unison of the metrical psalm was to be heard. " Sternhold and Hopkins " was published when Puritanism was still a diversified body of opinion, but the metrical psalms came into their own when, and where, Puritanism was an army on the march ; first in the kirks of John Knox's Scotland and then in the meeting-houses of Cromwell's and Milton's England.

I say this because it is in this way that psalmody can be fitted into a story that is really about hymnody. If what I have just written is true, psalmody was essentially the hymnody of wrath and war. As much as the early Lutheran hymnody, this was the song of an embattled army. It was really the intense, objective and godly wrath of the Psalter that drove the metrical psalms home and embedded them in the minds of Englishmen and Scotsmen. The great stories that are told about the psalms in metre are not told of the psalms we sing now as our favourites— the 23rd and the 84th ; they are told of the fighting psalms, the 76th and the 124th and the 68th.[19] And the story came full circle when the members of the House of Commons, on May 8th, 1945, after Mr. Churchill had announced the end of hostilities with Germany, went to their prayers at St. Margaret's, Westminster, and stood up to sing :

Now Israel may say, and that truly
    If that the Lord had not our cause maintain'd,
    If that the Lord had not our right sustain'd,
When cruel men against us furiously
Rose up in wrath to make of us their prey ;

Then certainly they had devour'd us all,
    And swallowed quick for ought that we could deem ;
    Such was their rage, as we might well esteem.
And as fierce floods before them all things drown,
So had they brought our soul to death quite down.

This association of hymnody with the zeal of the Lord's
people for righteousness and victory, here corrupt, there
regenerate, was carried over into the age of English
hymnody, and we shall hear more of it.

CHAPTER 7

Liberation

WATTS AND WESLEY

BUT there is one great limitation of psalmody, and against this limitation a powerful voice was raised in the opening years of the eighteenth century. Indeed, it was in the very year (1690) following the proclamation of the Toleration Act which called an armistice between Puritan and Anglican, that a young man called Isaac Watts protested against the dullness and crudity of expression, and the total lack of the New Testament Gospel in the contents of the Psalms. Being challenged by his father on the spot to write something better, he came back with this :

> Behold the glories of the Lamb
> Amidst his Father's throne ;
> Prepare new honours for his name
> And songs before unknown.[20]

Here was a decently educated and thoughtful young man, who knew his Authorized Version and his Milton, who was offended by the gawkiness of Barton's Psalms, and who could do better himself. But more and more as he grew older the theological question presented itself to him : why may we no longer sing to Christ as God ? When Christ makes all things new, why must our praises remain in the Old Covenant ? And so, at the age of 31, in 1705, he published his first book of hymns, *Horae Lyricae*. It contained among other things these lines :

God is a name my soul adores,
  The almighty Three, the eternal One ;
Nature and grace, with all their powers
  Confess the Infinite unknown.

Thy voice produced the sea and spheres,
  Bade the waves roar, the planets shine ;
But nothing like thyself appears
  Through all these spacious works of thine.

Who can behold the blazing light ?
  Who can approach consuming flame ?
None but thy wisdom knows thy might,
  None but thy word can speak thy name.*

And its concluding hymn has these lines :

God is in heaven, and men below ;
Be short our tunes, our words be few ;
A sacred reverence checks our songs,
And praise sits silent on our tongues.†

I quote these two hymns because, although they are not yet singing of Christ " as God " they set the key for Watts's work. Watts was the father, and also the liberator, of English hymnody, and the manner in which he used his new freedom was characteristic. He used it in order to express wonder. You might almost say that this was, on a small scale, Luther over again. Luther said, " Leave a man free to be forgiven." Watts, who was Calvinist rather than Lutheran, said, " Leave a man, leave a church free to worship and to wonder at the almighty power and grace of God." The quality which is common to all Watts's work, even the most trifling and incompetent of his verses, is this wonder, which is the essence of John Calvin's message. Let a man wonder and share his wonder with his fellows in the church—thus said Watts, and where did he get this but from the Psalms themselves ? Where is there such cosmic vision, such pure and self-denying wonder as there ?

* *C.P.*, 32, verses 1, 2 and 6.   † *C.P.*, 7, verse 5.

The Lord reigneth ; let the earth rejoice : Let the multitude of the isles be glad thereof.

Clouds and darkness are round about him ; righteousness and judgment are the habitation of his throne.

A fire goeth before him, and burneth up his enemies round about. . . .

The voice of the Lord is upon the waters : the God of glory thundereth ; the Lord is upon many waters.

The voice of the Lord is powerful. The voice of the Lord is full of majesty. . . .

Out of the depths have I cried unto thee, O Lord.

Lord, hear my voice ; let thine ears be attentive to the voice of my supplication.

If thou, Lord, shouldest mark iniquities, O Lord, who shall stand ?

But there is forgiveness with thee, that thou mayest be feared.

Watts protested against the lack of Christian Gospel in the Psalms, but he took from them that quality of wonder which made him, even at his least inspired moments, a man with the poet's touch.

The next year (1707) he completed the first edition of his *Hymns and Spiritual Songs*, containing 210 hymns and 12 doxologies ; this he enlarged in 1709 to contain 345 hymns and 15 doxologies. In 1715 he produced a little volume for children entitled *Divine Songs for Children,** and in 1719 his version of the Psalter, containing over three hundred psalm-versions in the old psalm-metres.

It is in the 1707 book that he rises to his greatest heights. It is here that we find the supreme English hymns, " When I survey the wondrous Cross ", " Give me the wings of faith ", " There is a land of pure delight ", and " Join all the glorious names ".

The *Psalms*, or, to give them their full title, *The Psalms of David Imitated in the Language of the New Testament*, have received some notice on an earlier page. Here we find that second national anthem of ours, " Our God, our help in

* See below, page 250.

ages past ", not to mention " Jesus shall reign ", " Give to
our God immortal praise " and " How pleased and bless'd
was I ".   First and last, Watts composed about 750 hymns,
and on the whole it must be said that of all our hymn writers
he scaled the greatest heights and plumbed the most bathetic
abysses.   But whether he was on the mountain-top or
whether he was floundering in the bog, he remained
wondering.

> Were the whole realm of nature mine,
>   That were a present far too small ;
> Love so amazing, so divine
>   Demands my soul, my life, my all.

How many youthful imaginations have been caught by that
word " amazing "—so blunted and cheapened by the
corrosive vulgarity of modern journalism, but here so solemn
and so august.

He finishes his great doxology to the Trinity with these
lines :

> Where reason fails with all her powers,
> There faith prevails and love adores.*

This, be it noted, was the work of the man who was to write
a textbook on Logic [21] which was to be for a hundred years
the standard work on the subject in the Universities of
England.

We shall have to come back to Watts again, but we will
leave him for the moment, having made just this one point,
that the liberation of English hymnody was, for him, the
setting free of the English Protestant Christian to wonder
and adore.

This was the august inception of the English classical
tradition of hymnody.   But it was not yet fully matured.
Before our English treasury of hymnody could achieve the
maturity and catholicity which is its great glory the Calvinist

* *C.P.*, 220, verse 4.

stream of psalmody had to be joined by the warm stream of Lutheran devotion. It is the secret of the richness of our heritage that it is equally indebted in its greatest period to both traditions.

The Calvinist stream came in through Watts, the Lutheran stream through the Wesleys. The name of that young Englishman whom we left on the steps of the Moravian chapel at Herrnhut was John Wesley, and provided that we are clear about the limitations of classical Moravianism, and say nothing to make it appear that John and Charles Wesley were in any sense disciples of Zinzendorf, we are entitled to lay plenty of emphasis on the importance to the Wesleys of their visits to the model village of Herrnhut. We must say that the evangelical faith of the Wesleys had nothing in common with the artificial introversions and enthusiasms of decadent pietism, but we can still admit that when the Wesleys heard the hymns at Herrnhut they found the answer to one of their great questions. By 1738, the year of their conversions, it had been troubling them these ten years and more. How was this zeal for the Gospel, long cherished in their hearts and nurtured in small coteries like the Holy Club at Oxford, to come to life among the English people at large? How was what might be a snobbery of cliquey spirituality to be transformed into an overflowing of love? What had gone wrong in Georgia and made John Wesley so conscious of failure? The answer, if we may say this without over-simplifying history, came when they heard the people at Herrnhut singing the German original of this:

> Thou hidden love of God, whose height,
>   Whose depth unfathomed no man knows,
> I see from far thy beauteous light,
>   Inly I sigh for thy repose.
> My heart is pained, nor can it be
> At rest till it finds rest in thee.*

* *Verborgne Gottesliebe du*, by Gerhard Tersteegen, translated by John Wesley. *C.P.*, 469.

Thus the Wesleys resolved that their people should sing their way to revival. This was how, in the new pentecostal age of religious enthusiasm, men and women should be added in thousands to the church. But the Wesleys were no pietists. The hymns of pietism provide a manual of specialized Christian devotion ; the hymns of the Wesleys provide a system of catholic Christian doctrine.[22]

But Wesleyan hymnody—by which for the moment I mean the six thousand-odd hymns of Charles and the translations of John—can be regarded as the hymnody of enthusiasm and even hysteria by the undiscerning.[23] When a modern novelist like Howard Spring (for example) wants to throw a little colour into the picture of some wretched street in Ancoats or Bradford, he makes somebody sing Charles Wesley : when George Eliot[24] wants to throw a strong, primitive religious faith into relief against high church formalism and inanity in the nineteenth century she makes somebody sing Charles Wesley. The hymnody of the Wesleys not only is, but is generally felt by English people in their bones to be, the result of enthusiasm, the negation of the institutional and formal aspects of churchmanship, and an unrivalled agent in inducing the experience of conversion. Those who see in conversion nothing but a pathological condition will see in Wesley's hymns a strong force driving people to hysteria and sensationalism.

Now the epithets we have so far applied to Wesleyan hymnody—the complimentary ones and the derogatory ones—would be consistent with the massed singing of songs that were idolatrous and pernicious. And perhaps those whom we mentioned in our first chapter as being the people who hate hymnody are thinking a good deal of Wesleyan hymnody. Those who regard the Wesleys as arch-peddlers of dope to the people are just those who heard Wesleyan hymnody in their youth in the Howard Spring atmosphere, and who therefore associate it with the seamy side of that ecclesiastical patronage which was an evil by-product of the Wesleyan revival among the working classes. Wesleyan hymnody is so powerful and so persuasive in its impact that there are many who are embarrassed by its fulsomeness and put off by its insistence on the security of the believer.

> He breaks the power of cancelled sin,
>   He sets the prisoner free,
> His blood can make the foulest clean,
>   His blood availed for me ;

these are mighty words, but there are many who say, " Why cannot the man leave himself out of the picture for once ? " There are not a few who hear through these words the insufferable superiority of the saved which has, as any minister who has worked in an industrial district in one of our great cities could tell you, brought the Gospel into disrepute among the poor.

This can be said, and is said ; but it is wrong. It is, at best, based on a perversion of Wesley, not on Wesley. There is in the hymns of the Wesleys a quality of thought and of poetic power which commands the attention, engages the affection, and in the end informs the thought and speech of men like the late George Sampson * and the late Bernard Manning.† For it happened that Methodist hymnody was founded by a man who combined with a revivalist enthusiasm two cooling and moderating disciplines—that of poetry (the poetry, be it recalled, of the most artificial of English periods), and that of Biblical theology. Therefore, where perhaps English hymnody might have been launched by some illiterate, irresponsible and opportunistic hysteric, it came in fact from a man who could throw off, at five minutes' notice, this kind of thing :

> Jesus, the first and last,
> On thee my soul is cast :
> Thou didst the work begin
> By blotting out my sin ;
> Thou wilt the root remove,
> And perfect me in love.

* See *A Century of Divine Songs* (1943).
† See *The Hymns of Wesley and Watts* (1942).

Yet when the work is done
The work is but begun :
Partaker of thy grace,
I long to see thy face ;
The first I prove below,
The last I die to know.*

That reads at first like an ecstatic sacred epigram. It is, by the way a whole hymn, unabridged. But consider how much there is in it of the Bible.

I am Alpha and Omega, the beginning and the ending, saith the Lord, which was, and which is, and which is to come (*Revelation* i. 8. Line 1).

Cast thy burden upon the Lord, and he shall sustain thee (*Psalm* lv. 22. Line 2).

He which hath begun a good thing in you will perform it unto the day of Jesus Christ (*Philippians* i. 6. Line 3).

According unto the multitude of thy tender mercies blot out my transgressions (*Psalm* li. i. Line 4).

Every plant, which my heavenly Father hath not planted, shall be rooted up (*St. Matthew* xv. 13. Line 5).

Till we all come in the unity of the faith and of the knowledge of the Son of God, unto a perfect man, unto the measure of the stature of the fulness of Christ (*Ephesians* iv. 13. Line 6).

I have finished the work which thou gavest me to do. (*St. John* xvii. 4. Line 7).

(Line 8 is *Philippians* i. 6 again.)

Ye are all partakers of my grace (*Philippians* i. 7) with who am . . . a partaker of the glory that shall be revealed (*I Peter* v. i. Line 9).

They shall see his face, and his name shall be in their foreheads (*Revelation* xii. 4. Line 10).

Now we see as in a glass darkly ; but then face to face ; now I know in part, but then shall I know even as also I am known. (*I Corinthians* xiii. 12. Lines 11–12).

So in twelve lines we have Old Testament, Epistle and Gospel. Sometimes we have interpretation, sometimes only the verbal echo of the Scriptures. But the discipline of the

* *C.P.*, 764.

Bible is always there.   And then, to cool what might become the exuberant ardour of the religious feeling, there are
the purely artificial disciplines of eighteenth-century poetry,
the play on words, the neat antithesis, the careful rhyme.
The hymnody of the Wesleys, whether it was in this exquisitely simple vein or whether it was the majestic vision of
some of the longer and great hymns, is always intellectually
disciplined, always anchored down to Christian doctrine,
and always leads the believer away from himself in the end
to the communion of saints and the eternal Life.   Consider
" Jesu, lover of my soul ", " Love divine, all loves excelling ",
and " O thou who camest from above " * if you would
find a combination of rich scriptural allusion, sound and
catholic doctrine, and a persuasiveness of expression that
conceals both.   Consider, above all, that masterpiece of
condensed theology, " Hark, the herald angels sing " :

> Veiled in flesh the Godhead see,
> Hail the incarnate Deity !
> Pleased as man with man to dwell,
> Jesus, our Immanuel. . . .
>
> Mild he lays his glory by,
> Born that man no more may die ;
> Born to raise the sons of earth,
> Born to give them second birth.

One mystery after another rolls glibly off your tongue, and
you do not realize what you are singing ; you do not realize
it all at once, but one day you do.   That is just what
Wesley hoped for.   These hymns were composed in order
that the men and women whom Hogarth depicted in his
terrible pictures might sing their way not only into experience but also into knowledge ; that the cultured might have
their culture baptized and the ignorant might be led into
truth by the gentle hand of melody and rhyme.   This
disciplined fervour was what made it possible for English

* *E.H.*, 414, 437, and 343.

hymnody to have a classical age before it fell into corruption and decay.

The two streams, then, are the (ultimately) Calvinist and the (ultimately) Lutheran, coming through Watts and Wesley. Perhaps if we place two Passiontide hymns side by side we shall effectively show how the same august subject appeared to the two masters, and in what way their techniques were precisely complementary. Here is Watts :

> Alas, and did my Saviour bleed !
> And did my Sovereign die ?
> Would he devote that sacred head
> For such a worm as I ?
>
> Was it for crimes that I had done
> He groan'd upon the tree ?
> Amazing pity ! grace unknown !
> And love beyond degree !
>
> Well might the sun in darkness hide
> And shut his glories in,
> When God, the mighty Maker, died
> For man, the creature's, sin.
>
> Thus might I hide my blushing face,
> While his dear cross appears ;
> Dissolve my heart in thankfulness,
> And melt my eyes to tears.
>
> But drops of grief can ne'er repay
> The debt of love I owe ;
> Here, Lord, I give myself away ;
> 'Tis all that I can do.*

And here is Wesley :

> O Love divine, what hast thou done ?
> The immortal God hath died for me !
> The Father's co-eternal Son
> Bore all my sins upon the tree ;
> The immortal God for me hath died !
> My Lord, my Love is crucified.

* *Hymns and Spiritual Songs*, 1707, book II, no. 9, omitting verse 2 (bracketed in the original). *C.P.*, 130.

Behold him, all ye that pass by,
   The bleeding Prince of life and peace !
Come, sinners, see your Maker die,
   And say, was ever grief like his ?
Come, feel with me his blood applied :
My Lord, my Love, is crucified.

Is crucified for me and you,
   To bring us rebels back to God :
Believe, believe the record true,
   Ye all are bought with Jesu's blood.
Pardon for all flows from his side :
My Lord, my Love is crucified.

Then let us sit beneath his Cross,
   And gladly catch the healing stream,
All things for him account but loss,
   And give up all our hearts to him ;
Of nothing think or speak beside,
My Lord, my Love, is crucified.*

Both men are stricken and dumbfounded by the Crucifixion ;
both are saying the same thing—total surrender by God
demands as its response total surrender from his creatures.
But how differently they say it.   Watts calls all nature to
share his grief ; his mind worries all the time at the hideous
paradox of it all.   If such a lie could come to life as that the
Maker should die for the creature, then the sun cannot dare
to shine on the scene.   His surrender is abject, it is the final
act of a divine tragedy.   " 'Tis all that I can do."   For
Wesley the feeling uppermost is gratitude.   " My Love is
crucified " echoes an ancient Greek father,[25] and Wesley,
like the Greek Christians, never lets his hearer's *mind* relax
for an instant.   What does this mean for us ? he says.   In
his third verse he becomes didactic—this is for me, *and for
you*.   " Then let us sit beneath the cross, and gladly catch
the healing stream "—the end is the end of Divine Comedy :
" . . . Who for the *joy* that was set before him endured the
Cross, despising the shame."   Wesley is emotional—he uses

* *Methodist Hymn Book*, 186.

that " Is it nothing to you ? " phrase from Lamentations, which Watts never uses.   But all the time he is teaching because he believes that the truth will make men free and joyful.

And you noticed, of course, the worm in Watts's hymn ? Worms are not things of beauty, and enough jokes have been made about their appearance in hymns for us to by-pass that aspect of them here.   But the worm is a familiar part of Watts's scenery.   Watts, the cultured Calvinist, is conscious of the magnificence and grandeur of God, and of man's insignificance and smallness—and the organized magnificence of the physical universe in Watts's day was still something of a new discovery.   Wesley, seeing the world of Hogarth, sees man not as a puny reptile but as an uncontrolled and rebellious giant, the multitude of whose sins is yet unable to defeat the love of God.

More generally, Watts's hymns were designed to be sung in church and were inspired in church ;   their infinite capacity for bathos was the result of his instinctively working in church metres and in language which would not offend the congregations of Above Bar, Southampton, and Mark Lane, London.   Wesley's hymns were written for private devotion and for the enormous open-air congregations to which he and his brother ministered ;   so for the Wesleys the church discipline was tempered by the educated devotional tradition of the Holy Club on the one hand and the enthusiasm of mass-preaching on the other.   Watts's people would have been impatient of anything that cost them much trouble in understanding the words or learning the tunes. Wesley's people were, in the one context, educated enough to pick up new metres and tunes, and in the other, enthusiastic enough to sing anything that met their fervid emotional needs.

We have, therefore, established Watts as the father of the liturgical hymn and Wesley as the father of the enthusiastic or devotional hymn in our language.   In the next two generations we shall see the two traditions sometimes merging and sometimes running independently.   How this came to pass will serve for a new chapter.

CHAPTER 8

Victory

THE GREAT CENTURY, 1750–1850

THESE two traditions—the " church " tradition and the devotional tradition, we see carried on in the later years of the eighteenth century. Perhaps one of the outstanding examples of both is in the Olney Hymns, a book written, according to the custom of local hymn-books still prevailing at the time, for the parish church of Olney and published in 1779. The curate of Olney was John Newton,[26] whose romantic conversion is one of the great stories of our subject. Newton had been a sailor ; at one time he had been little less than a pirate, and he had assisted in the evil traffic of slave-dealing. His first thirty years were dark and unedifying in the extreme, but two things brought him to see a great vision of the love of Christ—the love and constancy of his fiancée, Miss Mary Catlett, and Thomas à Kempis' *Imitation of Christ*. Newton knew what it was to be shipwrecked and deserted and desperate ; and it was after a storm at sea that had made him sure that he would never see land or home again, but from which he was delivered, that he turned to the Gospel. His conversion occurred some years before he abandoned the business of slave-trafficking by sea ; and it is not surprising that when he sought ordination in the Church of England he had difficulty in finding a bishop who would look at him. In the end he was ordained and given the perpetual curacy of Olney, where he worked devotedly for seventeen years until, in 1781 at the age of 56, he was presented to the rectory of St. Mary Woolnoth, in London. His trusted assistant at Olney was William

Cowper, the poet, and it was Cowper's genius for poetry that gave Newton the idea of compiling a new hymn-book for the prayer-meeting at Olney ; not, be it noted, for the church services, but for a weeknight evangelical meeting which he had started and which met with such great success that they had to move from the small church room to the great room in the " Great House "—the manor of Olney.

Cowper started on his task, and wrote 68 hymns of surpassing excellence, a number of which we all know and love (" God moves in a mysterious way ", " Hark, my soul, it is the Lord ", " Sometimes a light surprises " and " O for a closer walk with God " come immediately to the mind). But Cowper was overtaken at this point by one of his periods of mental darkness, and Newton had to take up the tale himself. Newton with characteristic industry and abandon wrote 280 hymns to complete the book.[27]

Now in this combination you might say that Newton, though he comes second in time, was the Watts and Cowper the Wesley. Newton, energetic, spirited, indomitable, sure of conversion and implacably zealous for souls, was the typical Calvinist Anglican of the time. He was bursting with religious experience and could always spare time to help anybody. It was in his Calvinism that he was like Watts ; for he was the sort of person who is happy with Calvinism—the extrovert, the man of action. He wrote his hymns because there was nobody else to write them. They never rise to Watts's heights nor sink to his depths ; some of them come off magnificently, most of them are in a high degree tedious and didactic. He thought of the hymns as a means of making the church people sing and of engraving the truth of the Gospel on their hearts. He hacked them out of commonplace material and never wrote a line of verse apart from them.

Cowper was as different from this as he could be. He was never sure of his salvation ; he could remember no conversion ; he had lived a sheltered, tentative life, and his soul was full of subtlety and hesitation. His gifts were

never the social gifts ; he never had spiritual energy to spare
—he had not enough to keep himself going for long.   His
hymns are hymns of passionate Christian experience, the
hymns of the introvert.   " God moves in a mysterious way "
is the only outward-looking hymn he ever wrote, the only
hymn of simple devotion.   He wrote didactically here and
there, but what we know and revere him for is his ministry
to the hesitating and sensitive Christian soul.   He was
essentially a solitary person, and although he was vastly, and
tragically, influenced by Newton's Calvinism, it is a
question whether he would have retained his sanity if he
had been supported instead by Wesley's assurance of salvation.   The following is a typical hymn of Cowper which
Newton could never have written :

> The Lord will happiness divine
>   On contrite hearts bestow ;
> Then tell me, gracious Lord, is mine
>   A contrite heart or no ?
>
> I hear, but seem to hear in vain,
>   Insensible as steel ;
> If aught is felt, 'tis only pain
>   To find I cannot feel.*

Let us compare Newton and Cowper on a similar theme, if
we can ; Newton, of course, set himself to write material
that would be complementary to Cowper's ; but here and
there they overlap.   Here, then, is Newton, the sailor-
parson, singing of redemption :

> Begone, unbelief, my saviour is near
> And for my relief will surely appear.
> By prayer let me wrestle and he will perform ;
> With Christ in the vessel I smile at the storm.
> His love in time past forbids me to think
> He'll leave me at last in trouble to sink :
> Each sweet Ebenezer I have in review
> Confirms his good pleasure to help me quite through.†

* *Olney Hymns*, 9 (Poetical Works of Cowper), verses 1 and 2.
† *Olney Hymns. C.P.*, 396, verses 1 and 3.

With this rugged confidence, contrast this of Cowper :

> The billows swell, the winds are high,
> Clouds overcast my wintry sky ;
> Out of the depths to thee I call—
> My fears are great, my strength is small.
> Though tempest-toss'd and half a wreck,
> My Saviour through the floods I seek ;
> Let neither winds nor stormy main
> Force back my shatter'd bark again.*

We need say no more here about Newton and Cowper, except to remind the reader of those great and joyful hymns of Newton that are part of every protestant Christian's vocabulary—" How sweet the name of Jesus sounds ", " Glorious things of thee are spoken ", and " Come, my soul, thy suit prepare ".†

I say that Cowper was the Wesley and Newton the Watts of this combination, then, not wishing to find any correspondences between the temperaments of the two pairs, but looking only to the essential gregariousness of Newton's outlook and the essential solitariness of Cowper's experience, and to the fact that Newton at his best was always a writer for the church, while Cowper excelled in the hymn of personal devotion.

The congregational tradition of hymns written for the settled church rather than for revival or for personal devotion was really carried to its conclusion, as might be expected, in the Church of England. Watts was followed in Independency by Philip Doddridge, of whom more in a moment ; Wesley was followed within his own fold by Cennick and Madan. The overflowing of the streams of militant Calvinism and of Methodism into the Anglican Church brought in the Olney hymnists and such lesser writers as Hart and Kelly. But of these, and of that far more excellent genius, James Montgomery, I want to say more in another place. For the present we shall follow this story of the development

---

* *Olney Hymns* (Cowper), 37.   † *E.H.*, 405, 393 and 377.

of devotional and liturgical hymnody in the Church of England.

During the whole of the eighteenth century and the first years of the nineteenth, hymn-singing was an unofficial, and, if anybody cared to press the point, an illegal activity in the Church of England. The rubrics provided for canticles, psalms, and anthems, but not for hymns in the services of public worship appointed in the Book of Common Prayer. On the whole, we may say that there were three exceptions to this strict rule which had begun to appear in the Church of England.

The first, and not unimportant, was the fact that the " Psalms " in use in the Church of England selections were tending more and more to be those of Isaac Watts and James Merrick [28] than of the Old or the New Versions. This meant that the church was already singing, for instance, " Jesus shall reign " and " Sweet is the work, my God, my King ". It had therefore abandoned literal adherence to Scripture in favour of that wide and liberal interpretation of the Psalter " In the language of the New Testament " which was Watts's, and to a less extent Merrick's, technique. This was an important concession.

Then, of course, there was the impact of the Methodists. John and Charles Wesley lived and died ordained ministers of the Church of England with no thought of founding a sect and every thought of reviving the Church of England. Many of their most able followers were similarly Anglican vicars, of whom the most celebrated was Martin Madan. Madan produced in 1760 a selection of psalms and hymns which included a number of hymns of Watts, Wesley, and Joseph Hart. Two or three other hymn-books appeared in the second half of the eighteenth century, including the *Olney Hymns* and two collections edited by Toplady (the author of " Rock of Ages "). This was all very illegal, but there were plenty of congregations who were prepared not to expose the offence.

I think that, thirdly, we must also take into account the

H.H.L.

G

fact that extra-liturgical services were becoming not only
common in the Church of England but were in fact the
source of all its evangelical power. Here again we cite the
Olney Hymns, which were compiled for the prayer-meeting.
The Wesleys always regarded their evangelical services as
extra-liturgical services of the Church of England ; [29]
though the bishops took a different view. It was with this
sort of worship, not with Mattins and Evensong, that hymn-
singing was associated in the Church of England during the
eighteenth century.

Another not inconsiderable force in this direction was the
services in the charity-hospitals in London and elsewhere,
which, under the guidance of zealous evangelical ministers
and musicians, were taking the lead in propagating
hymnody, and which were the source of several notable
hymns and tunes of which the most famous is " Praise the
Lord, ye heavens adore him ", which introduced Haydn's
tune AUSTRIA to this country just about the turn of the
century. [30]

But although music-books came out rapidly during the
second half of the eighteenth century, only a few hymn-
books appeared. It is the more surprising, therefore, that
between 1801 and 1820 no fewer than forty-two books of
hymns were published for use in Anglican churches up and
down the country.* This indicated a sharp rise in the
people's interest in hymnody, and this interest was not
uniformly friendly. There were some conservative spirits
who thought it a menace, and who began asking questions
about its legality.

The matter came to a head in the church of St. Paul,
Sheffield, whose vicar, Thomas Cotterill, along with another
prominent citizen named James Montgomery, had been
giving a strong lead in favour of hymnody. In 1819
Cotterill produced, for the use of his church, the eighth
edition of his *Selection of Psalms and Hymns*. The congregation regarded this as an intolerable imposition, and

* Julian's *Dictionary of Hymnology*, pages 331-43.

pressed the matter to a legal decision in the Diocesan Court at York. This brought into the story one of the great heroes of English hymnody, Archbishop Vernon Harcourt. The archbishop, before the trial came to a hearing, approached the vicar of St. Paul's, Sheffield, with a proposition in the following terms. " Withdraw that eighth edition and compile a ninth. Send it to me and undertake to cut out every hymn which I do not officially sanction. Dedicate the book to me. Then we have them ! " This Cotterill gratefully did, and the ninth edition was published in 1820. The archbishop's action amounted to a reversal of the legal prohibition of hymns in the Church of England, and opened the way for the great flowering of anglican hymnody in the nineteenth century.

Once the singing of hymns in the services prescribed by the Book of Common Prayer was thus legalized, Anglican hymn-writers took full advantage of their opportunity. And it was natural that they should fairly soon see the propriety of arranging their hymn-books, not haphazard as the early collections were arranged, nor along the lines of theological experience as were the Wesleyan books, but as companions to the Book of Common Prayer. Thus the stream of liturgical hymnody began to flow in full spate in the Church of England, and it was not long before the distinguished priests and prelates of the Church began to take the lead in writing hymns of this sort. I think here not so much of Bishop Heber, that hero and missionary, nor of the Irish Bishop Mant nor of Sir Robert Grant, all of whom made notable contributions which we shall have to notice ; but rather of Bishops How of Wakefield and Wordsworth of Lincoln and those translators who, under the impact of the Oxford Movement, with its new reverence for history and especially for the Middle Ages, translated for English singers many of the medieval office hymns—Caswall, Chandler, Jackson Mason, and J. M. Neale. From this liturgical movement in hymnody came, on the one hand, such excellent things as Wordsworth's " Hark, the sound of

holy voices " and How's " For all the saints ", and on the
other, those rather creaky translations of Ambrosian hymns
which have been so pungently criticized by the late Bernard
Manning as " fusty as a second-hand Lewis and Short ".[31]
Hymns Ancient and Modern [32] (1860) was the crown of this
movement, and in the later editions of that work—even to
the latest of 1950—we can see on the one side a faithful
following of the Book of Common Prayer and on the other
a rather hectic scramble by translators and authors to see
that no saint and no liturgical office is left without a hymn,
however pointless the hymn may in fact be.

Robert Bridges in his *Yattendon Hymnal* did something
towards saving English hymnody from this particular vice
of fustiness and " padding ", and the *English Hymnal* (1906)
produced many new translations of the ancient hymns, some
of them greatly improved, from the hands of such scholars
as R. M. Pope, Charles Bigg, and Percy Dearmer. *Songs
of Praise*, contemptuous of the High Church ideals to a large
degree, was none the less particular enough about the red-
letter saints to produce a number of brand-new hymns for
their festivals, some of which were singularly eccentric but
few of which were dull. One way and another we can
trace the efforts of the Church of England to supply the
needs of liturgy and also of a rising general culture by
examining the treatment, say, of the Office of Terce or of
some particular saint from the *Hymnal Noted* of 1852 to the
1950 *Hymns Ancient and Modern*. We counsel the reader to
do this with that enigmatic saint, Bartholomew, about
whom our knowledge is proverbially dim. If he looks at the
Saint Bartholomew hymns in the standard (1875 to 1916)
Hymns Ancient and Modern (419), in the *English Hymnal* (239),
in *Songs of Praise* (1931 edition, 236), and in the latest (1950)
Hymns Ancient and Modern (562), he will see how ignorance
is cloaked, always decently, by ponderousness, by ingenuity,*
by a neo-Anglican playfulness, and by a desperate candour.

All this has come a long way from Isaac Watts. The only

* The *English Hymnal* effort is an acrostic.

thing that Victorian hymnody of the Church of England has in common with his work is that it was designed for use inside and not outside the services of the Church. You might say that both Watts and the editors of *Hymns Ancient and Modern* saw a gap to be filled and conscientiously and laboriously filled it ; but it was one thing to equate, as Watts did, the gap with the whole of the Gospel, and another to make a sort of crossword-puzzle frame of the church's year and fill up the squares with *ad hoc* hymns. Watts ran to the bathos of exuberance and over-writing ; *Hymns Ancient and Modern* ran to the bathos of inanity. And so we come in the end to that delectable parody which Mr. Osbert Lancaster introduces into his *Drayneflete Revealed*, and which we cannot resist quoting here.

Hardly less illustrious, however, was Dr. Palinure, the celebrated Bishop of Horizon and the Isles. Born of humble Protestant stock on Lord Littlehampton's Irish estates of Spanielstown, his early promise soon attracted his Lordship's notice, and at his expense he was able to go first to Trinity College, Dublin, and later to Oxford. On leaving the University he became Personal Chaplain to his patron, who presented him with the living of Drayneflete at the first opportunity ; to this were added in the course of time the livings of Belching-cum-Sowerby, Blicester, Great Danehampton, Toad-in-the-Wold, St. Ursula-inside-the-Wardrobe and Stobdalkin in Co. Meath. As the years passed and his fame grew he became Canon of Christ Church, Archdeacon of Bloomsbury, Dean of Spanielstown, Chaplain-out-of-the-Ordinary to His Majesty, and finally Bishop of Horizon and the Isles. 'Today these distinctions are largely forgotten, but he lives in the memory of all as the author of that exquisite hymn (No. 882, Hymns Ancient and Modern) which starts :

> How little, Lord, we need below
> As through this vale of tears we go.
> He doth all worldly goods despise.
> Who striveth for a heavenly prize.*

* Osbert Lancaster, *Drayneflete Revealed*, John Murray, 1949, page 29. See below, page 299.

That, we feel, is the last word on the incredible facility and triteness of many of the hymns which appeared under this liturgical movement in hymnody.

It was not all dead wood, however. Wordsworth gave us " Gracious Spirit, Holy Ghost ", " O Day of rest and gladness ", " See, the Conqueror mounts in triumph ", and How, " It is a thing most wonderful " and " To thee, our God, we fly ". One of the happiest of this group, who filled gaps with something much better than paper-packing, was John Ellerton, who wrote " The day thou gavest ", " Saviour, again to thy dear name " and " O Strength and Stay " for evening, " Behold us, Lord, a little space ", an admirable and almost unique hymn for midday. He also has the distinction of having written two saints'-day hymns of high quality that really have something to say, " We sing the glorious conquest " * (St. Paul) and " O Son of God, our captain of salvation " † (St. Barnabas).

So much for the liturgical tradition. The devotional tradition of the Wesleys similarly gathered strength during the nineteenth century, and this in three ways.

First, there are the hymns of personal experience contributed by all manner of persons within and outside the Church of England. They find their zenith in H. F. Lyte's " Abide with me " and " Praise, my soul ". Lyte was an obscure country curate who has no claim to fame beyond his saintly character and a handful of hymns. But " Abide with me " ranks with the classics in every sense, and it has successfully stood up to harder working than perhaps any hymn in the language. This was written in 1847 [33]; before that time we have a long line of hymn-writers of experience, beginning perhaps with the broken ecstasies of Joseph Hart the Calvinist (1712–68) and Augustus Toplady (1740–78). John Keble's best-seller, *The Christian Year* (1827), was essentially a book of private devotion ; he published it only to please his father, but the proceeds from its sales enabled him to restore completely the fabric of his parish church at

* *Hymns A. & M.*, 406/541. † *Hymns A. & M.*, 413/550.

Hursley, Hampshire. This book yielded " There is a book, who runs may read " and two verses of " Blest are the pure in heart ". In the same succession stand Faber's hymns of Catholic devotion, " My God, how wonderful thou art " and " Workman of God, O lose not heart ", Newman's immortal " Lead, kindly Light ", J. E. Bode's " O Jesus, I have promised " written for his children's confirmation, and Anstice's " O Lord, how happy should we be ". These are all distinguished hymns of personal devotion, and behind them stand many others, usually of less merit.

The second division is the hymns of medieval devotion translated by Englishmen of the nineteenth century, the most notable of whom are Caswall, Neale and Littledale. Caswall has given us at least two red-hot hymns of this kind, " To Christ, the Prince of peace " and " Glory be to Jesus ", not to mention his exquisite paraphrase " Jesus, the very thought of thee ". Neale's translations were, as we have said, chiefly liturgical, but " Jerusalem the golden " and the other selections from his *Rhythm of St. Bernard of Morlaix* are more of the devotional kind. Littledale produced a number of undistinguished translations and one of priceless beauty, " Come down, O Love divine ",* from the Italian of Bianco of Siena. The best of these translations contributed much to the richness of Christian devotion in this period.

The third class of devotional hymns, perhaps artificially thus segregated, is the remarkable contribution of Christian women from Anne Steele (1716–78) to Christina Rossetti (1830–94). Of these I shall write later, and only say here that the quality of some of these hymns, such as Anne Steele's " Father, whate'er of earthly bliss ", Harriet Auber's " Our blest Redeemer ", Charlotte Elliott's " Just as I am ", Anna Laetitia Waring's " In heavenly love abiding ", Frances Havergal's " Lord, speak to me, that I may speak ", and Christina Rossetti's " None other Lamb ", places beyond question the judgment that the intimacies of devotion are

* *E.H.*, 152.

more movingly expressed during the whole of this period
by the women than by the men.

Let us, then, in conclusion, record what we may regard
as the crowning achievements of these two traditions.   The
liturgical tradition, we may judge, never rose higher than it
does in Dean Milman's glorious hymn for Palm Sunday :

> Ride on, ride on in majesty !
> Hark ! all the tribes " Hosanna " cry !
> Thy humble beast pursues his road
> With palms and scattered garments strewed.*

Here is a hymn by Thomas Haweis, an Anglican clergyman
with strong Methodist sympathies who was one of the
founders of the London Missionary Society.   He wrote the
tune RICHMOND (" City of God ") for these words, and here
are some of them in his original version :

> O thou from whom all goodness flows
>   I lift my heart to thee ;
> In all my sorrows, conflicts, woes,
>   Dear Lord, remember me.
>
> Temptations sore obstruct my way
>   And ills I cannot flee ;
> O give me strength, Lord, as my day ;
>   For good remember me.
>
> If on my face for thy dear name
>   Shame and reproaches be,
> All hail, reproach, and welcome shame
>   If thou remember me.[34]

As an example of what the Christian women of the nineteenth century could rise to, we cannot forbear quoting
a few verses of this great song of faith :

> The sands of time are sinking,
>   The dawn of heaven breaks ;
> The summer morn I've sighed for,
>   The fair sweet morn awakes ;

* E.H., 620.

Dark, dark hath been the midnight,
  But dayspring is at hand,
And glory, glory dwelleth
  In Immanuel's land.

The King there, in his beauty,
  Without a veil is seen ;
It were a well-spent journey
  Though seven deaths lay between ;
The Lamb with his fair army
  Doth on Mount Zion stand,
And glory, glory dwelleth
  In Immanuel's land.

The bride eyes not her garment
  But her dear bridegroom's face ;
I will not gaze at glory,
  But on my King of grace,
Not on the crown he giveth,
  But on his piercèd hand ;
The Lamb is all the glory
  Of Immanuel's land.[35]

CHAPTER 9

Wrath and Praise

I. THE CHURCH EMBODIED

I WISH now to go back to the days of Isaac Watts's youth and draw out another strand from our heritage of psalmody. At the end of Chapter 6 we said that English psalmody was, in its most characteristic moments, the hymnody not of liturgy or of personal devotion but of wrath and war. We shall go far astray if we think that the hymnody of the settled church and the songs of individual Christian piety were the only legacy left us by the psalmists and by Watts and Wesley. The church's war has been continuous, now on one front and now on another, and war, since the days of the Arians, has made people sing.

Let us consider then the campaign of the Church militant as it was being waged in the eighteenth and nineteenth centuries. We shall find that the terrain is importantly different from that of the seventeenth century. But we shall find a strain of sacred invective running through all our hymnody which we can trace straight back to the Covenanters.

We need only deal here with such of the church's controversies as gave rise to hymnody, and we can therefore gratefully pass by the barren theological controversies of the early eighteenth century in which Watts himself was not too creditably engaged. Nobody wanted to sing about that, and so we can leave it.

Watts, indeed, is not a great source for hymns of war and passion. His campaign is still of the seventeenth-century pattern. The enemies of Christ are the Pope and the Turk, and he belabours them with some force and without much grace. We have in his works, and in those of his later contemporaries, a number of hymns for the Fifth of November and a good deal of slanging of the papists and the infidels. Except in his invention of hymnody, Watts was for his day remarkably old-fashioned and conservative.

But we have already hinted at the point of keenest controversy in dealing with the Wesleys. They fought on two fronts, it will be recalled—the doctrinal and the social. Of the doctrinal controversy with Calvinism we shall say something in a moment, but for the present, let the reader kindly recall the pictures of Hogarth. Now as a matter of fact there is not much in Wesley about all this. The Wesleys wanted their people to sing of Christ, not of the world's darkness. But there is a good deal in an older writer whose august name we have as yet scarcely mentioned—Philip Doddridge. We justify a neglect of him which will have surprised a learned reader by asserting, what you would not guess from the few hymns of Doddridge's which are at all well known at present, that his real contribution to our story was his hymns on the social applications of the Gospel ; the hymns of wrath aroused by contemplation of the hideous miseries of the English poor and the ignorance of the Gospel in foreign lands.

Philip Doddridge (1702–51) was Congregational minister at Castle Hill Independent Chapel in Northampton, and was the founder and director of an academy associated with that church for the training of young nonconformists who were refused, because of their nonconformity, admission to the English universities. He was a man of deep learning and simple piety who in his short life made an ineffaceable impression on English Christianity. He is the author, of course, of " O God of Bethel " (which we know in a considerably altered version), " Hark, the glad sound, the Saviour comes ", and " Ye servants of the Lord ". He wrote in all about 370 hymns, which were published after his death by his friend Job Orton (1755), who diligently collected and edited them from Doddridge's scattered manuscripts. He wrote them all to be sung after the sermon in his church, and prefixed his text to each hymn. His technique, diction and theology he borrows from Watts ; but his subject-matter shows that he was, unlike Watts, in the heat of the battle all the time. Like Watts, he finds his true pleasure in praising, and many of his hymns are on the theme of God's Providence. He has none of Watts's poetry, and is usually far more impersonal than Watts had been. But in his concern for social necessities he goes far beyond his distinguished predecessor, and when he is dealing with these things he takes fire. Even in " Hark, the glad sound " you have it—

> He comes, the broken heart to bind,
> The bleeding soul to cure,
> And with the treasures of his grace
> To enrich the humble poor.*

The whole hymn is a close paraphrase of the quotation of *Isaiah* lxi. in *St. Luke* iv. : but all the time he insists on its social message. The hymn is entitled, not, as in most modern hymn-books, " Advent ", but " Christ's Message ". He never meant it to be confined to the season of Advent.

Here are two verses from his hymn on " The Good Samaritan." (*Luke* x. 30–37):

> Father of mercies, send thy grace
> All-powerful from above
> To form in our obedient souls
> The image of thy love.
>
> When the most helpless Sons of Grief
> In low distress are laid,
> Soft be our hearts their Pains to feel,
> And swift our hands to aid.†

The most beautiful of all his hymns on this subject, which we conjure the reader to look up in full at the reference, ends with this verse :

* *Hymns* (1755), 203. *E.H.* 6, verse 3.
† *Hymns* (1755), 205, verses 1 and 3.

Thy face with reverence and with love
I in thy poor would see ;
O let me rather beg my bread
Than hold it back from thee ! *

For his missionary zeal, consider these lines :

Why then, almighty Saviour, why
Do wretched souls in millions die ?
While wide th' infernal tyrant reigns
O'er spacious realms in ponderous chains.

Awake, all-conquering arm, awake,
And hell's extensive empire shake ;
Assert the honours of thy throne,
And call this ruined world thine own.†

It is not difficult to see through the quaint language to the passion of this. This is the first missionary hymnody, and it antedates by two generations the era of triumphant missionary expansion.

We said that Wesley is not often in this mood ; but we find it memorably here and there :

Arm of the Lord, awake, awake !
Thine own immortal strength put on :
With terror clothed, hell's kingdom shake,
And cast thy foes with fury down.‡

and

" Come, Lord ! " thy glorious Spirit cries ;
And souls beneath the altar groan :
" Come, Lord ! " the bride on earth replies ;
And perfect all our souls in one.§

* *Ib.*, 188. *C.P.*, 669, verse 5.

† *Hymns* (1755), 121, verses 2 and 4. Compare *C.P.*, 319, " Triumphant Sion ".

‡ *Methodist Hymn Book*, 486, verse 1. *C.P.*, 499 (here slightly altered). This hymn was sung at the opening of the Wesleys' New Room at Bristol in 1739 ; it clearly refers to the whole dominion of Satan, not only to the necessity of foreign missions.

§ *Methodist Hymn Book*, 814, verse 2. The reference is to *Revelation* xxii. 17.

But in the latest (1933) edition of the *Methodist Hymn Book*, of 22 hymns in the Missionary section only three are by Wesley (our first quotation is not one of them), and they are chiefly aspiring rather than, in Doddridge's sense, wrathful.

Another early and distinguished writer of hymns for the Church Militant was William Williams of Pantycelyn. We know him best for " Guide me, O thou great Jehovah " and his best-known missionary hymn is " O'er those gloomy hills of darkness ".* He is ecstatic rather than angry, but one of his less-known hymns has this powerful verse :

> Free my soul from sin's foul bondage :
> Hasten now the glorious dawn ;
> Break proud Babel's gates in sunder ;
> Let the massive bolts be drawn.†

But in his wrath and passion for social righteousness and for missionary extension, Doddridge was well before his time. It is not until the nineteenth century that we find more hymns comparable with his. Chartism and Christian Socialism brought a ripe harvest in hymns of social endeavour, of which the first, and perhaps the greatest of all, was Ebenezer Elliott's great song beginning

> When wilt thou save the people ?
> O God of mercy, when ?
> Not kings and lords, but nations ;
>   Not thrones and crowns, but men !
> Flowers of thy heart, O God, are they ;
> Let them not pass like weeds away,
> Their heritage a sunless day,
>   God save the people ! ‡

And so on, to that last impassioned cry in the third verse—

> The people, Lord, the people !

* *C.P.*, 320.
† *Church Hymnary* (1927), 384, verse 2, translation by William Howells.
‡ *C.P.*, 567. Here as in most modern books the third line of the first verse is altered to " The people, Lord, the people ".

These lines, later to be magnificently set to music by Josiah Booth, were the battle-cry of the " hungry forties ", and we still sing them.   I remember them missing fire only once, when a minister, enthusiastic in the social implications of the Gospel, chose it on the Sunday following the tragic abdication of King Edward VIII.   " Not kings and lords " rang falsely then—and it is the weakness of these battle-songs that they may be carried by their passion beyond the bounds of catholicity, and be found in unguarded moments to proclaim sectionalism and injustice.

Charles Kingsley took up the tale manfully in some of his religious poems, not all of which he ever expected to hear sung.   His hymn for hospitals : " From thee all skill and science flow " is widely loved, and so it should be, as one of the few successful hymns that mention science at all.   This, however, is obviously a *pièce d'occasion* :

> Gather you, gather you, angels of God—
>   Freedom and mercy and truth ;
> Come, for the earth is grown coward and old,
>   Come down and renew us her youth,
> Wisdom and sacrifice, daring and love
> Haste to the battlefield, stoop from above
>   To the day of the Lord at hand.
>
> Gather you, gather you, hounds of hell,
>   Famine and plague and war ;
> Idleness, bigotry, cant and misrule,
>   Gather and fall in the snare !
> Hireling and Mammonite, bigot and knave,
> Crawl to the battlefield, sneak to your grave,
>   In the day of the Lord at hand.* 36

More modern times have given us some great hymns of wrath in this same strain.   One of them, surely, is Rudyard

---

* From *Andromeda and Other Poems* (1858) in the group called " Poems connected with 1848–9 " (the year of Revolutions).   It appears as a hymn at *Songs of Praise* (1931), 310.   We quote the second and third verses, the third being modestly starred in that hymn-book.

Kipling's *Recessional*, which, though dealing with another subject, has all the passion and all the shakiness of " When wilt thou save the people ". Kipling, the poet of imperialism, asked to write something for the Diamond Jubilee of Queen Victoria in 1897, produced this majestic song of national penitence. The man whom everybody connected with the lines " East is East and West is West ", wrongly attributing to him an unholy acquiescence in the colour-bar on that ground, could write this :

> Far called, our navies melt away,
>   On dune and headland sinks the fire ;
> Lo, all our pomp of yesterday
>   Is one with Nineveh and Tyre.
>   Judge of the Nations, spare us yet,
>   Lest we forget, lest we forget.

And then that verse with the two terrible lines—

> Such boastings as the Gentiles use
> Or lesser breeds without the Law.*

Once again, it is wrath—this time the remorseful wrath of the conqueror who sees the ineffaceable evil that he has wrought and pleads for forgiveness—and it here over-reaches itself into an expression that is, for most of us, either unintelligible or unbearable. The lines have now, per-haps, passed into history ; but they are a good man's monument.

Greatest of all, catholic in every good sense, soaring above sectionalism and yet firmly based on the earth is G. K. Chesterton's hymn, " O God of earth and altar ", which for economy of words and straight-hitting diction eclipses everything in the literature. Chesterton was, as his critics have often remarked, the poet *par excellence* of war. He was always fighting, fighting, you might say, with sword

* *E.H.*, 558.

or bludgeon or broken bottles. Here he fights with the
whole armour of God.

> O God of earth and altar
>   Bow down and hear our cry ;
> Our earthly rulers falter,
>   Our people drift and die.
> The walls of gold entomb us
>   The swords of scorn divide ;
> Take not thy thunder from us
>   But take away our pride.
>
> From all that terror teaches,
>   From lies of tongue and pen ;
> From all the easy speeches
>   That comfort cruel men ;
> From sale and profanation
>   Of honour and the sword ;
> From sleep and from damnation
>   Deliver us, good Lord.* [37]

With this we may compare Henry Scott Holland's hymn,
" Judge eternal ", less angry, less forcible, but still strong
and vital in defence of national righteousness, and the burn-
ing lines of Thomas Hughes, the author of *Tom Brown's
Schooldays*, beginning " O God of Truth, whose living
Word ", and rising to white-hot anger at one point—

> *We* fight for truth ? *we* fight for God ?
>   Poor slaves of lies and sin ;
> He who would fight for thee on earth
>   Must first be pure within.†

Perhaps it is natural that men should feel less wrathfully
about the missionary cause of the church than about the
necessity of relieving social evils. This was not, as we saw,
true of Doddridge, who contemplated the lot of the heathen
with anger no less warm than that which he felt at the
condition of the English poor. But missionary hymns that

* *E.H.*, 562, verses 1-2.   † *E.H.*, 449, verse 4.

sound this note are rare. The only familiar one is also one of the earliest, Bishop Heber's "From Greenland's icy mountains". There is real passion here :

> Can we, whose souls are lighted
> With wisdom from on high,
> Can we to men benighted
> The lamp of life deny?
> Salvation! O Salvation!
> The joyful sound proclaim,
> Till each remotest nation
> Has learned Messiah's name.*

More often the missionary cause has led men to see visions of the last days in which " every knee shall bow ". In this strain Montgomery has some great lines—

> Baptize the nations! far and nigh
> The triumphs of the Cross record ;
> The name of Jesus glorify
> Till every nation call him Lord ! †

and an even wider cosmic vision in " Hark the song of jubilee ".‡

Here is Benjamin Gough on the same subject :

> The Lamb who bore our sorrows
> Comes down on earth to reign ;
> No sufferer now, but victor
> For evermore to reign ;
> To reign in every nation
> To rule in every zone ;
> O world-wide coronation !
> In every heart a throne ! §

We could quote many more excellent hymns of the same kind, Oakley's " Hills of the North ",|| for example, and

---

* E.H., 547, verse 3 ; but there, as in most books, " Ceylon " has become " Java ". † C.P., 323, verse 5.
‡ C.P., 325, quoted in full below, page 315.
§ C.P., 334, verse 4. || C.P., 337.

Lewis Hensley's beautiful lines beginning " Thy kingdom come, O God " * (so unjustly censured by the editor of *Songs of Praise*). But the general point is clear enough— that the wider mission of the Church Militant has caused men to see visions rather than to rise in wrath.

It must be remembered, of course, that while the hymns of social service are written often by those who are actively engaged in that kind of work, whether parsons like Kingsley or journalists like Chesterton, missionary hymns are commonly not written by missionaries. The great exception was, of course, Bishop Heber. His diocese was Calcutta (and in those days it included Australasia), to which he was sent at the age of 39, and where only four years later he died, worn out with devoted service. What Heber saw was enough to provoke the passion of " From Greenland's icy mountains " ; and anybody who has read the lives of John Williams or David Livingstone or Robert Morison knows that missionary work is a matter not only of preaching a creed but of risking being eaten by cannibals ; the " wood and stone " to which the heathen bows down can come to life not only in falsehood and vanity but also in unspeakable cruelty. A modern liberalism has made hymn-writers reluctant to speak of the heathen by that name and has led to a certain romantic diffuseness in some of our missionary hymns. But we cannot complain of diffuseness in these splendid lines, written by a doctor who served for years with the London Missionary Society in India and is now in general practice in the industrial environs of Chesterfield. These have the authentic ring :

> Spirit of peace, for healing grace
>   A parched world waits in dry despair ;
> Break through the clouds that hide thy face,
>   For hope unconquered knows thee there ;
> Humble our pride and come as guest
> Most hidden and most manifest.

* E.H., 554. Cf. *Songs of Praise Discussed*, p. 172.

Spirit of truth, thy blinding light
  Must needs be tempered to our eyes ;
Yet dawn upon our darkened sight
  With freedom as our dearest prize.
With torch of truth held high in hands
Help us to free the fear-bound lands.*

The distinguishing mark of all these hymns has been that they have been *part of* the controversies with which they are associated. In this they all followed, in some measure, the lead which Doddridge had given.

It is natural, then, for us to pass from these to two other kinds of hymn. There are the hymns which, written in time of controversy or distress, seek to rise above the controversy and to give comfort rather than exhortation ; and there are the hymns which issue from, or which cause, controversy of the doctrinal kind.

The first part of this judgment will recall to the reader the hymns we quoted from the time of the Thirty Years War, where we found one which was, virtually, part of the controversy, and two which rose above it in prophecy or in consolation. And just as the hymns of controversy in England came from the Calvinist roots, so the hymns of comfort and prophecy tended to come from the Wesleyan. We have seen how relatively little of the actual controversy with ignorance and superstition there is in the text of the Wesleys' hymns. But there is, conversely, much prophecy in them, much lifting up of the weak and comforting of the fallen. Consider, for example, Charles Wesley's *Hymns to be sung in a Tumult,* published in 1744. The "tumult" in question was the sinister shadow of the Young Pretender, with its possibilities of new setbacks to English Protestantism and English democracy. The people of this country were worried by the possibilities of the Pretender's success in a way comparable to the fear of a Nazi invasion in 1940, and for them Wesley wrote this small book of hymns. The

* " Spirit of flame " by Arthur H. Driver, *C.P.*, 348, verses 2 and 3.

most celebrated of these was " Ye servants of God ",*
which we usually sing in four verses, but which originally
contained these as the second and third :

> Men, devils engage, the billows arise,
> And horribly rage, and threaten the skies ;
> Their fury shall never our steadfastness shock
> The weakest believer is built on a rock.

> The waves of the sea have lift up their voice
> Sore troubled that we in Jesus rejoice ;
> The floods they are roaring but Jesus is here ;
> While we are adoring he always is near.

It then continues in the familiar way—

> God ruleth on high almighty to save. . . .

The hymn is thus really less a hymn of pure praise than one
of refuge, recalling *Psalm* xciii. :

> The floods have lifted up, O Lord,
> The floods have lifted up their waves ;
> The Lord on high is mightier than the noise of many waters ;
> Yea than the mighty waves of the sea.

The American hymn-writers have given us two well-
known hymns that are the outcome of conflict and distress,
both of them from the American Civil War of 1861–6. The
most celebrated is Julia Ward Howe's " Mine eyes have
seen the glory ", which comes straight from the great
controversy over the liberation of the slaves.

Mine eyes have seen the glory of the coming of the Lord ;
He is trampling out the vintage where the grapes of wrath are
stored ;
He hath loosed the fateful lightning of his terrible swift sword ;
His Truth is marching on.

* *C.P.*, 66.

He is coming like the glory of the morning on the wave ;
He is wisdom to the mighty, he is succour to the brave ;
So the world shall be his footstool, and the soul of time his
   slave :
   　　Our God is marching on.*

These words were written for the tune " John Brown's
Body " after Mrs. Howe had visited the camp of the Army
of the Potomac in 1861 and heard it there.　She had
already been working a decade and more in the cause of
the abolition of slavery.　The lines are full of wrath, and
are given a dark colour in the midst of their triumphant
pomp by the reference in their second line to the terrible
passage in *Isaiah* lxiii. which tells of the divine wrath, and
begins

Who is this that cometh from Edom ? this that is glorious
in his apparel, travelling in the greatness of his strength ? I
that speak in righteousness, mighty to save.
Wherefore art thou red in thine apparel, and thy garments
like him that treadeth the winefat ? I have trodden the wine-
press alone ; and of the people there was none with me : for I
will tread them in mine anger, and trample them in my fury.
. . For the day of vengeance is in my heart.

Three years later, when the war had reached its crisis,
was born another hymn of a very different kind, serene,
prayerful, dignified, and in its context infinitely moving.
It is the work of a 24-year-old graduate of the Divinity
School, Cambridge, Massachusetts, written for his Gradua-
tion just before he was ordained to the ministry of the
Second Unitarian Church, Brooklyn.　John White Chadwick wrote of this hymn, " The smoke of battle hung over
the mighty hosts for six days, while the North remained
in a state of suspense bordering on agony ; but Grant wrote
to the Government at Washington, ' I propose to fight it

* *C.P.*, 170, verses 1 and 4.

out on this line, if it takes all summer.' " This was the young man's vision :

> We would be one in hatred of all wrong,
>   One in our love of all things sweet and fair,
> One with the joy that breaketh into song,
>   One in the grief that trembleth into prayer,
> One in the power that makes the children free
> To follow truth, and thus to follow thee.*

Those lines were often sung, particularly by the singers of the B.B.C. services, during the second World War.†

The two great world wars have not given many great hymns to our treasury ; this, perhaps, partly because by the twentieth century the treasury was already so well filled that it was difficult for a new hymn to achieve greatness in the popular imagination. The locust-eaten years were, however, not entirely barren, and I should like to quote three hymns, none of them well known, one from the former war, one from the early days of the uneasy peace, and one from the second war.

Here are lines written by one of the most distinguished of Congregational ministers, Henry C. Carter, then of Emmanuel Church, Cambridge, in 1917. He was all his life one of the most devoted upholders of the Gospel of peace, and amidst all the jingoism and clamour of those days, he wrote this, on the Christian's spiritual armour :

> Give me, O Christ, the strength that is in thee
>   That I may stand in every evil hour ;
> Faints my poor heart except to thee I flee,
>   Resting my weakness in thy perfect power.
>
> Give me to see the foes that I must fight,
>   Powers of the darkness, throned where thou shouldst reign ;
> Read the directings of thy wrath aright,
>   Lest, striking flesh and blood, I strike in vain.

* *E.H.*, 384, verse 3.
† For further matter on American hymns, see Chapter 17.

Give me to wield the weapon that is sure,
   Taking through prayer thy sword into my hand.
Word of thy wisdom, peaceable and pure,
   So, Christ my conqueror, I shall conqueror stand.*

It was never sung ; indeed, it lay buried in its author's papers until it was unearthed and submitted to the committee preparing the latest hymn-book for Congregationalists. But now, in the days of wrath that are on us again, it has already proved its worth.

Perhaps the most popular hymn that came out of the first Great War was Blake's *Jerusalem*, as discovered by Parry ; Parry had a genius for finding strange and mysterious words for his settings—see his *Songs of Farewell*, for example —and here he made Blake into something Blake himself would have been horrified to be, the author of a popular national song. The music was written originally for a celebration in the Albert Hall of the achievement in 1916 of women's suffrage, but it soon became one of our national anthems. We can therefore justifiably regard it as a hymn of the twentieth century. Its last four lines, beginning " I will not cease from mental fight,' had been already made famous by the journal of the Guild of St. Matthew, a Christian Socialist society, which printed in heavy type under the title in every issue :

I will not cease from mental fight
   Nor shall my sword sleep in my hand,
Till we have built Jerusalem
   In England's green and pleasant land.†

After the first World War was over, the era of mass public meetings was well established, and patriotic songs of an exalted kind began to appear in considerable numbers. One of the more celebrated was Clifford Bax's " Turn back, O man ", and several others can be found in the " National "

---

* *C.P.*, 532, verses 1, 2 and 4.
  † The other notable hymn of the Great War was Arkwright's " O valiant hearts ".

section of the larger edition of *Songs of Praise*. I believe the finest of them all was written by another great advocate of the cause of international peace, Laurence Housman. He wrote these lines for H. R. L. Sheppard's " Life and Liberty" Movement, in 1919, and it was sung at a mass meeting of that movement in the Queen's Hall to the music by Geoffrey Shaw given in *Songs of Praise* :

Father eternal, ruler of creation,
  Spirit of life, which moved ere form was made,
Through the thick darkness covering every nation,
  Light to man's blindness, O be thou our aid :
    Thy kingdom come, O Lord, thy will be done.

Races and peoples, lo, we stand divided,
  And, sharing not our griefs, no joy can share ;
By wars and tumults love is mocked, derided ;
  His conquering cross no kingdom wills to bear.
    Thy kingdom come, O Lord, thy will be done.*

And from the second World War, I ask leave to quote this, written in the dark days of 1942 :

O Christ our Lord, O Christ our King,
Who back the gates of Hell didst fling,
Whose place upon creation's throne
By Easter triumph was made known,
Rule now on earth from realms above,
Subdue the nations by thy love.

O vindicate against men's greed
The weak whose tears thy justice plead.
Thy pity Lord, on men who lie
Broken by war and tyranny.
Show them the Cross which thou didst bear,
Give them the power which conquered there.

Let those who now usurp thy throne
Acknowledge thou art Lord alone.

* *Songs of Praise*, 326, verses 1 and 2.

Cause those whose lust torments mankind
Thy wrath to know, thy mercy find.
Make all this rebel world proclaim
The mighty power of thy dear name.

So shall creation's bondage cease,
Its groans and pangs give birth to peace ;
And all the world, redeemed by thee,
From agony and death be free.
O haste the time, make short the days
Till all our cries dissolve in praise.[38]

This fine expression of Christian intercession in time of war may fittingly bring this chapter to a close. We must now turn to those hymns of controversy which issue from the more difficult ground of religious strife.

CHAPTER 10

Wrath and Praise

11. THE CHURCH EMBATTLED

WE did our best in our second chapter to engage the reader's sympathy with those who regard religious controversy as not unimportant. And perhaps we are able to say that the days are passing in which sincerity was thought to be the highest of the virtues, and in which it was proper to believe that it mattered not what you believed so long as your acts were honest. Controversy within religious groups, as distinguished from controversy between religious and irreligious, has much about it that repels the honourable layman ; it frequently brings to the surface a scum of technical verbiage for which the layman has no use ; and his own security has usually made it unnecessary for the layman to engage in such disputes himself, so that he rarely sees that that very security was usually won as the result of fightings and sufferings.

The religious controversies which have affected the story which we are now telling of hymnody since 1700 are the controversies between the Wesleyans and the Calvinists, the controversies produced by the Oxford Movement, the discussions over natural religion in the middle of the nineteenth century, and the dispute which has continued for a considerable time since about 1850 between high and low churchmen, biblical and non-biblical theologians, critics and conservatives.

That makes an uncommonly unpromising start ; it sounds, you will say, very unreal and academic. But it is, for a beginning, the story of " Rock of ages ".

Augustus Montague Toplady, the author of this immortal hymn, was born in 1740 and became vicar of Broadhembury in Devon, where he remained until he died of consumption at the age of 38. His later years he divided between a faithful ministry and a good deal of writing, not a little of which contains some of the most acrid controversy which has ever defaced the history of English Christianity. Toplady could write ; that is to say, he could write prose, for he was no poet. His was a facile pen, and it gave expression to the workings of a wondrously controversial and contentious mind. This formidable armament was directed upon John Wesley and all he stood for.

He thus describes John Wesley's headquarters, the Foundery Chapel in Moorfields :

" Its chief ingredients are : An equal portion of gross Heathenism, Pelagianism, Mahometism, Popery, Manichaeism, Ranterism, and Antinomianism ; culled, dried and pulverized, *secundum artem* ; and, above all, mingled with as much palpable Atheism as you can possibly scrape together from every quarter."[39]

In another place he writes :

" Whereunto shall I liken Mr. John Wesley ? And with what shall I compare him ? I will liken him to a low and puny tadpole in divinity, which proudly seeks to disembowel a high and mighty whale in politics " * [40]

the reference here being to an alleged plagiarism by Wesley of a pamphlet by Dr. Johnson.

Toplady found time, in his country parish, to write scores of pages of this kind of thing, analysing Wesley's arguments phrase by phrase and arguing at enormous length his own contentions. His quarrel with Wesley was, in the background, doctrinal, and in the foreground as personal as any quarrel between two men has ever been. He accuses Wesley of contempt for the Church, of wanton schism, of setting himself up as a religious dictator (he often

* *Works* (1849), page 729.

calls him " Pope John ") and of blasphemous misadminis-
tration of the Sacraments.   But all this is because in the
first place Wesley published an attack on Toplady's Calvinistic doctrines.   The argument here is not unimportant ;
these two men between them were hammering out the question, " Is God responsible for evil ?   Has man free will ? "
Wesley said that all men *must* be saved by God's mercy.
Toplady said that to give men free will and say they *must*
be saved is to rob God of free will, and that this is worse
than to rob man of it.   Wesley tired of the argument first,
Toplady became more and more scandalous, and the outcome of the argument was singularly barren, even though
it was dealing with questions that have occupied the attention of honest Christian philosophers all through the ages,
and are occupying them still.   Barren it was, except in one
particular.

Perhaps the most grotesque article Toplady ever wrote
was one entitled " Questions and answers relative to the
National Debt ", which he wrote for a journal in 1775.   It
is in the form of a dialogue, and begins in the following
cheerful fashion :

Q. 1.   Supposing this debt to be only 130 millions of pounds
sterling at present (although it is much more) and that it was
all to be counted in shillings : that a man could count at the
rate of 100 shillings per minute each day till he had counted
the whole ; how much time would he take in doing it ?
Ans. 98 years, 316 days, 14 hours and 40 minutes.
Q. 2.   The whole of this sum being 2600 millions of shillings,
and the coinage standard being 62 shillings in the Troy pound,
what is the whole weight ?
Ans. 41 million, 935 thousand, 484 Troy pounds.
Q. 3.   How many carts would carry this weight, supposing
a ton in each ?
Ans. 20,968 carts.

And so the dialogue between the Vicar and the genius in
mental arithmetic goes on, establishing in turn how far the
shillings would stretch if laid side by side, how many men

would be required to carry the weight, how long such a procession would be, and what is the interest on it at $3\frac{1}{2}$ per cent. From this he deduces that the national debt will never be paid until there is " more money in England's treasury than there is at present in all Europe ".

From this he proceeds to the " Spiritual improvement of the foregoing ", which begins with a catena of Scripture quotations about the impossibility of our paying our debts to God, but passes soon to an even more severe test in mental calculation.

Q. Supposing a person was to break the law but once in 24 hours ; to how many would his sins amount in a life of ten, twenty, thirty, forty, fifty, sixty, seventy, or eighty years ?

This the pupil may be assumed to have answered correctly. The sum is then developed on the basis of two sins a day, one sin an hour, one sin a minute, and finally one sin a second ; and the interlocutor is satisfied only when he has elicited from his pupil the happy thought that in a life of eighty years a man would have, on this basis, committed 2,522,880,000 sins. Then comes a quick fire of theological questions. When shall we be able to pay off such a debt ?— Who can do us any good ? Are we not lost ? And in the end the author leaves his fantastic dialogue and runs straight into these words—

O thou covenanting, thou incarnate, thou obeying, thou bleeding, thou dying, thou risen, thou ascended, thou interceding Son of God ! not all the seraphs thou hast created, not all the innumerable saints thy love hath redeemed, will be able to comprehend, much less to display, along the endless line of eternity itself, the length, the breadth, the depth, the height of a sinner's obligations to thee.* [41]

And then—

* *Works* (1849), pages 448–50 ; where, however, the hymn is not quoted.

A LIVING AND DYING PRAYER FOR THE HOLIEST BELIEVER IN THE WORLD

> Rock of ages, cleft for me,
> Let me hide myself in thee ;
> Let the water and the blood
> From thy riven side which flowed
> Be of sin the double cure ;
> Cleanse me from its guilt and power.

Thus, in the excellent words of a modern commentator, is the " scorn of man turned to his praise ".* The whole episode is described by another commentator as an example of sin-obsession.† This I believe to be a false diagnosis. The whole article is a piece of bitter theological satire ; Toplady is not obsessed with sin, though he is undoubtedly obsessed with the sins of John Wesley. But the point here is that " Rock of ages ", which is part of the folk-song of the religiously unlettered of today and one of the half-dozen best loved hymns in the world, which was the favourite of Mr. Gladstone and which Professor Saintsbury has called a " really great poem ", came out of this muddy and obscure controversy and from a mind that could be so grievously distorted by personal envy and malice. And yet Toplady must not be written off as a madman or even as " fanatical in a gross Calvinism " ; when he lay dying, still a young man, and somebody suggested that he would recover, he replied, " No, no, I shall die. No mortal could endure such manifestations of God's glory as I have done, and live." ‡ A year later, " Rock of Ages " went into the first edition of Wesley's *Hymns for the People Called Methodists*.

Let us turn now to a controversy which comes much nearer to our own day—that aroused by the Oxford Movement.[42] This movement, whose most distinguished leaders

---

* W. S. Kelynack, *Companion to the new School Hymn Book of the Methodist Church*, page 326.

† Percy Dearmer, in *Songs of Praise Discussed* (1933), pages 336–8.

‡ *Ib.*, page 338.

were E. B. Pusey and John Henry Newman, was the source
of what we now know as " Anglo-Catholicism ", and the
controversy that still exists between " High " and " Low "
in Anglican circles dates from those days.   The Movement
is historically dated from Keble's Assize Sermon of 1833.
Very briefly, the objects of those who launched it were the
revitalization of the Church of England by reopening some
of the channels between it and the pre-Reformation Catholic
Church which had been stopped up by what they thought
to be wanton and now out-of-date acts of Puritanism.   A
new sense of history—frequently a romantic rather than a
critical sense—a new conception of the duties and status of
priests, new thinking about the Sacraments, new attention
to the details of worship, new thinking even about the
Thirty-Nine Articles and the liturgies of the Book of Common
Prayer—these were the issues in the air.   The group which
gathered round Newman while he was a Fellow of Oriel and
vicar of St. Mary's, the University Church of Oxford, saw
the Church of England dying of inanition because the sup-
plies of grace that could come from the past and from
Catholic doctrine had been cut off.   Inasmuch as these
reformers considered all Puritanism to be barren of nourish-
ment for the English Church, and therefore ranged themselves implacably against nonconformist practices, they must
be called a " party " ; but a great deal of what they did
came to stay, and when you see the vicar preaching in a
white surplice and the choir seated in the east end of the
" lowest " of evangelical Anglican churches, you are looking
at the effects of the Oxford Movement.

The controversy was passionate and protracted.   On the
whole the Christian Socialists were against the reformers,
regarding them as fiddling while Rome burned.   Their new
attitude to Roman Catholicism was also unpalatable to a
large section of public opinion.   But the point for us is that
in 1833 this group of people were sure that England was
sinking into religious barbarism, and that they alone could
save it.

From this movement came a great outpouring of hymns, on some aspects of which we have already commented ; the liturgical interest of the reformers was, of course, responsible for all that led up to *Hymns Ancient and Modern* (which in its first days was a very " High Church " book indeed). Especially the new interest in medieval history caused the emergence of a number of translations of old hymns ; indeed, anything in Latin was good enough, even if, as in " The strife is o'er " * and " Conquering Kings their titles take ",† the Latin was scarcely a hundred years old.

You might say, too, that the hymns of Newman were a by-product of the movement, inasmuch as Newman's genius, in his Anglican days before 1845, was so strong a factor in its growth. But the two that are well known are essentially devotional hymns, not connected directly with the controversy. " Lead, kindly Light " ‡ was never meant to be a hymn ; it was written at sea in 1833 at a time of great strain and weakness, and is simply a personal prayer of surpassing and haunting beauty which we all want to make our own. " Praise to the Holiest ",§ written in 1865, is an episode in Newman's *The Dream of Gerontius*, there appearing without the repetition of the first verse ; the criticism of Bernard Manning that its last verse, " And in the garden secretly " is a sad anticlimax applies only to the hymn as used in public worship ; in the context it disappears.

But the movement did produce one real battle-hymn ; this was Philip Pusey's " Lord of our life, and God of our salvation ", which we have already mentioned as being derived from the old battle-hymn of Löwenstern which had appeared almost two centuries before during the Thirty Years War.‖ As is pointed out by modern commentators,¶ the history of this hymn is remarkable. It appeared in

* *E.H.*, 625. † *E.H.*, 37. ‡ *E.H.*, 425.
§ *E.H.*, 471. ‖ See above, page 43.
¶ *Songs of Praise Discussed*, page 192.

1834, the year after the triumphant passing of the Emancipation Bill, at a time when Christian social activity was in
the ascendant and when the Church still had a great hold
on the people.   Nor can we say that Pusey was looking
forward a hundred years to the sinister results of the Industrial Revolution ; for it was not in the nature of the Oxford
Reformers in this sense to look forward, and he wrote himself
of this hymn, " It refers to the state of the Church, that is to
say, the Church of England, in 1834—assailed from without,
enfeebled and distracted within, but on the eve of a great
awakening." [43]

> See round thine ark the hungry billows curling ;
> See how thy foes their banners are unfurling ;
> Lord, while their darts envenomed they are hurling,
>   Thou canst preserve us.

The answer is, of course, that this is an imaginative hymn,
that the German of Löwenstern had linked up in Pusey's
mind with the great new controversy ; and that the enthusiasm of the early years of the Oxford Movement painted its
enemies, its critics, and the actual debilities of the English
Church blacker than history would allow.   And it was, of
course, the fact that most of the new social reforming zeal
had come not from the earlier generations of the Church of
England but from the Wesleyan influence on it.   Those
whose loyalty bound them to the Church of England as a
family to a mother were inclined to think that unless some
new vitality came into the Church of England from an
indigenous source, the country had better go Methodist.
These were the thoughts behind this hymn ; but they are
small compared with the thoughts that come out of it.
Like all great hymn-writers, Pusey wrote more than he knew
here, and this has become one of the great battle-hymns of
the fighting church, sung as heartily by any nonconformist
or evangelical as it ever was by those for whom it was
specially intended.

Rather like this is the story of Faber's " Faith of our

fathers " ; * this was originally a hymn written for the
newly-emancipated Catholics of England and Ireland, with
the refrain

> Faith of our fathers, holy Faith
> We will be true to thee till death.

It was, of course, a cry of triumph over Protestant oppressors,
but within a couple of generations it was being sung heartily
by Congregationalists from Horder's *Worship Song* (1905).
Like all Faber's work it is richly sentimental, and it seems to
have passed out of use now.   But it is another example of a
hymn of controversy rising above the sounds of the battle.

This brings us to the third great controversy, which has
had several ramifications, but which is still very much with
us.   It is the controversy between those who are offended
by traditional statements of belief and those who are
offended by any assault on them.   The advance of the
critical faculties of thinking people in the ages of science,
reason, and " enlightenment " which began slowly in the
days of Isaac Newton, and was vastly accelerated in the
days of the Industrial Revolution, caused a sharpening of
the cleavage between those whom we may roughly call
conservative and liberal in theology.   The parties diversified themselves further, of course, fundamentalists standing
well to the right of the conservatives and radicals as far to
the left of the liberals.   But in every department of theology
and religious experience questions were being asked during
the nineteenth century, and the battle was on between those
who asked them and those who considered it profanity to
ask them.   We will give three examples of the effect this
had on hymnody.

One of the controversies which shook the Church of
England to its foundations during the 'sixties was that which
resulted from Bishop Colenso's publication of his commentary on the Pentateuch in 1862, in which he challenged
most of the presuppositions on which readers and students

* *Methodist Hymn Book*, 548.

of Scripture had been working up till then. What shook the church at that time had become, forty years later, commonplaces of Higher Criticism ; but at the time there were many who felt that a theory of criticism that would challenge the preaching presuppositions of, for example, F. W. Robertson was a blow at the people's faith. Colenso was at the time Bishop of Natal—he was called by his people " Sobantu ", which means " father of the people ". He was zealous in the exposure of corruption in the colony and had made himself greatly loved in all parts of his work. But his Biblical criticism, and his attacks on the sacramental system contained in his commentary on *Romans* (1861) brought forth from Bishop Gray of Capetown not only a stern rejoinder but an order depriving him of his see. This order was countermanded in the law courts in 1866, and Colenso lived another seventeen years in the administration of his episcopal duties.

Although all this happened in Africa, there were many troubled minds at home ; and in defence of Gray's orthodoxy while the controversy was still in progress, Samuel John Stone, a young clergyman of 27, wrote " The church's one foundation " in 1866. Its third verse recalls the controversy forcibly :

> Though with a scornful wonder
>   Men see her sore oppressed,
> By schisms rent asunder,
>   By heresies distressed ;
> Yet saints their watch are keeping ;
>   Their cry goes up, " How long ! "
> And soon the night of weeping
>   Shall be the morn of song.*

The remarkable compression of theological thought in the first verse of this hymn should be noticed. It is a monument of orthodoxy, and was written as a defence against that free thinking which was soon seen to be a necessity, but whose undisciplined waywardness has led the church since into

* *E.H.*, 489, verse 3.

much perplexity. None the less, the hymn, sometimes dropping the " schisms " verse, remains an anthem of praise in all Christian churches, established and nonconformist.

Many of the leaders of liberal thought at this time were Americans and Unitarians, and one of the most striking manifestations of militant liberalism was a little collection called " Hymns of the Spirit ", published in 1864 by Samuel Johnson and Samuel Longfellow. Longfellow was a Unitarian minister, and Johnson was a loosely-attached member of the Unitarian community. The object of this book, as plainly set out in the preface, was to exclude all hymns which by their traditional phraseology or out-of-date thought-forms would offend the sensibilities of a cultured liberal Christian. This meant, in effect, the dropping of the dogmatic, the scriptural, and the symbolic. To fill the gaps the two men contributed hymns of their own. Two of those on the church are worth quoting, inasmuch as the doctrine of the church was a keen point of controversy in these circles. The question was whether the Church comprised all men of goodwill, or whether creed or covenant should be required of its members. This was Johnson's answer :

> City of God ! how broad and far
> Outspread thy walls sublime ;
> The true thy chartered freemen are
> Of every age and clime. . . .
>
> How purely hath thy speech come down,
> From man's primeval youth !
> How grandly hath thine empire grown
> Of freedom, love and truth.*

And here is Longfellow in the same collection :

> Her priests are all God's faithful sons,
> To serve the world raised up ;
> The pure in heart her baptized ones,
> Love, her communion-cup.†

* *E.H.*, 375, verses 1 and 3.   † *C.P.*, 249, verse 3.

These two authors wrote smoothly and gracefully, and their
lines, especially Johnson's, have filled the needs of many
who were impatient of the traditional views of the church.
But the deliberate discarding of the New Testament doctrine
of the Church was an act of controversy.

The same line was taken by the Quaker Whittier, rather
more decidedly, in this verse from his " Our Master " (the
source of " Immortal love, for ever full ", and " O Lord and
Master of us all ") :

> Our Friend, our Brother, and our Lord,
>   What may thy service be ?
> Nor name, nor form, nor ritual word,
>   But simply following thee.*

and a rather infelicitously sectarian thrust at established
orthodoxy has long been popular among Congregationalists :

> We rear no altar—thou hast died ;
>   We deck no priestly shrine ;
> What need have we of creature-aid ?
>   The power to save is thine.†

Here, I fancy, controversy has, as we have noticed before,
slipped over into distortion and extremism.   But Johnson's
" City of God ", with its romantic appeal to young minds,
has established itself well above the clamour of dispute.
And those who are disconcerted by the verse quoted above
can always turn to Muirhead's answer, written from the
High Church point of view for the *Yattendon Hymnal* :

> The church of God a kingdom is
>   Where Christ in power doth reign ;
> Where spirits yearn till seen in bliss
>   Their Lord shall come again.

> An altar stands within the shrine,
>   Whereon, once sacrificed,
> Is set, immaculate, divine,
>   The Lamb of God, the Christ.‡

* *Congregational Hymnary*, 167, verse 5.
† *C.P.*, 272, verse 3.   ‡ *E.H.*, 488, verses 1 and 3.

Nothing could be clearer in sacramental doctrine than that.

Finally, we ought to turn to the one example in our story of a controversy of considerable size being started by hymns. Of course, controversy on the local scale, and occasionally small dogmatic controversies, are not unknown in regard to hymns. Some hymns provoke considerable dispute, especially among those whose duty it is to compile hymn-books. But the only time when such dispute has reached the national level was the occasion of what is called the *Rivulet* controversy of 1856.

The best account of this queer business is given in the late Albert Peel's *These Hundred Years*; this is a history of the first century of the Congregational Union of England and Wales (1831–1931), and if you are familiar with the dyspeptic architecture of the headquarters of that Union in Farringdon Street you might expect this to be a very tedious book indeed. As a matter of fact, it is extremely well, not to say racily, written, and admirably sets forth a chapter of church history that any English Christian ought to be familiar with. The title of the chapter dealing with the Rivulet Controversy is "Almost Wrecked"; and indeed it was over a handful of hymns that the Congregational Union very nearly foundered.

The *Rivulet* was a small book of hymns, subtitled *Hymns for Heart and Voice*, written by the Rev. Thomas Toke Lynch, a Congregational minister. Readers who know only Anglican books will probably not know the contents of this book, but the best known of them are "Gracious Spirit, dwell with me" * and "Dismiss me not thy service, Lord".† The *Rivulet* came out in 1855, and the first reviews were favourable. But in early 1856 a harshly dissentient voice was heard, that of the editor of the *Morning Advertiser*, James Grant, who said that the volume "might have been written by a Deist, and a very large proportion might be sung by a congregation of Freethinkers", that it

* *C.P.*, 213.   † *E.H.*, 555.

had " not one particle of vital religion or evangelical piety ",
and that it was " pervaded throughout by the rationalist
theology of Germany ".

Fifteen of the best known ministers in London, including
Thomas Binney, author of " Eternal light ! Eternal light ! "
wrote in protest against this judgment. This brought on to
the scene a new figure beside whom James Grant himself
seemed to shrink considerably. For John Campbell, editor
of *The British Banner* and the *Christian Witness* (the first and
only Congregationalist national weekly), was the greatest
power nonconformist journalism had in those days : and
nonconformist journalism in 1856 was not a force to be
trifled with. " Crude ! " said he. " Disjointed, unmean-
ing, un-Christian, ill-rhymed rubbish." " Incomparably
the most unspiritual publication of the kind in the English
tongue." On seven consecutive Thursdays Campbell tore
and stamped on this apparently inoffensive little book until
the denomination was set by the ears, and even the *Nonconformist*, from remoter height, was demanding the end of
Campbell's " uncouth despotism ".

In the end, largely owing to the peacemaking genius of
Binney, Congregationalism's greatest liturgist of the nineteenth century, Campbell resigned and the controversy died
down ; but the " Almost Wrecked " of Dr. Peel's title
implies that the discussion was so bitter that it nearly broke
down the machinery of the Union at its annual Assembly.

What then was the trouble ? The trouble was that
Lynch showed in his hymns an appreciation of nature which
his worthy contemporaries found quite outrageous. The
book was a book of religious verse, which could be sung if
anybody wanted to sing it. It was not intended to be a
comprehensive hymn-book, but rather to fill some gaps in
current hymnody. Current dissenting hymnody, let it be
remembered, was pretty heavy. Its chief ingredient was the
psalms and hymns of Isaac Watts, and it was heavily loaded
with eighteenth-century Calvinism. The *Congregational
Hymn Book* of 1836 could almost be accused of subscribing to

the gnostical heresy of the damnation of matter, so frightened
was it of any hymn about God's creation. Lynch's subject
matter was not less startling than his style. The ceremonious solemnity and dogmatic predictability of the
eighteenth-century hymn-writers had not prepared the
conservatives of 1856 for this :

> O where is he that trod the sea ?
>   O where is he that spake—
> And demons from their victims flee,
>   The dead their slumbers break ;
> The palsied rise in freedom strong,
>   The dumb men talk and sing,
> And from blind eyes, benighted long,
>   Bright gleams of morning spring.*

There is a vivid picture ; the tenses are confused and it
does not run very smoothly ; but it is a picture. In the
third verse this hymn rises to one couplet of pure inspiration :

> O where is he that trod the sea ?
>   'Tis only he can save ;
> To thousands hungering wearily
>   A wondrous meal he gave ;
> Full soon, celestially fed
>   Their rustic fare they take ;
> 'Twas springtide when he blest the bread,
>   And harvest when he brake.†

But that was not an age when, if an author's sympathies
were undogmatic, the powers that were would forgive him
a few bad lines. Nowadays Lynch's bad lines are still the
bar to his being sung much outside his own denomination.
But if we are to estimate the quality of his thought, and see
an example of the strain which his contemporaries found so
exasperating let us look at what may be his finest hymn.
Look well at it, for it is disappearing from the hymn-books :

* *Congregational Hymnary*, 102, verse 1.
† *Ib.*, verse 3.

Lift up your heads, rejoice, redemption draweth nigh ;
Now breathes a softer air, now shines a milder sky ;
The early trees put forth their new and tender leaf ;
Hushed is the moaning wind that told of winter's grief.

Lift up your heads, rejoice, redemption draweth nigh ;
Now mount the laden clouds, now flames the darkening sky ;
The early scattered drops descend with heavy fall ;
And to the waiting earth the hidden thunders call.

Lift up your heads, rejoice, redemption draweth nigh ;
O note the varying signs of earth and air and sky.
The God of glory comes in gentleness and might
To comfort and alarm, to succour and to smite.

He comes the wide world's King, he comes, the true heart's
    friend,
New gladness to begin, and ancient wrong to end ;
He comes to fill with light the weary waiting eye ;
Lift up your heads, rejoice, redemption draweth nigh.*

" Where are we, in April or November ? " chided the
orthodox Calvinists, forgetting for a moment the mighty
paradox of the Lord's coming which is so often set out in
Scripture—is it springtime or is it a thundery summer ?
" The day of the Lord is darkness, and not light " ; " Comfort ye, comfort ye, my people." To those who had been
surfeited with Watts (there were four hundred of Watts's
hymns in the current hymn-book) the delicacy of Lynch's
poetic form and allusion, the rapier-thrust of that paradox at
the end of the third verse, the subtle working out of the
propositions of the first two verses in the last two were all
hidden. Lynch never wrote a perfect hymn, perhaps never
a great hymn, but the controversy cleared the air, and
Lynch is the hero of the nature-hymn and one of the first
hymn-writers to take seriously the claims of poetic criticism
in his writing. We will leave him preaching one Sunday
morning on the subject of a bunch of flowers, thus defying
the Calvinists who would not consider the lilies.

* *Congregational Hymnary,* 76.

This has taken us as far as it is profitable to go in the matter of hymns and controversy.   But it is perhaps fitting to close by quoting two verses of a hymn which, like that which closed our last chapter, will not be well known in this country.   It is the only translation extant of a hymn written by a leader of the German Confessional Church under persecution.   This comes indeed from the controversy that the Church is waging in our time with the most dangerous organized opposition it has encountered since the days of Diocletian.   The original is by Heinrich Vogel, German Protestant leader and martyr.

> O faithless, fearful army,
>   For you the Lord doth fight ;
> Through oceans dark and stormy
>   He cleaves his path of light.
> The Lord has shown you favour,
>   He comes before you call.
> The God who is your Saviour
>   Will never let you fall.
>
> The Saviour's Incarnation,
>   His people's righteous dress ;
> Our glory and salvation
>   Are Christ, when we are his,
> The warrior true and glorious
>   Who has God's battle won ;
> Lord Christ, for us victorious,
>   Thy perfect work is done.*

* H. Vogel, *The Iron Ration of a Christian*, translated by W. A. Whitehouse (S.C.M. Press, 1941), page 224.

CHAPTER 11

Interlude

THE TYPICAL ENGLISH HYMN-WRITER

THE reader was warned in the Preface that this is not a history of hymnody. This chapter will be the last of what could possibly be called the " historical " chapters, and it will be devoted to a summary of the tendencies which I have tried to draw out of the history in the preceding pages. I have been at some pains to show that hymns have been written either for the adornment and enrichment of the liturgy of a settled church, or for the heightening of devotion and the enhancing of evangelism, or as the result of controversy on a small or large scale. Hymns have sprung from man's wrath, his piety, and his need of his neighbour expressed in churchmanship. Broadly speaking, I doubt if any hymn ever written falls far outside the bounds of those categories. The best way in which to sum all this up, before going on to some special aspects of the subject, is to consider the work of one hymn-writer who seems to embody all the tendencies, general and special, which we have observed ; that writer is James Montgomery, who was born at Irvine in Ayrshire in 1771, and died at Sheffield in 1854 at a ripe old age. He was thus a contemporary of John Wesley, who was born in 1703, and of Bishop How, who died in 1897.

I have written at some length elsewhere on Montgomery's work, and I propose to be brief here, and only to make the point that a summary of what we have found to be the essential connection between hymns and human life is to be better found in his work than in any consideration of twentieth-century tendencies.

First, consider his life.   His father was an Irish Moravian
minister in Scotland, but he was educated at a Moravian
settlement in Yorkshire, while his father and mother went
as missionaries to the West Indies.   He became a shopkeeper
at Mirfield, near Huddersfield, but in 1792 moved to
Sheffield, where he became an assistant in the shop of one
Mr. Gales, printer and bookseller.   Gales was proprietor
of a radical journal known as the *Sheffield Register*, and when
he made Sheffield too hot to hold him, Montgomery, aged
23, took his place as editor.   He had already developed
gifts for writing, and, changing the name of the paper to the
Sheffield Iris, he went ahead in the same advanced political
vein.   For his published opinions he spent two short terms
in prison.   The paper made its way, however, through the
rocks and shoals of current political opinion, and Montgomery made a name for himself.

In 1814, aged 43, he became a member for a time of the
Wesleyan Society, but three years later the course of his
religious life was given another turn by the arrival in Sheffield of Thomas Cotterill, who was the new vicar of St. Paul's
Church.   Of the controversy over Cotterill's hymn-book we
have already had something to say ;   Montgomery was in
this up to the neck, and began to write hymns for this
book and for wider use also.   He printed a version of fifty-
six of the Psalms under the title *Songs of Zion* (1822) and
three years later the *Christian Psalmist*, in which most of his
best work appeared, and to which he prefaced an introduction which was the first English work on hymnology.
He collected all his hymns, numbering 355, in one volume
in 1853.   In his later years he became a communicant
member of St. George's Church, Sheffield, whose vicar,
Mercer, was another distinguished hymnologist.

That life, then, contains as it were symbolically many
of the elements which we have been noticing on our way ;
he was descended from an Irish minister, and later connected with the Moravians, then with the Wesleyans, and
finally with the Church of England.   He was a man of

controversy and a fighter ; he was the son of a missionary ; he was a man of integrity and devotion ; and he had the true literary gift. Without any question, on the verdict of posterity, Montgomery was the greatest of Christian lay hymn-writers.

In modern hymn-books Montgomery usually has a good, though not over-generous, representation. The *English Hymnal* gives him ten places, the latest *Hymns Ancient and Modern,* eleven.

In doctrine, Montgomery's surviving hymns hold the balance, in their congregational and churchmanlike emphasis, between the cosmic impersonality of Watts and the fiery experience of Wesley. Even his literary style owes something to both and strikes a mean between them. In his psalm-versions he has something of the gaucherie of Watts, in his hymns of experience he has not a little of Wesley's intimacy.

The hymns of Montgomery that have had an uninterrupted career from their earliest days until now are "Hail to the Lord's Anointed ", "Songs of praise the angels sang ", and "For ever with the Lord ". Not far behind these in popularity are "According to thy gracious word ", "Stand up and bless the Lord ", and "Prayer is the soul's sincere desire ". Perhaps he never wrote anything so stirring to the imagination as "Our God, our help in ages past " or "Jesu, lover of my soul ", or "Rock of ages ". His name would not appear in anybody's list of the half-dozen greatest hymns. But it is just this touch of the commonplace, this avoidance of the extreme, this solidity of doctrine and catholicity of experience that gives Montgomery this pivotal place in hymnody. His work is good, sound, hard-wearing stuff with a touch of the genuinely inspired here and there that makes us able to regard him as *the* typical English hymn-writer. Julian's *Dictionary* says that about a quarter of his work was in common use in 1891. When one recalls that he was not, like Watts or Wesley, the peculiar property of any one denomination, this gives a good indication of the degree to which he has been found indispensable.

Many of Montgomery's hymns are the kind of thing that editors like Garrett Horder and Percy Dearmer, looking out for striking poetry, passed over as commonplace, for which the liturgical editors of the Church of England, their books already filled with a good deal of padding, could find no room, and which has been, for the Methodists, overshadowed by the towering rhetoric of Charles Wesley. But few editors have been able to resist the magic of this :

> Lift up your heads, ye gates of brass,
>   Ye bars of iron, yield,
> And let the King of glory pass,
>   The Cross is in the field.
>
> A holy war his servants wage,
>   Mysteriously at strife,
> The powers of heaven and hell engage
>   For more than death or life.
>
> Ye armies of the living God,
>   His sacramental host,
> Where hallowed footsteps never trod
>   Take your appointed post.* 44

Let Montgomery, then, be accepted as " the typical English hymn-writer ".

‡ *E.H.*, 549, verses 1–3.

PART TWO

THE PEOPLE IN THE STORY

CHAPTER 12

The Cloister and the Hearth

BISHOPS, PRIESTS, AND DEACONS

HAVING given some account of the circumstances, experiences, and necessities which have brought forth our hymns, let us now address ourselves to the question, " What sort of people wrote our hymns ? "

It is natural that most of our hymn-writers were clergymen or nonconformist ministers ; the parson and the minister are in the best position for seeing the necessities of their people in this respect, and if they happen to be (as commonly they used to be) of a literary turn, in the best position for meeting them. But the next chapter will show how great has been the contribution of the laity to our heritage.

We will, then, with decent submission, begin with the ordained ministry of the Church of England, and in that Church with those who were, or became, bishops.

The episcopal contribution to our hymnody is not, by the standards of eighteenth-century prolixity, very large, but it has been both successful and influential. There are thirty-three bishops, four of them American, whose names are honoured for hymns in more or less common use in this country. Of the Americans we shall say something in a later chapter ; but it is worth noticing at the beginning that of the twenty-nine English bishops, only six were born before the year 1807. This is a striking confirmation of what we said at an earlier stage, that after the twofold awakening which the Church of England underwent in the authorization of hymnody in 1821 and the Oxford

Movement from 1833 onwards, it was the clergy who not only encouraged but actually led the way in hymn-writing.

Without doubt the most influential of these eminent clergymen was Reginald Heber (1783–1826), of Calcutta, who was Vicar of Hodnet in Shropshire at the time when most of his hymns were written. We have already observed his missionary zeal, but more notable even than this was his inauguration of the " romantic " school of hymn-writing. His life falls entirely within the long life (1770–1850) of the poet William Wordsworth, and he has celebrated as beautifully as any Christian poet the revived respect for nature that had, already, by the first quarter of the nineteenth century, become part of the English literary tradition. " Brightest and best of the sons of the morning " * is a capital example of this ; in that hymn Heber is not calling on the congregation to worship nature, but he provides for his theme a background of natural beauty. The hymn deals with the worship of the humble and contrite heart, but it was something new, in 1811, for Christians to sing of humility in terms not of minatory censure but of happy gratitude.

Heber's work was, of course, romantic in its fullest sense ; in a once-famous but now (I believe) little-used hymn, Heber throws all topographical accuracy to the winds in order to fill in his scenic background :

> By cool Siloam's shady rill
> How sweet the lily grows !
> How sweet the breath, beneath the hill,
> Of Sharon's dewy rose ! †

On this Dr. Millar Patrick has commented : " The first two lines of this hymn have been caustically described, by one who has intimate knowledge of the conditions in present-day Jerusalem, as containing ' the maximum of mis-statement in the minimum of space ' ".‡ And even if we judge a hymn-writer entitled to a certain poetic freedom,

---

* *E.H.*, 41.   † *Church Hymnary* (1927), 309, verse 1.
‡ *Supplement* to the *Handbook to the Church Hymnary* (1936), page 37.

when he goes so far from the truth as this he becomes vulnerable in an age when, in war and peace, everybody has been nearly everywhere. The same kind of criticism might be directed at a verse of one of his well-known hymns :

> They met the tyrant's brandished steel,
>   The lion's gory mane,
> They bowed their necks, the death to feel,
>   Who follows in their train ?

on the ground that his mane was not the most formidable part of the lion from the point of view of the unfortunate victim in the Roman arena.

But this is not of the essence of Heber. Here is what he wrote in 1811 in the preface to his first collection of hymns :

No fulsome or indecorous language has been knowingly adopted ; no erotic addresses to him whom no unclean lips can approach ; no allegories, ill understood and worse applied.

Heber was substituting for the imagery of pietistic devotion that of created nature ; and even though Lynch did get into trouble for writing in just Heber's style forty years later, and even though the technique was much abused, Heber did deliver the English hymn from the sourness which was overtaking the devotional hymns of decadent Wesleyanism. Heber's attitude to nature can be well seen in the last verse of " I praised the earth ", one of his most moving hymns :

> O God, O good beyond compare,
> If thus thy meaner works are fair,
> If thus thy beauties gild the span
> Of ruined earth and sinful man,
> How glorious must the mansion be
> Where thy redeemed shall dwell with thee ! *

Even his " Holy ! Holy ! Holy ! ",† one of Tennyson's favourites, though it is a hymn of pure adoration, praises

---

* *Hymns Ancient and Modern* (revised 1950), 173, verse 3.
† *E.H.*, 162.

God less as the awful King of the Calvinists than as the Lord " perfect in power, in love and purity ", surrounded with all the more attractive elements in the scenery of the apocalyptic heaven. This is Heber's most famous hymn, but we honour him also for " God, that madest earth and heaven ", " Bread of the world ", and " When spring unlocks the flowers ".* Heber's final collection came out posthumously in 1827 ; Montgomery's best collection appeared in 1825. Between them, these two authors, the one from the aristocracy of the north Midlands and the other from the industrial tumult of Sheffield, launched Anglican hymnody on its victorious progress.

Heber is the only bishop whose work influenced the course of English hymnody ; but some of the other bishops have made famous contributions. There is John Cosin of Durham (1594–1672), the eldest of them, who wrote the translation of *Veni Creator* beginning " Come, Holy Ghost, our souls inspire ", † which was one of the two hymns authorized in the 1662 Book of Common Prayer. Then there is Thomas Ken (1637–1711) of Bath and Wells, who while he was a court-chaplain refused to provide lodging in his house for Nell Gwynn and thereby won unexpectedly the respect of King Charles II and a bishopric ; his morning and evening hymns,‡ written for the boys of Winchester College, are both classics. Richard Mant (1776–1848), of Down and Connor with Dromore in Ireland, gave us " Bright the vision that delighted ".§

These three come from the earlier generations. Three others of Victorian days have produced well-known hymns. Christopher Wordsworth (1807–85) of Lincoln is the archetype of the nineteenth-century bishop hymnographer. His hymns were almost entirely seasonal, never highly inspired, always sound, usually a little commonplace. The best known is " Gracious Spirit, Holy Ghost ",‖ which is characteristic not only in being written for a season of the

* *E.H.*, 268, 305, and 299.   † *E.H.*, 153.
‡ *E.H.*, 257 and 267.   § *E.H.*, 372.   ‖ *E.H.*, 396.

church's year but also in its close adherence to Scripture. This latter quality is well seen in " Hark, the sound of holy voices ",* whose famous verse about being " sawn asunder, slain with sword " is a paraphrase of *Hebrews* xi. 37. In the same metre is the Easter hymn, " Alleluia, Alleluia ",† which is one of the few which have come to terms with the mysterious passages about the seed and the harvest in *St. John* xii. 24 ff. and *I Corinthians* xv. 37, 42-4. " See the Conqueror ", his Ascensiontide hymn, is full of didactic material from the Old and New Testaments, especially in two verses which have recently disappeared from *Hymns Ancient and Modern* :

Now our heavenly Aaron enters with his Blood within the veil ;
Joshua now is come to Canaan and the kings before him quail ;
Now he plants the tribes of Israel in their promised resting-
    place ;
Now our great Elijah offers double portion of his grace . . .

He who walked with God and pleased him, preaching truth
    and doom to come ;
He, our Enoch is translated to his everlasting home.‡

Wordsworth is essentially the teacher and pastor in his hymns, and they have proved well-wearing material of an undistinguished kind.

   Bishop How of Wakefield (1823-97) is another Words-worth, a little gentler in his idiom.   One verse that he wrote for children has authentic and wistful beauty :

> It is a thing most wonderful,
>   Almost too wonderful to be,
> That God's own Son should come from heaven
>   And die to save a child like me.§

How wrote on the spacious style and loved long hymns. That one, " For all the saints ", and " To thee our God

* *E.H.*, 198.   † *E.H.*, 127.
‡ *Hymns Ancient and Modern* (standard edition), 148, verses 4 and 5.
§ *E.H.*, 597, verse 1.

we fly ",* although surviving as long hymns, are all shortened in modern books from their original length. His pressure was always low enough to allow of a sustained effort.

Edward Bickersteth (1825–1906) of Exeter was one of the most evangelically-minded of the nineteenth-century bishops, and was responsible for *Hymns Ancient and Modern's* chief competitor, the *Hymnal Companion*. This book contains a large number of his own hymns, very few of which come above the second-rate, and only one of which has made much impression on Christians at large. But that one, " Peace, perfect peace ", has become a classic. Its second line has repelled some, but the little series of epigrams has much that is precious.

> Peace, perfect peace, by thronging duties prest ?
> To do the will of Jesus, this is rest.
>
> Peace, perfect peace, with loved ones far away ?
> In Jesus' keeping we are safe, and they.
>
> Peace, perfect peace, our future all unknown ?
> Jesus we know, and he is on the throne.
>
> Peace, perfect peace, death shadowing us and ours ?
> Jesus has vanquished death and all its powers.†

Now that it has been rescued from bondage to an unhappy tune, it has much to say. One evening in the winter of early 1941 the Archbishop of York (William Temple) conducted a broadcast service. To the blacked-out citizens of London, " pressed by thronging duties " all day, separated from loved ones in the evening, overshadowed by death at night, these lines, which he caused to be sung, brought home the Gospel more fully than any words, even from that eloquent and devoted shepherd of the Church, could have done. Few men were less sentimental than Dr. Temple, but he knew that a hymn which at some times might be

---

* *E.H.*, 641 and 565.   † *E.H.*, 468, verses 2, 4, 5, and 6.

sentimental would thus speak to the condition of be-
leaguered Englishmen.

The other bishops have made less extensive contributions
to our hymn-books. Jeremy Taylor (1613–67) of Down
and Connor is remembered for " Draw nigh to thy Jerusalem " * which we quote in our last chapter. Archbishop
Richard Whateley (1787–1863), that attractive Irishman
with the mordant wit who, when the Duke of Wellington
was elected Chancellor of the University of Oxford, applied
for the command of the Horse Guards, comes into this story
for the verse " Guard us waking " which he added to Heber's
" God that madest earth and heaven ".† Heber's lines,
by the way, are said to have been written on hearing the
tune " All through the night ", and the complete hymn was
first, and is now usually, sung to that melody.[45] Whateley's
verse begins with a rendering of the ancient prayer, " Save
us, O Lord, waking . . ."

Another Irish archbishop who wrote hymns was Richard
Trench (1807–86) ; " Let all men know that all men move
under a canopy of love " ‡ is his best known, but worth
remembering also are the gentle lines beginning

> Make channels for the streams of love
> Where they may broadly run,
> And love has overflowing streams
> To feed them every one.§

Bishop Armstrong of Grahamstown (1813–56) is still
honoured for a hymn for clergy, " O thou who makest
souls to shine ",‖ and another bishop of a foreign see,
Edward Cotton of Calcutta (1813–66) is known for " We
thank thee, Lord, for this fair earth ".¶ J. R. Woodford
(1820–85) of Ely is best remembered for two excellent
translations, " God from on high hath heard " ** and
" Thee we adore, O hidden Saviour ".††

* *C.P.*, 121. † *E.H.*, 268. ‡ *Songs of Praise*, 505.
§ *Congregational Hymnary*, 516.
‖ *Hymns Ancient and Modern*, 353/471.
¶ *Songs of Praise*, 691. ** *C.P.*, 82. †† *E.H.*, 331.

Two English primates have each a small niche in hymnody. W. D. Maclagan (1826–1910) of York for " The saints of God, their conflict past " * and E. W. Benson (1829–96) of Canterbury for the Rogationtide hymn " O Throned, O crowned with all renown ".† William Stubbs of Oxford (1825–1906) belongs to the same generation, and his lines beginning

> Lead me, Almighty Father, Spirit, Son,
> Whither thou wilt, I follow, no delay ‡

are worth pondering.

The bishops of later generations have been less prolific than their predecessors, but they kept up a good succession. Outstanding among their hymns are " O thou, who gavest power to love ",§ a marriage hymn by Mandell Creighton (1843–1901) of London, and " Before thy throne, O God, we kneel " ‖ by Boyd Carpenter of Ripon (1841–1918). Handley Moule of Durham (1841–1920) wrote " Come in, O come, the door stands open now " ¶ which has the distinction of being one of the three English hymns translated in the current hymn-book of the Evangelical Lutherans of Germany.

In our final group come the episcopal authors of some excellent modern hymns. Here are the opening lines of one by Bishop Boutflower (1863–1942) which appears in the new *Hymns Ancient and Modern* :

> O joy of God, that comest in the morning,
>   For thee, unsunned, we wait and eastward gaze,
> Lift on our dark the splendours of thy dawning,
>   Flood all our being in the feast of praise.**

J. H. B. Masterman of Plymouth (1867–1933) is now well

* *Hymns Ancient and Modern*, 428/572.
† *Hymns Ancient and Modern* (standard edition), 505.
‡ *Oxford Hymn Book*, 237.   § *E.H.*, 347.
‖ *Methodist Hymn Book*, 884.   ¶ *Ib.*, 472.
** *Hymns Ancient and Modern* (revised), 404.

known for "Almighty Father, who dost give the gift of life
to all that live ",* but perhaps even more excellent was a
hymn of his for use in time of war beginning

> O Saviour Christ, our sins again
> Have nailed thee on thy cross of pain.
> And in the darkness thou dost plead
> For all thy world's exceeding need.†

Bishop Palmer of Bombay wrote a translation of *Lobe den
Herren* beginning " Praise thou the Lord, O my soul, let
thy song upward soaring ",‡ and the late J. R. Darbyshire,
Bishop of Glasgow and Archbishop of Cape Town, wrote
several manly hymns, of which the best is probably, " Who
dreads, yet undismayed dares face his terror ",§ a really
penetrating hymn about St. Thomas the Doubter.   Bishop
Burroughs of Ripon has a good young people's hymn in
Songs of Praise beginning " Lord God, from whom all life ",‖
and G. K. A. Bell (1883–1958) sometime Bishop of Chichester
has in the same book some excellent lines beginning " Christ
is the King !   O friends, rejoice ".¶   The long procession
ends with the name of the Bishop of Truro, Dr. E. R.
Morgan, who contributed a splendid Eucharistic hymn to the
most recent edition of *Hymns Ancient and Modern*, beginning

> Thee, living Christ, our eyes behold
>   Amid thy church appearing,
> All girt about thy breast with gold
>   And bright apparel wearing.**

If we may briefly refer to the musical contribution of our
English bishops to our hymn-books, we shall be able to
complete a case for saying that the most implacable opponent

---

* *Ib.*, 583.   † *Congregational Hymnary*, 563.
‡ *Clarendon Hymn Book*, 238.
§ *Hymns Ancient and Modern* (revised), 534.
‖ *Songs of Praise*, 343.   ¶ *Ib.*, 242.
** *Hymns Ancient and Modern* (revised), 422.

of prelacy could not compile an effective hymn-book which had no bishop's name in its indexes. The two best-known episcopal tunes are QUAM DILECTA * (We love the place), by Bishop Jenner of Dunedin, and NEWINGTON † (Thine for ever) by Archbishop Maclagan ; Maclagan wrote several other tunes as well, nor must we forget the excellent tunes of Thomas Banks Strong, Bishop of Oxford, which appear in the *Oxford Hymnal*. The best known of these is HEBDOMADAL,‡ for " Praise to the Holiest ", so named because it was composed during one of the less lively sessions of the Hebdomadal Council.

Before we leave the exalted culture of the Precincts we had better take a glance at the hymns that have come from the deaneries. The earliest dean-hymnographer, if we leave out John Donne,§ is Samuel Crossman. When he wrote " Jerusalem on high " ‖ and " My song is love unknown " ¶ he was not a dean, for he only reached the deanery of Bristol a few weeks before he died. But those two hymns are firmly established. So far as we can discover " Jerusalem " is comparatively rarely sung now, although it was once much more popular ; " My song is love unknown ", on the other hand, only rarely found in nineteenth-century books and never earlier, has only become really popular since it was set in *Songs of Praise* to John Ireland's beautiful tune, LOVE UNKNOWN.¶ It has been, however, well loved by Nonconformists since its inclusion in the *Congregational Church Hymnal* of 1887.

William Bullock, Dean of Halifax, Nova Scotia, wrote the greater part of " We love the place, O God " ;** we have just mentioned its tune, and may comment here on the strange providence which produced so simple and innocent a hymn from such a collocation of ecclesiastical dignities.

---

* *E.H.*, 508.   † *C.P.*, 252.   ‡ *Oxford Hymn Book,* 279.
§ Donne's " Wilt thou forgive that sin " (*E.H.*, 515) is believed to have been sung in St. Paul's during the period following the Restoration ; but it is a personal meditation rather than a hymn.
‖ *E.H.*, 411.   ¶ *C.P.*, 128.   ** *E.H.*, 508.

Dean Milman of St. Paul's wrote " Ride on, ride on in majesty ",* which, rather than any of his other hymns, entitles him to high honour. But the most celebrated hymnographical dean was Alford of Canterbury, who has given us, among other things, " Ten thousand times ten thousand ",† " Come, ye thankful people, come ",‡ and " Forward ! be our watchword ".§ Alford was keenly interested in the subject ; two things are worth recording about him here. One is that he took no responsibility for the alterations made to " Come, ye thankful people " in the first and subsequent editions of *Hymns Ancient and Modern* and the other concerns " Forward ! be our watchword ". It seems that he was invited to write a processional for some high occasion in Canterbury Cathedral, and that he wrote one—in his study. The precentor who had commissioned the hymn pointed out that admirable though it was, its rhythm was unsuitable for singing on the march. The dean's reply was to write another—in the cathedral. He paced round the aisles at processional-speed, and the result was the hymn which is still greatly loved by those who want a really long hymn for a festival procession. Taken together, these two stories show the dean as an honest man who could distinguish between courteous criticism and editorial ruthlessness.

Arthur Penrhyn Stanley, Dean of Westminster, made a few hymns of an original kind ; they have not had a long life, but the best known is probably his hymn for the Feast of the Transfiguration,

> O Master, it is good to be
> High on the mountain here with thee.

This is an excellent piece of allusive and cultivated writing ; but it has been not unreasonably pointed out that the singer

* *E.H.*, 620.   † *E.H.*, 486.
‡ *E.H.*, 289 (compare *Hymns Ancient and Modern*, 382/482).
§ *E.H.*, 642.

needs a good deal of erudition to catch the allusions in its second verse :

> O Master, it is good to be
> With thee, and with thy faithful three ;
> Here, where the Apostle's heart of rock
> Is nerved against temptation's shock ;
> Here, where the Son of Thunder learns
> The thought that breathes, the word that burns ;
> Here, where on eagle's wings we move
> With him whose last best creed is love.*

It is beautifully done, and Peter and James stand out fairly clearly ; but the last couplet makes what would now be thought a rather large assumption concerning the authorship of the Fourth Gospel. Another hymn of his, in the same rather ponderously ceremonial style, is

> The Lord is come, on Syrian soil
> The child of poverty and toil.†

It is not unfitting that the Transfiguration should have been dealt with also by a dean of the next generation, John Armitage Robinson of Wells, whose hymn, " 'Tis good, Lord, to be here ",‡ stands next to Stanley's in the *English Hymnal*, and deals with the subject much more simply. By Armitage Robinson's day the age of academic prelacy had passed, and we have seen in our account of the bishops what a good effect this had in letting the air in on Anglican hymnody.

Dean Plumptre, also of Wells, wrote several hymns of good quality, one of which seems due for a long stay. " Thy hand, O God, has guided " § has been given the promise of a long life by Basil Harwood's tune THORNBURY, and an excellent hymn of aspiration to church unity it is, with its stirring refrain, " One Church, one Faith, one Lord ". Like Alford, he is responsible for a popular Anglican processional, " Rejoice, ye pure in heart ", ‖ which is nowadays

---

* *E.H.*, 235, verse 2.   † *E.H.*, 48.   ‡ *E.H.*, 236.
§ *E.H.*, 545.   ‖ *E.H.*, 644.

set to a grand tune (ICH HALTE), but which is a very good
example of the skill by which a leisured Anglican dignitary
of the nineteenth century could spin out a very thin thread
to a very generous length.   A reviewer of the 1950 revision
of *Hymns Ancient and Modern*, remarked that some of the
processional hymns at the end of that book are so long that
the people would need to walk about in order to keep
awake ; [46] we may think this a rather generalized criticism,
but it is certainly true of Dean Plumptre's processional that
while the choir is presumably on the move, the sense in the
words is as completely static as could well be achieved in
forty lines of writing.

The last of our deans is the recent Dean of Durham,
Dr. Alington, sometime Head Master of Eton.   His hymns
come partly from the school and partly from the cathedral.
Several of them are in the latest *Hymns Ancient and Modern*,
of which the best known, which has been in circulation for
twenty years and dates from his Eton days, is the Easter
hymn, " Good Christian men, rejoice and sing ".*   All his
hymns show clean writing of the unemotional sort we expect
from an Anglican dignitary who has been a schoolmaster.
We shall refer to him again.

So much for the bishops and deans.   We gather that
archdeacons and chancellors have been too busy to write
hymns†—though we must raise a salute for Archdeacon
Edmund Prys, who, holding the livings of Maentrog and
Penrhyndeudraeth in the early seventeenth century, produced in 1621 the only Welsh metrical Psalter, and gave the
world two immortal psalm-tunes, ST. MARY and SONG 67.‡
Coming now to the rank-and-file ministry of the Church
of England, we have a good list of hymn-writers upon

* *Hymns Ancient and Modern* (revised 1950), 603 ; *C.P.*, 149.
† Since this was written, Dr. Adam Fox, author of several hymns in
the revised *Hymns Ancient and Modern*, has become Archdeacon of Westminster ; we are glad of this reason for modifying our generalization.
‡ *E.H.*, 84 and 197.

whom, although they are all worthy men, we need not dwell at length.   For who, if not a bishop, shall write hymns for his church but the parish priest ?   Here again, of course, it is the nineteenth century that gives the Anglican clergy their chance to enrich hymnody, and to this work they gave themselves with energy.

Before 1800 only three clergymen of the Church of England come into our story ; but they are a powerful trio. First there is John Mason (1645–94), Rector of Water Stratford.   He has the distinction of being the compiler of the first hymn-book called *Songs of Praise*, and although this was not, of course, a hymn-book in the modern sense, it did contain some lyrics that have commended themselves to our own generation.   The best known of these is " How shall I sing that majesty ",* but not less distinguished for tenderness and subtlety is " My Lord, my Love was crucified ", whose last eight lines run as follows :

> I bless thy wise and wondrous love,
>   Which binds me to be free ;
> Which makes us leave our earthly snares,
>   That we may come to thee ;
> I come, I wait, I hear, I pray,
>   Thy footsteps, Lord, I trace ;
> I sing to think this is the way
>   Unto my Saviour's face.†

Mason had a short and turbulent life.   Towards its close " he had a vision of Jesus wearing a glorious crown, and with an aspect of unutterable majesty.   He spoke about this and preached a sermon, ' The Midnight Cry ', proclaiming the nearness of the approach of the second Advent.   A report spread that this would be at his own village : Water Stratford was crowded with people, who brought in furniture and provisions ;   extraordinary scenes of singing, leaping, and dancing took place, and in the midst of excitement the old man passed away, still testifying that he had

* *E.H.*, 404.   † *C.P.*, 605, verse 3.

seen the Lord, and that it was time for the generations to tremble ; but his last words were, ' I am full of the loving-kindness of the Lord '." [47]   If this strange story be taken along with the ecstatic diction of his hymns, Mason may be called something of a mystic and something of an enthusiast ; his was clearly one of those generous souls who could find no words or acts in this life by which to glorify his God.

> Thousands of thousands stand around
>   Thy throne, O God most high ;
> Ten thousand times ten thousand sound
>   Thy praise ; but who am I ? *

> To whom, Lord, would I sing, but thee,
>   The maker of my tongue ?
> Lo, other lords would seize on me,
>   But I to thee belong.
> As waters haste into their sea,
>   And earth into its earth,
> So let my soul return to thee
>   From whom it had its birth.†

The second of the three clergymen is Nicholas Brady, an Irish Protestant who was an active supporter of King William III. With another Irishman, Nahum Tate (who became Poet Laureate in 1692), Brady collaborated in the *New Version* of the Metrical Psalter, to which we have already referred. Just which psalms or lines were written by Brady remains undiscoverable, although of the hymns that followed the psalms it is generally thought that " While shepherds watched " ‡ is entirely the work of Tate. Brady's most notable charge in this country was the rectory of Stratford-on-Avon.

Third in the trio stands John Newton, of whom we have already said enough. His Olney Hymns represent one of the most important single contributions made to our hymnody. As the author of " How sweet the name of Jesus sounds ",§

---

* *E.H.*, 404, verse 1.   † *Songs of Praise*, 675, verse 3.
‡ *E.H.*, 30.   § *E.H.*, 405.

" Glorious things of thee are spoken ",* " Come, my soul, thy suit prepare ",† and " Begone, unbelief ",‡ he has a good claim to be the leader of the English clerical school of hymn-writers.

Somewhere between the great days of the evangelicals and the Oxford Movement stand two hymn-writing parsons, Edward Cooper, author of " Father of heaven, whose love profound ",§ and John Marriott, [48] author of " Thou, whose almighty Word ".|| The two hymns, though widely different in subject matter, have this in common, that they are cast in what became about that time a rather conventional trinitarian form—four verses, one for each Person of the Trinity, and one for the undivided Godhead. Edmeston's " Lead us, heavenly Father " ¶ is on the same pattern, without the last verse. Cooper was Rector of Yoxall, Staffordshire, and his hymn first appeared in a private collection in 1805. Marriott was Vicar of Cotesbach, near Lutterworth ; he moved to Devonshire for his wife's health, and there, in the neighbourhood of Exeter, held several curacies in plurality with that at Cottesbach. The hymn was written in 1813, with the tune of the National Anthem in mind ; but it was not heard in public until six weeks after the author's death, when, on 12 May 1825, it was read, and made a great impression, at a meeting of the London Missionary Society.

The nineteenth century provides a long list of clerical contributors to the treasury ; many of these we have mentioned in speaking of the Oxford Movement. There was Keble at the head, author of " There is a book, who runs may read " ** and " Blest are the pure in heart " ; †† there followed him J. H. Gurney, Vicar of St. Mary's, Bryanston Square (" We saw thee not when thou didst come "),‡‡ J. S. B. Monsell, Vicar of Guildford, (" Fight the good

* *E.H.*, 393.   † *E.H.*, 377.   ‡ *C.P.*, 396.
§ *E.H.*, 387. || *E.H.*, 553.   ¶ *E.H.*, 426.
** *E.H.*, 497.   †† *E.H.*, 370 (verses 1 and 3 only by Keble).
‡‡ *E.H.*, 509.

fight " * and " O worship the Lord in the beauty of holiness "),† G. R. Prynne of Plymouth (" Jesu, meek and gentle "),‡ Godfrey Thring, brother of Edward Thring of Uppingham, Prebendary of Wells (" Fierce raged the tempest ",§ " The radiant morn hath passed away ",‖ " From the eastern mountains ") ¶ and John Ellerton of Crew (" The day thou gavest ",** " Saviour, again to thy dear Name ",†† and others mentioned on page 84). Lewis Hensley, Vicar and Rural Dean of Hitchin, Hertfordshire, wrote " Thy kingdom come, O God ",‡‡ and T. B. Pollock of St. Alban's, Birmingham, wrote a number of metrical litanies that have had some vogue. In more recent times we have had the translation of St. Francis's Canticle of the Sun beginning " All creatures of our God and King " §§ from W. H. Draper, who became Master of the Temple, and the splendid work in the reformation of English hymnody of Percy Dearmer, Canon of Westminster, beginning with the *English Hymnal* in 1906 ; in that book are several of his hymns, and in *Songs of Praise*, its wayward successor, a very large number, many of them discreetly superscribed only by initials such as " A. F." and " A. G." Finally we must mention the work of Canon G. W. Briggs of Worcester, who has carried on the Dearmer tradition, not, however, failing to add a considerable evangelical leaven to the somewhat exquisite mixture which Dearmer had left ; Canon Briggs has written many hymns, of which " Christ is the world's true light " and " Now is eternal life " ‖‖ are among the finest.

But we have left unmentioned the two greatest names of all. Thomas Kelly, son of an Irish judge, ordained in 1792, later inhibited for methodistical sympathies, founder of a sect which died with him, is honoured for the memory of his universal and unfailing kindliness and for three of his

* *E.H.*, 389. † *E.H.*, 42. ‡ *E.H.*, 415.
§ *E.H.*, 541. ‖ *E.H.*, 279. ¶ *E.H.*, 615.
** *E.H.*, 277. †† *E.H.*, 273. ‡‡ *E.H.*, 554.
§§ *C.P.*, 31. ‖‖ *C.P.*, 172 and 420. Cf. page 310 below.

765 hymns. His work is usually commonplace, and is extensively used now only by the Plymouth Brethren. But three of his hymns on the crucified and exalted Christ remain well known and loved, " Look, ye saints, the sight is glorious ",* " We sing the praise of him who died ",† and " The head that once was crowned with thorns ".‡ Of these the first is a slightly crude but magnificently ecstatic utterance, the second a great classic, the third, in our judgment, the greatest of English hymns (see below, page 315).

But none of these, nor even " How sweet the name of Jesus sounds ", has reached the popularity of " Abide with me ",§ which is the work of H. F. Lyte of Brixham. There is no need to emphasize further what this hymn has meant to Englishmen during its hundred years of life. In it this obscure and humble curate has ministered to a parish as wide as the English-speaking world. Of the popularity of his other famous hymn, " Praise, my soul ",‖ we give much evidence in Chapter 19.

* *C.P.*, 164.   † *E.H.*, 510.   ‡ *E.H.*, 147.
§ *E.H.*, 363.   ‖ *E.H.*, 470.

CHAPTER 13

The Manse, The Mission, and The Presbytery

NON-ANGLICAN MINISTERS AND CLERGY

ANGLICAN hymnody has its classical age in the nineteenth century, and if I have to tell the story of how Anglican bishops and parsons of that period wrote their hymns, I am telling a story of the most conventional and unemotional society in the world. I have drawn off all the fire of the story for my chapters on the church's wars, in which I could write of Philip Pusey and Charles Kingsley as hymn-writers. But although there was much to be done, and although the late Anthony Trollope is not to be exclusively relied on as an authority for the church's behaviour during the Victorian Age, the fact remains that if we are writing about parsons, *qua* parsons, as hymn-writers, we are writing about a set of men whose lives were abundantly serene and without traces of dramatic conversion and spiritual tumult. The fact is that in the nineteenth century the F. W. Robertsons and F. D. Maurices, the men of urgency and action, did not write the hymns. Hymn-writing was the work of liturgists, not the uninhibited outpourings of the newly converted. Hymns have traditionally been for the Church of England a matter less of driving home the Gospel message of repentance than of adorning the liturgy ; of this I shall say more at a later stage.* It follows then that we can do little more than enumerate the men and their hymns, and can tell few stories about the men's lives that may have anything to do with their hymns.

* Chapter 19, at the end.

147

When we turn to the hymns of the Nonconformist ministry, we move into a different world altogether. For one
thing, we move back into the eighteenth century, since this
was their classical age. For another, we move into the
atmosphere of conversion and enthusiasm, of dark doctrines
and solemn covenants. For a third and more general consideration, we move back into an age of less literacy, less
easy communication, less universal printing, and less opportunity for mediocrity. Newton and Toplady fall outside
the generalization we have just made about the Anglican
hymn-writing parsons simply inasmuch as the one was
writing to order for an illiterate congregation which would
learn the faith in no other way ; and the other was writing
from a burning conviction arising from his extreme Calvinist
experience. In the main, of course, the average Anglican
parson of the eighteenth century was better at writing textbooks or even novels than at writing hymns ; and it is the
ministers of the Baptists and Independents, and the Wesleyan
preachers, who led the way.

Although Isaac Watts and Philip Doddridge, of whom we
have already said enough, were the fathers of English
Protestant hymnody, it was a Baptist who, a generation
earlier, published the first English church hymns. He was
Benjamin Keach, who in 1673 introduced at his church in
Southwark the custom of singing a hymn at the close of the
Lord's Supper, in imitation of Christ and the Apostles as
recorded in the New Testament. These hymns he composed himself, and they were published in the fourth edition
of his *War with the Powers of Darkness* in 1676. About 300 of
his hymns were collected and published in 1691. None of
these has survived in common use.

In the generations contemporary with and subsequent to
that of Watts, however, there are several people whose
hymns have survived and whose stories are worth repeating.

Take for example Simon Browne, an Independent minister
who was a near neighbour and a younger contemporary of
Watts. He has left us a beautiful hymn of the Holy Spirit

which, somewhat edited, we know as " Come, gracious
Spirit, heavenly Dove ".* Browne, during his ministry in
London, was overtaken one night by a highwayman who
attempted to rob him. In the ensuing fight Browne knocked
the man down and killed him. For the last years of his
life the incident preyed on his mind until he became convinced that he was a murderer. He died at fifty-two
virtually insane. This may be not a very religious experience—but it is the characteristic reaction of a Calvinist-
trained mind to such a crisis as this. That was the sort of
age and spiritual climate in which these men were living.

Or take Joseph Hart (1712–68), whose 222 hymns are
now hardly heard except among the Baptists, but who
wrote in the preface to his collection of hymns (1759) an
account of his spiritual journey which is in its way a little
classic. He tells us minutely of the stages by which, from
his twenty-first to his forty-fourth year, he was brought to
surrender himself to the Gospel. Bunyan himself plumbed
no greater depths of despair and compassed no wider areas
of scepticism than did Hart, who was an intellectual and a
man of some means. In the end, after writing his hymns,
Hart became minister of the Independent Chapel in Jewin
Street, London, where he served for eight years until he
died. " Come, ye sinners, poor and wretched " † and the
better-known " Come, Holy Spirit, come " ‡ are the fruit
of this intense personal experience of conversion ; they and
their fellows mark for him the border-country between
conversion and evangelism.

Here, again, is a boy born of lowly parents in a Norfolk
market town, apprenticed at 15 to a hairdresser in London ;
the hairdresser found him more inclined to read books than
to attend to his duties ; his mother nursed the ambition
that he should become a clergyman of the Established
Church. At 17 you can see him spending a Sunday making
merry in the country. He and his friends have been pestered
by an old woman who insists on telling their fortunes ; they

* C.P., 205.　　† Methodist Hymn Book, 324.　　‡ C.P., 206.

find that it will make for better entertainment if they make the old woman drunk before she talks. As a result, the boy hears that he will live to see his children and grandchildren. He falls silent and turns away : this is a warning—that so gracious an announcement should come from a source so squalid and so heartlessly degraded by his own act. A few Sundays later he heard George Whitefield preaching with his usual minatory power on the text " O generation of vipers, who hath warned you to flee from the wrath to come ? " ; this, understandably, threw him into despair. Three years later he wrote in one of his books an inscription in Latin which, being translated, reads :

Born again on the Sabbath day, 24 May, 1752, by the powerful preaching of George Whitefield. Having tasted for three years and seven months the pains of renewal, I found full and free absolution, through the precious blood of Jesus Christ (Tuesday, December 10, 1755), to whom be honour and glory for ever. Amen.

This was the story of Robert Robinson (1735–90), the author of " Come, thou Fount of every blessing " ; * nor is that the end. He was called to the oversight of a Calvinistic Methodist congregation at Mildenhall, Suffolk, in 1758 ; within a year he had become minister of an Independent congregation at Norwich (the church now known as " Old Meeting "). A few months later he was invited to a Baptist Church at Cambridge as supply-preacher, and in 1761 he took full pastoral charge of the church. He was thus Methodist, Congregationalist, and Baptist within two years ; but Baptist he thereafter remained. He was a conspicuous orator, but never lost his sense of the imminence of judgment, and went through long periods of spiritual darkness. One day, towards the end of his life, when he was sadly conscious of moral regression, he was travelling in a stage-coach. A lady beside him was reading a book, and she drew his attention to verses in it which particularly

* C.P., 442.

pleased her. Seeing the verses, he tried to turn the con-
versation, but the lady insisted, and at last he burst out in
distress, " Madam, I am the unhappy man who wrote that
hymn many years ago ; and I would give a thousand
worlds, if I had them, to enjoy the feelings I had then ! "
One verse was

> Come, thou fount of every blessing,
>   Tune my heart to sing thy grace ;
> Streams of mercy, never ceasing,
>   Call for songs of loudest praise.

They still appear in some of our hymn-books ; usually their
crude phrases have to be editorially smoothed, but the
passion is still there. " Mighty God, while angels bless
thee ",* less passionate, and far more polished, is his other
well-known hymn.

Another Baptist minister who was notable in his day for
his hymns was Samuel Medley (1738–99), who after a short
period in the Navy was converted at 21 by a sermon of Isaac
Watts's which was read to him, and became Baptist minister
at Watford and at Byrom Street, Liverpool. His hymns
are still used by the Baptists, but they have found little
favour beyond that denomination.

In the nineteenth and twentieth centuries a few notable
contributions have been made by ministers of reformed
Nonconformity to English hymnody. The Congregationalists have played a more conspicuous part here than the
Baptists. From Congregationalism comes Andrew Reed's
" Spirit divine, attend our prayers ",† recently making its
debut in *Hymns Ancient and Modern*, long treasured by his
own denomination. Then there is the redoubtable Thomas
Binney, who wrote " Eternal Light ! Eternal Light ! " ‡
while he was minister at Newport, Isle of Wight, before he
became minister of the King's Weigh House Chapel in

* *C.P.*, 68.
† *Hymns Ancient and Modern* (1950), 239 : *C.P.*, 210.
‡ *C.P.*, 21.

London. Binney was a leader of the movement in Congregationalism away from the crudities and liturgical
slovenliness of latter-day Calvinism towards a mode of
worship that left fuller play for the liberal, aesthetic, and
ceremonious elements. His revival of liturgy at the King's
Weigh House paved the way for the spectacular liturgical
splendours of that Church in the days of Dr. W. E. Orchard,
who was minister there until 1931, and who subsequently
became a Roman Catholic. Binney's preface to Baird's
A Chapter on Liturgies and his address *On Poetry and Devotion*,
given to the Congregational Union in 1843, are classics of
liturgical literature. This sensitive approach to the mys-
teries of the faith is well reflected in the one hymn by
which he is remembered—

> O how shall I, whose native sphere
>   Is dark, whose mind is dim,
> Before the Ineffable appear,
> And on my naked spirit bear
>   The uncreated beam.
>
> There is a way for man to rise
>   To that sublime abode ;
> An offering and a Sacrifice,
> A Holy Spirit's energies,
>   An advocate with God.
>
> These, these prepare us for the sight
>   Of holiness above ;
> The sons of ignorance and night
> May dwell in the eternal light
>   Through the eternal love.*

This has something of Heber's romantic [49] and subtle touch ;
it was written on contemplating a particularly impressive
sunset. But it adds to that romanticism a touch of Calvinist
austerity and self-abasement that makes it one of the noblest
and most sympathetic expressions of the " numinous " in
our language.

* *C.P.*, 21, verses 3–5.

Josiah Conder, Congregationalism's great pioneer-editor, was a layman, and comes into the next chapter. His son, the Rev. E. R. Conder, who was Chairman of the Congregational Union in 1873, is the author of one of the loveliest children's hymns ever written, which is also one of the very few which treat of the " hidden years " of the life of Jesus ; it begins :

> Ye fair green hills of Galilee
>   That girdle quiet Nazareth,
> What glorious vision did ye see
>   When he who conquered sin and death
> Your flowery slopes and summits trod,
> And grew in grace with man and God ? *

Romantic again, of course—the hills are not notably green or flowery. But the message of the hymn is clear enough and if it makes a child think of Jesus walking on the South Downs, will not the prophet's agonized question

> " And did those feet in ancient time
>   Walk upon England's mountains green ? "

have an answer in a young heart that is worth the price of a topographical pedantry ?

Moving on another generation, we come to the august names of C. H. Spurgeon, John Hunter, Sylvester Horne, and W. Y. Fullerton, each of whom gave us at least one hymn. Charles Haddon Spurgeon, the greatest preacher the Baptists ever produced, and one of the greatest in our language, wrote, as a young man, a bravely simple hymn which, because of a rather saccharinous first line, has had less success that it deserved.

> Sweetly the holy hymn
> Breaks on the morning air ;
> Before the world with smoke is dim
> We meet to offer prayer.

* C.P., 106.

Upon the battle-field,
Before the fight begins,
We seek, O Lord, Thy sheltering shield
To guard us from our sins.

O hear us then, for we
Are very weak and frail ;
We make the Saviour's Name our plea,
And surely must prevail.*

This will not do for a respectable congregation whose first appearance before God on a Sunday is timed for eleven in the morning.   But I can remember how, after often scoffing at the hymn for its poor opening, it came alive for me ; being involved in the London Commando Campaign of April, 1947, a form of evangelism which had always terrified me, I recall being heartened by some of these lines when our group sang them in an early morning service of preparation from which we were to be sent out to the factories, shops, and taverns of a London industrial area.

Dr. John Hunter was one of Binney's successors at the King's Weigh House, but his most notable ministries were in Scotland.   He edited *Hymns of Faith and Life* in 1886—a typical hymn-book of the new liberal Congregationalism— and himself wrote a tiny hymn of two verses which was never openly ascribed to him until after his death.   It is a perfect example of the Christian lyric-epigram (which we have already seen above, page 69, in Charles Wesley's " Jesus, the first and last ") :

Dear Master, in whose life I see
All that I would, but fail to be,
Let thy clear light for ever shine
To shame and guide this life of mine.

Though what I dream and what I do
In my weak days are always two,
Help me, oppressed by things undone,
O thou, whose deeds and dreams were one ! †

* *Methodist Hymn Book*, 732, verses 1, 3, 5.   † *C.P.*, 462.

Both the scholarly Scot, Hunter, and the fiery evangelist, Spurgeon, are exquisitely simple when they sing.

Sylvester Horne (1865–1914), whose early death robbed Congregationalism of one of its most brilliant ministers, was minister at Whitefield's Tabernacle, Tottenham Court Road, from 1903 until 1914. During those years he also found time to be Chairman of the Congregational Union (1909), to sit in Parliament as Liberal M.P. for Ipswich (1910), and to write the famous hymn, " For the might of thine arm we bless thee ". The hymn is a rousing one and full of the atmosphere of adventurousness which was characteristic of Horne's life and thought.

The hymn is, as a matter of fact, based on some lines of Mrs. Hemans (1794–1835), which began " For the strength of the hills we bless thee, our God, our fathers' God ". Mrs. Hemans was fond of writing romantic verse about people and places in foreign parts whether or not she had actually visited them, and the martial courage of the Vaudois, or Waldenses, a sturdily surviving, though often persecuted and usually half-forgotten little sect in northern Italy, took her fancy. She wrote the poem in celebration of them, and ended each verse with her first line. Horne cast his hymn into the same mould, and set it to a Vaudois tune with which he was acquainted.

A distinguished Baptist minister, William Young Fullerton, who was President of the Baptist Union in 1913, is to be remembered for a haunting meditation on the exalted Christ, whose first verse runs :

> I cannot tell why he, whom angels worship
>   Should set his love upon the sons of men,
> Or why, as Shepherd, he should seek the wanderers
>   To bring them back, they know not how or when.
> But this I know,. that he was born of Mary,
>   When Bethlehem's manger was his only home,
> And that he lived at Nazareth and laboured,
>   And so the Saviour of the world is come.*

* *Methodist Hymn Book*, 809, verse 1.

This is usually sung to the " Londonderry Air " and has become very popular at missionary gatherings.

More recent still are hymns by two Congregational ministers, " For those we love within the veil ",* by W. Charter Piggott, who was minister at Streatham Congregational Church, and Basil Mathews' happy missionary hymn, " Far round the world thy children sing their song ".† Both of these have made their way far beyond their own denominations.

Henry Carter has already been mentioned as the author of " Give me, O Christ, the strength that is in thee ", and Henry Arnold Thomas, minister at Highbury, Bristol, until 1923, is the author of a hymn which we quote in full in our last chapter.‡

Finally we must mention the doyen of Congregationalist hymn-writers, Howell Elvet Lewis, who died in 1953 at the age of 93.   Elfed, as he was known in Wales, was minister at King's Cross Congregational Church from 1910 to 1940, but in his native Wales he achieved the highest distinction as hymn-writer and poet.   He was the most venerated figure at the National Eisteddfodau, and in 1948 was awarded the distinction of Companion of Honour for his services to English and Welsh literature.   His hymns were collected and published privately in 1948.   They are not yet widely known, but one of them, " Whom oceans part, O Lord, unite ",§ written forty years ago for the Colonial Missionary Society, has achieved wide popularity. The following verse, written in a Welsh metre to carry the massive Welsh tune CRUGYBAR, is worth quoting as an example of the austere grace of his style.

> The light of the morning is breaking,
>   The shadows are passing away ;
> The nations of earth are awaking,
>   New peoples are learning to pray.

* *C.P.*, 364.   † *C.P.*, 345.
‡ Page 312.   § *C.P.*, 343.

> Let wrong, O Redeemer, be righted,
> In knowing and doing thy will ;
> And gather, as brothers united,
> All men to thy Cross on the hill.*

From Reformed nonconformity we may turn to Methodism, and we shall find that although the enormous output of the Wesleys themselves has been somewhat oppressive to the creation of hymns by their followers, yet we have some notable contributions from some of their ministers and lay preachers.

The first lay preacher was John Cennick (1718–55), who became a lay preacher at the age of 24, and not long afterwards deserted the Wesleys for the Moravians. But he celebrated his conversion by writing, in those early years, a large number of hymns of which several have survived ; in these we find a captivating naïveté of expression which makes them excellently suitable for children and young people. The most celebrated is " Children of the heavenly King ",† though even more often sung in some quarters is probably his Grace before Meat beginning " Be present at our Table, Lord ". His morning and evening hymns, " Rise, my soul, adore thy Maker " and " Ere I sleep, for every favour " ‡ are much loved by Nonconformists, though their occasional quaintnesses of expression make them less welcome in Anglican circles. But perhaps he never wrote anything more charming than these little-known lines :

> Be with me, Lord, where'er I go ;
> Teach me what thou wouldst have me do ;
> Suggest whate'er I think or say ;
> Direct me in thy narrow way.
>
> Prevent me, lest I harbour pride,
> Lest I in my own strength confide ;
> Show me my weakness, let me see
> I have my power, my all, from thee.§

---

* *C.P.*, 342. Cf. nos. 343, 559, and 560 in that book.
† *E.H.*, 373.   ‡ *C.P.*, 595 and 619.
§ *Oxford Hymnal*, 186.

Cennick's style is an admirable foil to the dramatic power of the Wesleys.

A younger contemporary of his was Thomas Olivers, the Welsh cobbler, who wrote " The God of Abraham praise " *—a celebrated paraphrase of a Jewish liturgical chant ; we owe to him also the version of the tune which we usually sing to those words, and also the arrangement of a secular air which we associate with the most solemn of English advent hymns—" Lo, he comes, with clouds descending ".†

Mention of that hymn brings us to Martin Madan, who, although he was ultimately ordained in the Church of England, was converted by Wesley and was for a time one of his preachers.   Madan left no hymn that is now sung ; but we owe to him the final version of " Lo, he comes with clouds descending " that now appears in the *Methodist Hymn Book*,‡ and also, probably, the alteration of the first two lines in Charles Wesley's Christmas hymn whose first verse originally ran

> Hark, how all the welkin rings,
> Glory to the King of Kings ;
> Late in time behold him come,
> Offspring of a virgin's womb.§

Madan was editor of a famous and excellent collection of hymns, published in 1760, and it is possible that it was he who added the Alleluias to Wesley's Easter hymn, " Christ the Lord is risen today " and his Ascension hymn, " Hail the day that sees him rise ", since they both appear thus arranged for the first time in this book.‖

There are very few Methodists of later days who have contributed anything to the hymnody of communions outside their own.   Benjamin Rhodes's " My heart and voice

---

* *E.H.*, 646.   † *E.H.*, 7.

‡ *Methodist Hymn Book*, 264.

§ For the original version of its first thirty-two lines, see *E.H.*, 23.

‖ For these in their original form, but abridged, see *E.H.*, 135, and *Congregational Church Hymnal*, 160.

I'll raise " * is still sung with gusto in Methodism. E. J. Brailsford's beautiful lines on nature,

> All things that live below the sky
> Are brothers unto me †

have deservedly found favour elsewhere. R. M. Pope's translation of a Latin hymn, " Ye clouds and darkness, hosts of light ", has a well-deserved place in the *English Hymnal*.‡ G. O. Gregory, a contemporary Methodist minister, contributes one hymn to the current *Methodist Hymn Book*,§ and wrote a stirring hymn for the London Commando Campaign (1947) to be sung (perhaps unfortunately) to the tune FINLANDIA. As a result, FINLANDIA was worked to a standstill as the theme-song of that evangelistic episode. But the hymn itself was singularly moving in its direct evangelical appeal.

Finally we must make honourable mention of the remarkable experiment in evangelism conducted by the Rev. Thomas Tiplady at the Ideal Mission, Lambeth. Seeking to bring home the Gospel to people whom he had to remind to refrain from smoking in church, Mr. Tiplady found the traditional hymns inadequate for his special need ; so he wrote his own, using simple modern language that might carry the truth home to the people he was serving. He has written a large number of these hymns, and the following two verses are a good example of his work :

> All ye who know that on the Cross
> Christ did salvation bring,
> Lift up your heart, lift up your voice,
> And make the whole world ring.

> The song of our redemption raise,
> And storm high heaven's gate,
> Till angels in amaze look out
> At man's exalted state.||

---

* *Methodist Hymn Book*, 115. † *Songs of Praise*, 445.
‡ *E.H.*, 54. § No. 757.
|| *New Hymns of Praise* (1944), 21, verses 1 and 3.

Of the less populous denominations, the first with which we ought to deal is that of the Roman Catholics ; for at the time when they were writing English hymns most energetically, the Roman Catholics were a very small minority in this country. The four most eminent were Faber and Caswall, who were prolific, and Matthew Bridges and Newman, who were not. Faber is the author, of course, of " My God, how wonderful thou art " * and of " Souls of men, why will ye scatter ? " ; † his avowed object, he says in the preface to his collected hymns (1850), was to do for English Catholics what the Olney Hymns had done for Protestants. His idiom was therefore unashamedly popular and sentimental. He is at his best in those two hymns, and at his worst perhaps in " Hark, Hark, my soul ", of which Archbishop Temple was heard to say in the course of an address delivered during the Mission to Oxford University in February, 1941, that for him its existence was " a minor but quite indisputable part of the problem of evil ". But we have not yet come to the stage when we want to talk about bad hymns, so we may record that Faber was a man of true devotion who knew how to write for the simplest people, and who deserves immortality for the lines

> How beautiful, how beautiful
>   The sight of thee must be,
> Thine endless wisdom, boundless power,
>   And awful purity.‡

Caswall occupied himself in translating Catholic hymns from Latin and other languages. Perhaps his best known is " Jesu, the very thought of thee ",§ to which we have already referred (page 29), but it may be that the strongest and finest is " My God, I love thee ",‖ derived from a poem in

---

* *E.H.*, 441.
† *E.H.*, 499. Original first verse at *Hymns Ancient and Modern*, 634/364.   ‡ *E.H.*, 441, verse 5.
§ *Hymns Ancient and Modern*, 178/189.   ‖ *C.P.*, 425.

Spanish uncertainly ascribed to St. Francis Xavier. It contains these verses :

> My God, I love thee—not because
>   I hope for heaven thereby,
> Nor yet because who love thee not
>   Are lost eternally.
>
> Not with the hope of gaining aught,
>   Not seeking a reward ;
> But as thyself hast loved me,
>   O ever-loving Lord.
>
> E'en so I love thee, and will love,
>   And in thy praise will sing ;
> Solely because thou art my God
>   And my eternal King.

The Spanish sonnet is passionate enough ; but between it and Caswall stood a cold little Latin translation beginning " O Deus, ego amo te ". Caswall's warmth of devotion brought the lines to life again, and at his best Caswall is unsurpassed in this gift for transmitting to our age the rich devotion of counter-Reformation Catholicism. Here, for example, are two verses from his " To Christ, the Prince of peace " :

> O Jesu, Victim blest,
>   What else but love divine
> Could thee constrain to open thus
>   That sacred heart of thine ?
>
> O wondrous fount of love,
>   O well of waters free,
> O heavenly flame, refining fire,
>   O burning charity ! *

Caswall also gave us the familiar translation from a German hymn which we know as " When morning gilds the skies ".†
  Of the other two celebrated Catholic writers we need not say much. Matthew Bridges wrote the first version of

* *Hymns Ancient and Modern,* 180/198.   † *E.H.,* 512.

" Crown him with many crowns " ; * but the version sung in Protestant churches today is largely altered by Godfrey Thring. Newman's " Praise to the Holiest " and " Lead, kindly Light " have already been mentioned.

More modern Catholic hymnody, together with some poems by Catholics of the seventeenth century now for the first time used as hymns, can be seen at its best in the latest (1940) *Westminster Hymnal*. Outstanding among the more recent authors there represented are Gerard Manley Hopkins (" Godhead here in hiding "),† G. K. Chesterton, and Monsignor Ronald Knox.‡

The Society of Friends has produced one or two hymn-writers of some distinction. That Society does not, in this country, use hymns at its services of worship (although it has long done so in America) ; but it has produced poets, and its widening activities during the last two or three generations, especially in the Adult School Movement, have produced a demand for hymns which has been well met in the *Fellowship Hymn Book* (1910 and 1933). The first Quaker hymn-book, published in 1874, was called *Hymns Selected for the Use of Young Persons*, and edited by John Ford. Three names may be mentioned. Bernard Barton is well remembered for " Lamp of our feet, whereby we trace ".§ Ernest Dodgshun (1876–1944) is best known for " What service shall we render thee ? ",‖ and F. J. Gillman (1866–1949), the most distinguished of them all, not only contributed several hymns to the *Fellowship Hymn Book*, but was one of the founders both of the Adult School Movement and of the Hymn Society.

Quaker hymns are, of course, a modern institution, and their theology tends always towards the liberal. The long-standing identification of the Society of Friends with both a high standard of culture and also leadership in the move-

---

* *Hymns Ancient and Modern*, 304/224, with which compare *C.P.*, 166.
† *Westminster Hymnal*, 72.
‡ The Catholic Apostolic Church is mentioned on page 210.
§ *C.P.*, 229.   ‖ *Fellowship Hymn Book*, 14.

ments for social reform in this country is reflected in their hymns, which are largely concerned with the social implications of the Gospel, and are always written with taste and poise. A verse or two of one of Gillman's best-known hymns will illustrate this judgment :

> God send us men whose aim 'twill be,
>   Not to defend some outworn creed,
> But to live out the laws of Christ
>   In every thought and word and deed.
>
> God send us men with hearts ablaze
>   All truth to love, all wrong to hate ;
> These are the patriots Britain needs,
>   These are the bulwarks of the State.*

Another reflection of the same social emphasis in Quaker hymnody is found in the fact that both editions of the *Fellowship Hymn Book* begin with a section on the Social application of the Gospel ; the first hymn in the older edition is " When wilt thou save the people ? ", and the first in the later edition is Blake's " Jerusalem ".

A high standard of culture and a reserved attitude towards dogmatic statements is also to be found in Unitarian hymnody of this country. It is in America, of course, that Unitarian hymnody has had its greatest influence ; but we have to remember with gratitude in our own country the names of James Martineau for " A voice upon the midnight air ",† Sarah Adams for " Nearer, my God, to thee ",‡ Stopford Brooke for " It fell upon a summer day ",§ Sir John Bowring for " In the cross of Christ I glory ",‖ and W. G. Tarrant for " Now praise we great and famous men ".¶ Nor must we overlook William Gaskell, the distinguished minister of Cross Street, Manchester, and husband of the famous novelist, who wrote " Though lowly here our lot may be, high work we have to do ".** The most literary

* *Fellowship Hymn Book* (1933), 55.
† *C.P.*, 123. ‡ *E.H.*, 444. § *C.P.*, 111.
‖ *E.H.*, 409. ¶ *C.P.*, 667. ** *C.P.*, 545.

hymn-book ever produced by a Nonconformist denomination, *Worship Song*, owes much of its quality to the large
number of hymns by otherwise unknown Unitarian authors
which appear in it.

The Plymouth Brethren have given us few hymns, although for their own use they have written and adapted
many. Their most distinguished hymn-writer was Sir
Edward Denny, whose hymn, " Light of the lonely pilgrim's
heart ",* written well over a hundred years ago, has just
made its first appearance in *Hymns Ancient and Modern*. The
other hymn-writer from the Brethren is Albert Midlane,
best known for " Revive thy work, O Lord ",† another late-
comer to *Hymns Ancient and Modern*, and for " There's a
friend for little children ".‡

Finally we must make mention of the Church of Scotland
in hymnody. We cannot, with the best will in the world,
make a long chapter of this, for the good reason that hymns
have been not yet a hundred years authorized in the Church
of Scotland. There has therefore been little time for that
Church to develop a distinctive line in hymnody ; but in that
little time much has been done.

The inheritance of the Church of Scotland is, in the last
resort, that Celtic Church which it shares with Ireland. It
is only recently, however, that the veil drawn over that
ancient inheritance by John Knox and the reformers has
been drawn back to the extent of allowing translations from
a few great Celtic hymns to appear in Scottish hymn-books.
Apart from Mrs. Alexander's " St. Patrick's Breastplate ",
we now have two fine hymns attributed to St. Columba,
" O God, thou art the Father " § and " Christ is the world's
Redeemer ".‖ Another distinguished and already popular
hymn from an ancient Celtic source is " Be thou my
Vision ",¶ which has the same sonorous language and
picturesque diction as " St. Patrick's Breastplate ".

* *Hymns Ancient and Modern* (1950), 209.
† *Hymns Ancient and Modern*, 766/362.   ‡ *E.H.*, 607.
§ *Church Hymnary*, 454.   ‖ *Ib.*, 179.   ¶ *Ib.*, 477.

But modern hymnody from the Kirk is very largely not credal, like these ancient hymns, but devotional, and its most famous exponent is without doubt Horatius Bonar. Most of his hymns were written as devotional verse before hymns were sanctioned in the Kirk. We now know him best for " I heard the voice of Jesus say " * and " Fill thou my life ".† Most of his work is patchy, and many of his hymns have to be abridged for congregational use ; the greater number of them have at least one appalling line.⁵⁰ But " I heard the voice " is a classic of personal devotion, and will live many generations yet. Hardly less celebrated than Bonar is George Matheson, far less prolific, but the author of " O Love that wilt not let me go ",‡ and of " Make me a captive, Lord ".§ The first of these is another devotional masterpiece. James Drummond Burns, author of " Hushed was the evening hymn ",‖ is still remembered with affection, and R. M. McCheyne, that powerful evangelist who lived to be only thirty, ought to be better known than he is for " When this passing world is done ".¶

There are few exceptions to the judgment that the native hymnody of nineteenth-century Scotland shows a decisive reaction against the austerity of the metrical psalms and paraphrases. There, all is outward-looking and formal. In the hymns the atmosphere is devotional and intimate to the point, occasionally, of stuffiness. The Scots ministers were at their best when they were writing intimately. One hymn of pure praise, however, stands out from the long tale of devotional hymns, and it is now among the popular classics ; this is Walter Chalmers Smith's " Immortal invisible, God only wise " **—a fine, simple hymn full of plump polysyllables and very popular with young people. And we would remind the reader of the verses which we

---

* E.H., 574.
‡ C.P., 774.
‖ C.P., 455
** E.H., 407.

† C.P., 22
§ C.P., 460.
¶ C.P., 772.

quoted at an earlier stage, " The sands of time are sinking ", which more than any other hymn seem redolent of the atmosphere of the Kirk at its least forbidding and most gracious.

CHAPTER 14

Men of Letters

IT might well be expected that those who made the pursuit of letters their life's work should have an eminent place in our story. As a matter of fact the combination of disciplines which makes a great poet also a great hymn-writer is very rare. The combination is only to be found in two Englishmen in the whole literature —William Cowper and Robert Bridges ; these, that is to say, are the only men who have made a considerable contribution both in poetry and in hymnody.

Although genuine hymn-writing is not entirely separated from the more generalized literary genius, we shall find that the group of authors we are about to mention turns out to be a group of men each of whom threw off a hymn or two as a by-product of his professional literary activity.

From the seventeenth century we have three outstanding names. The first and greatest is John Milton, whose psalm-versions, to which we have already made some reference, are sufficiently within the ethos of hymn-writing to be included here. " Let us with a gladsome mind ", " The Lord will come and not be slow ", and " How lovely are thy dwellings fair " are the three hymns which we have preserved from Milton by taking selections from his psalms, and all the adaptations are fairly modern. " Let us with a gladsome mind ", containing such delightful lines as

> The hornèd moon to shine by night
> 'Mid her spangled sisters bright

was a trifle too picturesque for the editors of *Hymns Ancient and Modern*, and so the first lines of Milton to be heard in

our public worship were contained in Baker's " Praise, O
Praise our God and King ",* which uses Milton's refrain

> For his mercies still endure
> Ever faithful, ever sure

(altering his *aye* to *still*), but for the rest substitutes a more
conventional hymn with a general emphasis on the season
of Harvest. Later books returned to Milton's hymn, more
or less adapted to the metre of a conventional tune in sevens,
and the other two selections came into general use about
the beginning of the present century.

John Bunyan also comes into our story for " Who would
true valour see ", written, it is true, not as a congregational
hymn but as the epilogue to a chapter in the *Pilgrim's
Progress* ; it does not, indeed, appear in the first (1678)
edition of that work, and, in Dr. Dearmer's words, " it seems
to have summed up his reflections on the whole book.
He dropped it into the second part as a kind of prelude to
the conclusion. He did not weave it into the narrative, or
put it into the mouth of one of his characters . . . it is
placed after Mr. Valiant-for-Truth's discourse, because his
name makes it appropriate there ; but it is not sung by
him." That quotation is from a long comment in *Songs of
Praise Discussed* † in which Dr. Dearmer defends his own
hymn, " He who would valiant be ", which uses a few lines
of Bunyan's but is really a new hymn. The reader should
refer to that article, which produces a strong defence of the
view that Bunyan's song was not meant for congregational
singing and is not suitable for it. The other view, taken by
most other editors of our own day, is that Bunyan's mind
and work are familiar enough to modern congregations to
make it tolerable to sing his words, " hobgoblins " and all,
in public worship. There is, one might say, no greater
effort of interpretation needed here than is required in the
singing of most of the Psalms and a good deal of Charles
Wesley. Much depends on whether you are prepared to

* *Hymns Ancient and Modern,* 381/481.   † Page 320.

raise Bunyan to that eminence which is entitled to this grace
of interpretation on the part of the congregation. For good
or ill, anyhow, most people now sing Bunyan more or less
as he stands ; but it has not been until the present century
that the Pilgrim Song has become familiar, and it owes
much of its popularity to the tune which Dr. Vaughan
Williams arranged originally for Dearmer's hymn.

Bunyan also gives us " He who is down needs fear no
fall ",* the song of the shepherd boy in part II of the same
book. The place of this in the story is, of course, quite
clear and the lines have become well established in modern
hymnody. Perhaps it is possible to mention here also,
while we are talking of Bunyan, a remarkable hymn written
by P. B. Clayton (the founder of Toc H) as a commentary
or summary of the *Pilgrim's Progress*, which is less widely
known than it deserves : it begins :

> Blest be the day when moved I was
> A pilgrim for to be.†

John Dryden, dramatist, satirist and Poet Laureate, has
left us " Creator Spirit, by whose aid ", an august rendering
of the *Veni Creator* which has come into use in some modern
books, slightly edited because of an unequal division of lines
among its stanzas. It is a very finished piece of writing of
which this, its fourth verse, is a sample :

> Plenteous of grace, descend from high,
> Rich in thy sevenfold energy ;
> Make us eternal truths receive,
> And practise all that we believe ;
> Give us thyself that we may see
> The Father and the Son by thee.‡

Dryden became a Roman Catholic on the accession of
James II (1685, his 54th year), and lived the rest of his life
in that faith.

---

* *Hymns Ancient and Modern* (1950), 301.
† *Songs of Praise*, 456.   ‡ *E.H.*, 156, verse 4.

Finally we ought to mention the other Poet Laureate, Nahum Tate, who is probably the author of " While shepherds watched their flocks by night ".* Tate was an erratic, person of rather scanty literary gifts, and apart from this hymn and from his collaboration with Brady in the *New Version* of the Metrical Psalter, he is forgotten now. Southey wrote of him, " he was a good-natured fuddling companion, and his latter days were spent in the Mint as a refuge from his creditors " (the Mint was in those days a sanctuary for debtors).

Tate, then, alone of these four authors, was sung in his own lifetime ; the others have only come into currency as a result of modern research.

In the next century, as a bridge between the days of the Psalters and those of classical hymnody, we have the first journalist hymn-writer, ancestor in this respect of Montgomery, Conder, and Chesterton—Joseph Addison, Editor of *The Spectator*. It is difficult to say of any other author that eighty per cent. of his work is in common use today, that, indeed, the whole of it appears in current hymn-books ; but it is true of Addison. He wrote five hymns, and four of them are in most books.

It must have been something of an experience to read in *The Spectator* for 26 July, 1712, an article on Divine Providence which closed with a versification of Psalm 23 beginning " The Lord my pasture shall prepare ". It was thus that Addison made his bow as a hymn-writer, and in this version we have a beautiful example of the ceremonious style of the Augustan Age of English letters. Here is its third verse :

> Though in a bare and rugged way
> Through devious lonely wilds I stray,
> Thy bounty shall my pains beguile ;
> The barren wilderness will smile
> With sudden greens and herbage crowned,
> And streams shall murmur all around.†

* *E.H.*, 30.   † *E.H.*, 491, verse 3.

As an object-lesson in styles it is worth comparing this paraphrase and adornment of the psalm with that written ʲust 150 years later by Sir Henry Baker :

> Perverse and foolish oft I strayed,
>   But yet in love he sought me ;
> And on his shoulder gently laid,
>   And home, rejoicing, brought me.*

Next, on the 9th of August, came an essay on " Gratitude " which closed with a more ambitious poem, running to thirteen verses, beginning " When all thy mercies, O my God ".† This always has to be shortened in modern books, though the whole of it appears in the *Scottish Psalter* among the *Hymns* appended to the *Paraphrases* ; but it is unequalled as a piece of spiritual autobiography, a song of gratitude for continued mercies all through life.

A fortnight later, on the 23rd, came his most celebrated hymn of all, after an essay on " Faith and Devotion ". Here Addison returns to the Psalms, and produces this majestic version of Psalm xix. 1–6.

> The spacious firmament on high
> With all the blue ethereal sky,
> And spangled heavens, a shining frame,
> Their great Original proclaim.
> The unwearied sun from day to day
> Does his creator's power display
> And publishes to every land
> The works of an almighty hand.‡

" If this be not poetry," wrote Lord Selborne, " I do not know what is."

The fourth hymn appeared a fortnight later, as " A divine Ode, made by a gentleman upon the conclusion of his travels ". All these hymns were signed only with the initial " C." ; but although the secret had got out before Addison's

---

* *E.H.*, 490, verse 3.　　　　　　　　† *E.H.*, 511.
‡ *E.H.*, 297, verse 1.

death it was Macaulay who in the *Edinburgh Review* in 1843 explained that it was indeed a voyage which almost ended in shipwreck that had caused Addison the experience which issued in the lines beginning " How are thy servants blest, O Lord ". A verse not usually sung nowadays gives away the secret :

> And though in dreadful whirls they hang
>   High on the broken wave,
> They know thou art not slow to hear,
>   Nor impotent to save.*

The fifth hymn is altogether less well known, probably because of its unhappy beginning. It appeared in October, 1712. It begins " When rising from the bed of death ", and contains these fine penitential lines :

> Then see the sorrow of my heart,
>   Ere yet it be too late ;
> And hear my Saviour's dying groans,
>   To give those sorrows weight,
> For never shall my soul despair
>   Her pardon to procure,
> Who knows thine only Son has died
>   To make her pardon sure.†

This, " The spacious firmament ", and " When all thy mercies " are three of the five hymns authorized to be added to the *Paraphrases* of 1781 by the Church of Scotland. One of the others is by John Logan, the other by Isaac Watts.

After Addison, who died in 1719, there is a long gap in the list of literary hymn-writers. The eighteenth century was notable for the divorce which took place in it of literary culture from religion. The last thing we should expect from the successful poets and authors of that century is the religious enthusiasm which at that time was associated with hymn-writing. The more generous crop of literary hymnographers in the following century may be ascribed partly to the romantic movement, partly to the authorization of

* *E.H.*, 542, verse 3.   † *E.H.*, 92, verses 5 and 6.

hymns in the Church of England, and partly to the new association of hymn-writing with a devotion less intense than that of the Wesleys and Newtons of the eighteenth century.

Passing over Cowper, the single literary hymnist of his generation, we must mention Sir Walter Scott, who gave us two hymns, one of which is frequently to be seen in modern books, " That day of wrath, that dreadful day " ; * this is a compressed version in twelve lines of the *Dies Irae*, magnificent in a literary sense, but a little over-intense in its prediction of final doom for indiscriminate congregational use. Less familiar but more attractive is :

> When Israel, of the Lord beloved,
> Out of the land of bondage came,
> Her fathers' God before her moved,
> An awful guide, in smoke and flame.†

The former hymn appears at the end of the sixth canto of *The Lay of the Last Minstrel* ; the second one is from chapter 39 of *Ivanhoe*, sung by Rebecca on the eve of her trial for sorcery. The former is, in Scott's characteristic fashion, redolent of the Middle Ages ; the latter is, in all the thirty-two lines of its original version, straight out of the Old Testament. It is now normally used as an expression of prayer for the recall of the Jews to Christianity. Its language is majestic and worthy of its celebrated author.

William Wordsworth has a place in hymnody for the sake of his " The Labourer's Noon-day Hymn ",‡ written in 1834. He took as his model the morning and evening hymns of Ken, and in his own introduction to the hymn on its first publication he tells of the children of a village school singing it with pleasure to the OLD HUNDREDTH—which was, of course, the tune first associated with Ken's hymns. Here are two of its eight verses :

* *E.H.*, 487.
† *Church Hymnary* (1930), 367, verse 1.
‡ *Hymns Ancient and Modern*, 639.

Look up to heaven ! the industrious sun
Already half his race hath run ;
He cannot halt or go astray,
But our immortal spirits may.

Help with thy grace, through life's short day,
Our upward and our downward way ;
And glorify us for the west,
When we shall sink to final rest.*

The next in this illustrious succession is the Irish poet,
Tom Moore, author of *Irish Melodies* and *Lalla Rookh*, and
friend and vindicator of Lord Byron. Moore, born four
years before Heber, has a romantic touch more colourful
than Heber's, and in his little volume, published in 1816,
entitled *Sacred Songs*, he has some of the most precious
examples of romantic hymnody.   Here are selections from
two of these songs :

When night with wings of starry gloom
    O'ershadows all the earth and skies,
Like some dark beauteous bird whose plume
    Is sparkling with unnumbered eyes,—
That sacred gleam, those fires divine,
So grand, so countless, Lord, are thine.†

There's nothing bright, above, below,
From flowers that bloom to stars that glow,
But in its light my soul can see
Some feature of thy deity ;

There's nothing dark below, above,
But in its gloom I trace thy love,
And meekly wait that moment, when
Thy touch shall turn all bright again.‡

The charge which some have brought against hymns of the
romantic kind is that they glorify God by selecting the
most attractive and convenient aspects of nature and

---

* *Songs of Praise*, 40, verses 4 and 6.   † *E.H.*, 298, verse 3.
‡ *Songs of Praise*, 679, verses 2 and 3.

deducing from them his love ; Tom Moore had an imagination more generous, and, as these lines show, he was of those who, loving nature, aspire to love *all* nature as God's creation. And of course there is much more poetry in a line of Moore than in many pages of the more prolific hymn-writers.

Then there is Thomas Carlyle, whom nobody would think of calling a poet, but whose translation of " Ein feste Burg " has that highest merit of translations, that it conveys not only the sense but the very personality of the author of its original. There is in " A safe stronghold " a good deal of that heroic blustering and holy boastfulness that was in Martin Luther the quality so greatly loved by his friends and detested by his enemies :

> And were this world all devils o'er,
>   And watching to devour us,
> We lay it not to heart so sore ;
>   Not they can overpower us.*

Even Elizabeth Wordsworth's excellent rendering † in the older editions of *Hymns Ancient and Modern* is more English than German. Carlyle's is perhaps the greatest translation in the whole field of hymnody.

We might possibly bring in at this stage James Montgomery as the second hymn-writer who was also a great journalist ; but we have given him enough space already. Of the same kind, however, was the Congregationalist Josiah Conder, owner and editor of the *Eclectic Review* and editor also of the *Patriot*. He was also a voluminous, though not now a celebrated, author, his *magnum opus* being *The Modern Traveller* in thirty volumes, with which was also associated his *Dictionary of Ancient and Modern Geography*. He edited the first hymn-book of the Congregational Union (founded in 1831) in 1836 and just failed to live to see its 1855 revision. Conder has a vigorous if rather uneven

* *E.H.*, 362, verse 3.
† *Hymns Ancient and Modern* (standard edn.), 678.

style in verse. His greatest and most famous hymn is " Bread of heaven, on thee we feed ",* which John Ellerton [51] said reads like a passage of Bonaventura. Not quite so well known, but nearly as worthy, is his " The Lord is King ".† Some of his most imaginative lines are to be found in " Beyond, beyond that boundless sea ", a hymn based on the theophany on Mount Horeb recounted in *I Kings* xix, whose first and last verses run :

> Beyond, beyond that boundless sea,
> Above that dome of sky,
> Farther than thought itself can flee,
> Thy dwelling is on high ;
> Yet dear the awful thought to me
> That thou, my God, art nigh.
>
> O not in circling depth or height,
> But in the conscious breast ;
> Present to faith, though veiled from sight,
> There doth his Spirit rest.
> O come, thou presence infinite,
> And make thy creature blest.‡

Here once again is the imaginative and romantic style ; this time it is theological romanticism rather than natural romanticism—God, that is, is seen in the human consciousness and need of him rather than in his works.

Moving on a whole generation we come to an interesting group of literary hymn-writers. Thomas Hughes, the author of *Tom Brown's Schooldays*, we have already mentioned for his own hymn, " O God of Truth ". George Macdonald, the Scottish novelist, began as a Congregational minister, holding a charge for a short time at Arundel in Sussex, but he made his name as a novelist of Scottish life in *David Elginbrod* and *Robert Falconer* and as a poet in *The Disciple* and *A Threefold Cord*. A few of the poems in *A Threefold Cord* have been used as hymns ; the most often quoted is that beginning with the verse

* *E.H.*, 304. † *C.P.*, 58. ‡ *C.P.*, 19, verses 1 and 5.

> They all were looking for a king,
>   To slay their foes and lift them high ;
> Thou cam'st a little baby thing
>   That made a woman cry.*

The others are " Our Father, hear our longing prayer " †
and " O Lord of life, thy quickening voice ".‡ George
Macdonald is not read much nowadays, but he has come to
life again in the work of the Oxford apologist, C. S. Lewis,
who in several places acknowledges his debt to Macdonald's
thought and works, and makes him one of the characters
in his *The Great Divorce*.

Contemporary with Macdonald was Francis Turner
Palgrave, immortal as the editor of *The Golden Treasury*.
Palgrave had just the kind of lyric genius that makes the
good hymn-writer ; he has little evangelical warmth, being
inclined rather to the unitarian elegances of his generation.
But one or two of his hymns have become well known, and
he rarely wrote one that had nothing to say. His best-
known hymn is " O thou, not made with hands ", an
admirable expression of the " liberal " view of the Church
which contains these two beautiful verses :

> Thou art where'er the proud
>   In humbleness melts down ;
> Where self itself yields up ;
>   Where martyrs win their crown ;
> Where faithful souls possess
> Themselves in perfect peace.

> Where in life's common ways
>   With cheerful feet we go ;
> Where in his steps we tread
>   Who trod the way of woe ;
> Where he is in the heart,
> City of God, thou art.§

* *Songs of Praise*, 668, verse 1.   † *C.P.*, 452.
‡ *C.P.*, 599.   § *E.H.*, 464, verses 3 and 4.

His other well-known hymns are " Thou say'st, Take up thy cross ",* " Lord God of morning and of night " † and " O Light of life, thou Saviour dear ",‡ which are relatively commonplace.   Much more full of character, and therefore (as it happens) less appealing to the theological climate of today, are the following lines which are worth rescuing for a moment :

> Christ in his heavenly garden walks all day,
> And calls to souls upon the world's highway ;
> Wearied with trifles, maim'd and sick with sin,
> Christ by the gate stands, and invites them in.
>
> How long, unwise, will ye pursue your woe ?
> Here from the throne sweet waters ever go ;
> Here the white lilies shine like stars above :
> Here in the red rose burns the face of Love.§

This is a long way from " That day of wrath, that dreadful day ".   We quote it not so much to commend its revival as to provide an exquisite example of the hymnody of Victorian elegance at a high level of devotion.   To show that Palgrave was not an incurable sentimentalist we had better quote a verse from his hymn of redemption beginning " Though we long, in sin-wrought blindness, from thy gracious paths have strayed " :

> Sudden, 'midst our idle chorus
>   O'er our sin thy thunders roll,
> Death his signal waves before us,
>   Night and terror shake the soul ;
> Till through double darkness round us
> Shines a star, and thou hast found us.‖

The next generation provides us with several distinguished names.   Gerard Manley Hopkins has already been mentioned ; his translation of Thomas Aquinas's *Adoro Te*

* *C.P.*, 524.   † *C.P.*, 598.   ‡ *C.P.*, 625.
§ *Worship Song*, 495, verses 1 and 2.   ‖ *Ib.*, 214, verse 3.

is little known as a hymn, but it is a classic. In the same
year (1844) was born Robert Bridges, late Poet Laureate,
whose distinction is that he did more than any other person
to raise English hymnody to the level of respectable literature, redeeming it from both the crudity of the eighteenth
century and the conventionality of the nineteenth. This
he did in the *Yattendon Hymnal* which he compiled for the
parish church of Yattendon, Berkshire. This book he fur-
nished with some classical hymns and a number of his own
compositions. One of these we quote in our last chapter,
and we doubt if anything more purely beautiful is to be
found in all hymnody. Other hymns from this collection
that have come into common use are " Happy are they ", *
" Thee will I love ",† and " Love of the Father, Love of
God the Son ".‡ Bridges was anxious not only to break
new ground in hymnody but also to bring back into use the
original versions of some of the ancient tunes from Germany
and Geneva. We owe to this small hymn-book and to
Bridges' writings on various occasions most of the impetus
which has so greatly raised the standard of English hymnody
in the present century. Bridges quite shamelessly invited
church people to tell him why he should sing in church what
insulted his intelligence, and when nobody would tell him,
provided better things with his own hand.

William Canton, born in 1845, was best known as a
journalist on the *Glasgow Herald*, as sub-editor of the *Contemporary Review*, as manager of the publishing firm of
Isbister, and as the author of a good deal of children's
poetry. He did not write any hymns in the strict sense, but
" Hold thou my hands " comes near enough to be included
here. This was written as the direct result of hearing a song
in *The Yeomen of the Guard*, by Gilbert and Sullivan : the
words " Hold thou my hands " from the song remained in
his mind, and eventually he wove the following lovely verses
round the phrase :

* *E.H.*, 398.   † *C.P.*, 430.
‡ *E.H.*, 438.

> Hold thou my hands !
> In grief and joy, in hope and fear,
> Lord, let me feel that thou art near ;
> Hold thou my hands.
>
> Hold thou my hands—
> These passionate hands too quick to smite,
> These hands so eager for delight ;
> Hold thou my hands ! *

This is very near the borderline of devotional poetry ; but it is not inappropriately printed near to " O love that wilt not let me go " in one modern hymn-book, a hymn with which it has a good deal in common.

John Oxenham, whose real name was W. A. Dunkerley, and whose son, Dr. Roderic Dunkerley, is a distinguished Congregationalist minister, is still well known as a novelist and poet. His best-known contribution to hymnody is " In Christ there is no east nor west ",† a capital expression of the humanistic optimism which wàs the keynote of much Christian devotion and preaching before the first Great War. The hymn was written some time between 1900 and 1913, and if it by-passes all the problems and ignores all the difficulties, it is none the less a hymn of good hope and sound aspiration.

John Addington Symonds, another leisurely man of letters, would have been surprised to hear his lines beginning " These things shall be "‡ sung as a hymn ; but they were included in Horder's *Worship Song* and in *Songs of Praise* and provide, once again from the age of optimism, a good song of faith and hope for young people.

The last literary name we have to mention is that of " Jan Struther ", domestically known as Mrs. A. K. Placzek. Her pen-name was derived from her maiden name of Anstruther. She was English born but lived in America, and was well known for her children's hymns in *Songs of Praise* before she became a celebrity with the novel, *Mrs.*

---

* *E.H.*, 403, verses 1 and 3.   † *C.P.*, 344.   ‡ *C.P.*, 583.

Miniver, from which a film was made which proved vastly popular in England during the Second World War. She has a happy facility in writing light pieces for young people, makes plenty of use of modified refrains, and deserves to be especially remembered for " Lord of all hopefulness " * and " Round the earth a message runs ".† ‡ Perhaps her most pleasing hymn, however, is a wedding-hymn, beginning " God, whose eternal mind ".§ At weddings (see Chapter 20 below) we tend to bring out the old war-horses and not to indulge in novelties, so this hymn has had little currency. But it is owed honour not only because it uses simple modern language but also because it is not one of those hymns which make us sing *about* the bride and bridegroom—an embarrassing and incongruous practice in public worship. Jan Struther's hymn has the following excellent lines :

> Grant that we may treasure less
> Passion than true tenderness,
> Yet never, Lord, despise
> Heart to sweetheart turning.
> Bless us, God of loving.

One supposes that most wedding congregations of the fashionable sort will be hard enough put to it to scramble through " Praise, my soul " and " Love divine ", and will have little time left for a brand-new tune ; but in this hymn we have a fruitful prayer or meditation for betrothed or married couples of every age.

So much, then, for the literary hymn-writers. In them we find what we expect to find—a high standard of elegance at the expense of the irresponsible ecstasies of the eighteenth-century evangelical preachers and the professional padding of the nineteenth-century liturgists. Cowper is again an exception to this, but broadly the situation is well summed up by saying that Addison has a healthy cooling influence on the age of Wesley, that Tom Moore's rich and passionate

* *C.P.*, 534. † *C.P.*, 728.
‡ See also below, page 257. § *Songs of Praise*, 282.

plea for respect for God's creation comes well after the dooms of Calvinism, and that the clean, if not theologically profound, thinking of Palgrave and Macdonald is a great relief after some of the stuffier products of the compilers of *Hymns Ancient and Modern.* Of the new attempts to bring poetry and hymnody close together we shall say something later.

CHAPTER 15

Distinguished Visitors

SOME of our favourite hymns come from the background of a more or less busy professional life. It is reasonable, perhaps, that the near-literary profession of the don and the schoolmaster should produce some fine hymns, and that in our hymn-books we should occasionally come across the name of some figure mighty in scholarship.

Most of the university readers and professors who concern us are men inspired by the nineteenth-century Anglican revival ; they are, of course, all Anglicans inasmuch as before 1870 membership of the Church of England was a necessary qualification for a university-chair at Oxford or Cambridge. But there is one distinguished name from the seventeenth century which appears in some of our hymn-books—that of Henry More, Fellow of Christ's, Cambridge, who was one of the leading Cambridge Platonists. This group of philosophers constituted the chief body of liberal reaction to both the fury of Puritanism and the bigotry of Laudian Anglicanism in the middle years of the seventeenth century ; John Milton, a Cambridge man, owed to them a good deal of the liberal inspiration which is shown in his political works. It was theological and philosophical, rather than political Liberalism for which in the main the Cambridge school stood, and their generous culture and restrained scholarship are admirably summed up in the lines of Henry More which one of our hymn-books preserves to us. It is from More's *Divine Dialogues with Divine Hymns* (1668), one of the books which John Wesley took with him to Georgia :

Wesley did in fact adapt one of More's hymns for his own 1780 collection. These are the lines :

> The Holy Son of God most high,
>   For love of Adam's lapsed race,
> Quit the sweet pleasures of the sky
>   To bring us to that happy place.

> The Son of God thus man became,
>   That men the sons of God might be,
> And by his second birth regain
>   A likeness to his deity.*

Most of that last verse is a paraphrase of a celebrated passage in the ancient Greek Church Father, Irenaeus of Lugdunum (*c*. 140–202), one of the first systematic exponents of the Christian Faith.[52] The lines of More carry on the tradition of philosophical rather than evangelical presentation, and excellently display the character of the quiet scholarship of his Cambridge group.

Next in order of time is one of the most eminent scholar-hymnographers, Timothy Dwight, President of Yale, who refashioned and extended the psalms of Isaac Watts for the use of American Christians in one of the pioneer hymn-books of the United States. We shall have to mention him again when we deal with the Americans.

If we do not count the Professor of Anatomy at Cambridge, Charles Collignon, who probably wrote one of our most famous hymn-tunes, University † (published about 1790), we come now to the nineteenth-century scholars who have enriched our hymn-books. One of the senior members of this group is Benjamin Hall Kennedy, Regius Professor of Greek at Cambridge, who published *The Psalter in English Verse* and *Hymnologia Christiana*, from the first of which (1860) comes " Hear thou my prayer, O Lord " in the *Methodist Hymn Book*.‡ Those who remember the early

---

* *Songs of Praise*, 80, verses 1 and 4.
† *E.H.*, 93.   ‡ No. 543.

stages of a classical education will be better acquainted with
the poems by Kennedy beginning

> *A, ab, absque, coram de*

and

> Common are *sacerdos, dux,*
> *Vates, parens, et conjux.*[53]

John Stuart Blackie, one of the most picturesque and
celebrated of Scottish professors, held the chairs of Greek
at Edinburgh, and Latin at Aberdeen, but found time to
write that happy paraphrase of the *Benedicite omnia opera*
beginning " Angels holy, high and lowly ".*

Another Cambridge don, T. R. Birks, Professor of Moral
Philosophy, lives on in " O King of mercy, from thy throne
on high " ; † and while we are at Cambridge we ought to
mention the Professor of Mathematics, who became Bishop
of Ely, Thomas Turton, who wrote several hymn-tunes, the
only survivor of which is ELY ‡—and a very worthy tune it
is.

The mighty name of F. J. A. Hort, partner of Bishop
Westcott in the famous critical edition of the Greek Testament, appears in our book for the sake of four lines only—
the doxology added to Ellerton's " O Strength and Stay ".§

The Faculty of Theology at Oxford has given us some
famous hymns. The Reader in Ecclesiastical History towards the end of the nineteenth century was William Bright,
best remembered for two Communion hymns, " And now,
O Father, mindful of the love ",|| " Once, only once, and
once for all ",¶ and for the morning hymn, " At thy feet,
O Christ, we lay ".** His predecessor, a younger man
than he, was Edwin Hatch, the author of " Breathe on me,
Breath of God ".†† His successor, Charles Bigg, gave us no
original hymns, but some distinguished translations, two of
which were mentioned in Chapter 2.

* *C.P.*, 39. † *Methodist Hymn Book*, 633.
‡ *C.P.*, 343. § *E.H.*, 271, verse 3. || *E.H.*, 302.
¶ *E.H.*, 327. ** *E.H.*, 256. †† *C.P.*, 216.

From the even more august height of the Regius Chair of Divinity we are benevolently regarded for a moment by Henry Scott Holland, who wrote only one hymn, but that a fine and famous one, " Judge eternal, throned in splendour ".*

Two Cambridge masters of recent times have given us good hymns ; A. C. Benson, the son of Archbishop Benson and Master of Magdalene, has us in his debt for " The spring again is here ",† and Henry Montague Butler, Head Master of Harrow and Master of Trinity, is remembered for a capital school hymn beginning " Lift up your hearts ".‡

Other scholars who have provided us with hymns and translations are F. C. Burkitt, Regius Professor of Divinity at Cambridge, who translated *Wachet Auf*§ (as we have already seen) and wrote " Our Lord, his passion ended ",‖ and more recently C. S. Phillips, Lecturer in Ecclesiastical History at St. Augustine's, Canterbury, who has several hymns and translations in the latest edition of *Hymns Ancient and Modern.*

This is a respectable showing for a group of men pre-occupied with the duties of academic appointments. Some of them were, of course, schoolmasters before they were professors—Henry Montague Butler, for instance, and Charles Bigg, who was Head Master of Brighton College. But the record of those who devoted their lives to school-teaching is scarcely less honourable.

The first in this bright succession is Henry Twells, Head Master of Godolphin School, London, who wrote a few very remarkable hymns. " At even, when the sun was set " ¶ (in which he wrote " ere " for " when ") is the best known, and he said that he wrote it while invigilating in a school examination. But more beautiful, though less known, is his devotional hymn beginning " Not for our sins

---

* *E.H.,* 423.   † *Methodist Hymn Book,* 965.
‡ *E.H.,* 429 (longer version at *C.P.,* 661).
§ *E.H.,* 12.
‖ *Hymns Ancient and Modern* (1950), 155.   ¶ *E.H.,* 266.

alone, thy mercy, Lord, we sue ", from which we cannot resist quoting two verses—

> The holiest hours we spend
>   In prayer upon our knees,
> The times when most we deem
>   Our songs of praise will please,
> Thou searcher of all hearts,
>   Forgiveness pour on these.
>
> And most, when we, thy flock,
>   Before thine altar bend,
> And strange, bewildering thoughts
>   With those sweet moments blend,
> By him whose death we plead,
>   Good Lord, thy help extend.*

Twells had an unusually vivid style. Sometimes it was too highly coloured to find favour with congregations, and the following lines, though they appeared in two editions of *Hymns Ancient and Modern*, remained virtually unknown. But they are a remarkable utterance and worth mentioning here.

> The voice says, Cry ! What shall we cry ?
> " All flesh is grass, and like the flower
> Its glories droop, its pleasures die,
>   Its joys but last one fleeting hour."
>
> The voice says, Cry ! Lord, we would cry,
>   But of thy goodness teach us how ;
> For fast the hours of mercy fly,
>   And, if we cry, it must be now ! †

This unusual approach to the opening passage of *Isaiah* xl, is characteristic of a most original mind.

It is fitting that the two hymns which every public school boy knows by heart, " Lord behold us " and " Lord dismiss us with thy blessing ",‡ should be the work of a

* *Hymns Ancient and Modern*, 528/324.
† *Hymns Ancient and Modern* (standard edn.), 686.
‡ *Ib.*, 576 and 577.

schoolmaster.   Their author, F. C. Buckoll, was an assistant
master at Rugby in the time of Thomas Arnold, and by his
hymns and translations laid the foundation of the *Rugby
School Hymn Book* which, published in 1831, was the first
of a long line of public school hymn-books.   One of his
most felicitous translations is the morning hymn, " Come,
my soul, thou must be waking ".*

One of the most famous of all our hymns, " Eternal
Father, strong to save ",† is the work of William Whiting,
who was Master of Winchester Quiristers' School.   Whiting
was no poet, and wrote no other hymns ; but this one, for
its unusual intention and its famous tune by J. B. Dykes, is
a national possession.

Eton has only, so far as we know, produced three hymn-
writers from its teaching staff.   One is A. C. Benson,
whom we have already mentioned.   Another is A. C.
Ainger, whose chief contribution to hymnody is " God is
working his purpose out ",‡ though in his shortened Latin
Verse dictionary, *Gradus*, he is second to B. H. Kennedy
in the memories of those who studied classics in their youth.
The other Eton hymnographer is the lately-retired Dean of
Durham, Dr. Cyril Alington, who before taking the deanery
was Head Master of Eton.   Several of his hymns have
found wide favour ; the best known is " Good Christian
men, rejoice and sing ".§

Returning to Rugby, we must make honourable mention
of the famous and well-loved assistant master, G. F. Bradby,
who has some lines in *Songs of Praise* beginning " Where is
death's sting ? " ‖ and P. H. B. Lyon, until 1947 Head
Master, whose " Lift up your voice, ye Christian folk " ¶
has become well known in choral festivals organized by the
Royal School of Church Music, and now has a place in
Hymns Ancient and Modern.

Finally we must mention Frank Fletcher, Head Master
of Charterhouse, for his excellent hymn for boys, " O Son of

* *C.P.*, 591.   † *E.H.*, 540.   ‡ *E.H.*, 548.   § *C.P.*, 149.
‖ *Songs of Praise*, 296.   ¶ *Hymns Ancient and Modern* (1950), 297.

Man, our hero strong and tender ",* and J. H. Skrine of Uppingham for " Lord of the brave ".†

Beyond these there are many names of modern public school masters and assistant masters whom we might mention for their contributions to the three editions of the *Public School Hymn Book* ; we have dealt only with those who have found their place in the hymnody of the church at large.

Scholars and schoolmasters alike have given us a good tradition of solid, craftsmanlike hymn-writing. It is only lately that " public school religion " has set its mark on the words and music of public school masters ; in the earlier generations such schoolmasters as were Christians were Christians and not " educationists " ; the more self-conscious attitude to education prevailing since the introduction of universal and compulsory education in this country was no doubt responsible for the marking off of public school religion into a distinctive sphere of its own ; certainly the " public school hymn " is a development of the twentieth century, and the schoolmasters of the nineteenth tended to write for the church in a way which gave no hint of their profession.

MEN OF PUBLIC LIFE

Not a few of our hymns are the work of distinguished public men. We may indeed, if we are allowed a moment's trespassing into Lord Ernle's province, say that the first congregational songs of English Protestantism came from court-life, inasmuch as Thomas Sternhold, who published the first English metrical psalms,[54] was Groom of the Royal Wardrobe.

But our earliest genuine hymn from a distinguished public servant is " O worship the King ",‡ written by Sir Robert Grant. Born in 1785, Grant entered Parliament in 1808 representing the Elgin Burghs ; thereafter he represented Inverness, Norwich, and Finsbury. In 1831 he became a Privy Councillor, in 1833 carried a Bill for the emancipation

* *C.P.*, 116.   † *C.P.*, 256.   ‡ *E.H.*, 466.

of the Jews, became Judge Advocate-General in 1832, and in 1834 Governor of Bombay, when he was knighted. He died four years later at the age of 59, and a medical college was erected in Bombay to his memory. He wrote a few other hymns, of which " Saviour, when in dust to thee " * is still in use ; but " O worship the King ", with its fine lofty phrases, is immortal. He wrote it towards the end of his parliamentary career in England.

Another distinguished M.P. who wrote hymns was Sir John Bowring, who was of Unitarian faith and had a varied career. He was born in 1792, and became a friend of Jeremy Bentham, which led to his becoming editor of the *Westminster Review*. In 1831 he failed in business and entered Parliament, where he represented successively the Clyde Burghs, Kilmarnock, and Bolton, and made his mark in the House by his strong defence of Free Trade. He was a keen economist, and it was he who obtained the introduction of the florin into the currency as the first step towards the decimal coinage for which he frequently pleaded. He was frequently sent by the Government on foreign travels for the investigation of commercial matters ; this because he knew two hundred different languages and could speak adequately in a hundred of them. He eventually became British Consul in Canton and then Governor of Hong Kong. In this last appointment he gained himself a bad reputation ; a neighbour, Sir Henry Parkes, Governor of Amoy, wrote of him " He is full of conceit and without any very clear idea of political principles on a large scale ". His high-handed policy in Hong Kong is regarded as the chief cause of the " Opium War " of 1856–8, and as a result a vote of censure was passed on him in the House of Commons which brought on a General Election. His policy was, however, carried on by his successor, Lord Elgin (whose name is associated with the strange episode of the Elgin Marbles). He died in 1872, his eightieth year. Two of his hymns are well known—" In the Cross of Christ I

* *E.H.*, 87.

glory ",* and " God is love ; his mercy brightens all the path in which we rove ".†

Next in order of time comes an author whose work we mentioned some time back—Philip Pusey, author of " Lord of our life and God of our salvation ". He was an elder brother of E. B. Pusey, the Tractarian leader, but did not himself take Holy Orders. He became a landowner and public figure in his family's estate at Pusey, Berkshire. He was a leading agriculturist and one of the founders of the Royal Agricultural Society. He sat in the House of Commons for Rye, Chippenham, Cashel and Berkshire, and was the first to introduce the term " tenant-right " into the House. Disraeli said of him, " both by his lineage, his estate, his rare accomplishments and fine abilities, he was one of the most distinguished country gentlemen who ever sat in the House of Commons ". He was a connoisseur of art and one of the founders of the London Library ; he was also one of our earliest hymnologists. He died in 1855, aged 56, and his great hymn was written in 1834.

The next M.P. for us to deal with is none other than the Rt. Hon. William Ewart Gladstone, the only Prime Minister who ever wrote a published hymn. It is a beautiful piece of work, and in honour to it and its eminent author we will quote part of it here :

> O lead my blindness by the hand,
>   Lead me to thy familiar Feast,
> Not here or now to understand,
>   Yet even here and now to taste,
> How the eternal Word of heaven
> On earth in broken bread is given.
>
> We, who this holy precinct round
>   In one adoring circle kneel,
> May we in one intent be bound,
>   And one serene devotion feel ;
> And grow around thy sacred shrine
> Like tendrils of the deathless vine.‡

* E.H., 409. † C.P., 54. ‡ E.H., 322, verses 1 and 2.

This tender and simple devotion was, of course, characteristic of our most outstanding Prime Minister between Chatham and Churchill.

One of Mr. Gladstone's sons, W. H. Gladstone, who was M.P. for Worcestershire and predeceased his father by eight years, wrote a number of hymn-tunes that are still well known, among which are OMBERSLEY and HAMMERSMITH.*

The list of M.P.s ends with Sir John S. Arkwright, M.P. for Hereford 1900–12 and Chief Steward of the City of Hereford, to whose hymn, " O valiant hearts " † we have already made some reference.‡

From the M.P.s it is but a short step to the non-parliamentary public servants, of whom we may mention two here, Sir Cecil Spring-Rice and Sir Henry Newbolt.   Spring-Rice, a choice spirit, began his public career as a clerk in the War Office, moved to the Foreign Office and became Private Secretary to Lord Granville.   In 1900, aged 40, he became British Chargé d'Affaires at Teheran, and the following year became British Commissioner of Public Debt in Cairo.   In 1903 he moved to the Embassy at Petrograd, and in 1906 he went back to Persia as Minister and Consul-General.   In 1908 he was Minister to Sweden and in 1912 gained his last appointment as British Ambassador to the U.S.A.   On the 12th of January, 1918, at the age of 58, he wrote the lines which have made him famous in the hymn-books beginning " I vow to thee, my country ".§   On the night of the 13th he died in Ottawa, and his biographer, Sir Valentine Chirol, wrote of him, " The vow recorded in these lines had been kept long before he put it into words, for he had served his country for a quarter of a century with ' the love that never falters '."

Sir Henry Newbolt was born in 1862 and practised for a time as a barrister.   After 1899 he held various adminis-

* *C.P.*, 23 and 284.   † *Songs of Praise*, 293.
‡ See also Thomas Hughes (page 95) and Sylvester Horne (page 155).
§ *C.P.*, 756.

trative posts, among which were Controller of Wireless and
Cables during the First Great War, and President of the
English Association (1927–8), having also been (1923)
Official Naval Historian.   He is probably best known for
the poem *Vitai Lampada* which coined the expression " play
up, and play the game ", but his other works were numer-
ous, and his *Naval History of the War* is an acknowledged
classic.   His only hymn is that which begins

> O Lord almighty, thou whose hands
>   Despair and victory give,
> In whom, though tyrants tread their lands,
>   The souls of nations live ;
>
> Remember not the days of shame,
>   The hands with rapine dyed,
> The wavering will, the baser aim,
>   The brute material pride.*

The tone of this hymn, which was written during the First
Great War and published in 1919, is not unlike that of
Kipling's *Recessional* ; a trace of imperialistic pride is
balanced in both by the sombre note of national penitence.

Of men in other walks of life who distinguished themselves
otherwise than as hymn-writers we may refer first to James
Edmeston the architect, who was the teacher of Sir George
Gilbert Scott [55] (grandfather of Sir Giles Gilbert Scott who
designed Liverpool Cathedral and, we are told, the standard
telephone call-box now in use) and who wrote upwards of
two thousand hymns.   He was a keen member of the
Church of England and a constant visitor at the London
Orphan Asylum.   He is the object of one of Dr. Percy
Dearmer's not infrequent barbs of criticism ; Dearmer
wrote, " it was his regrettable practice to write a hymn
every Sunday and read it at family worship ".   Of his
hymns it is true to say that all but two are not even re-
gretted.   " Saviour, breathe an evening blessing " † is still

* *C.P.*, 574, verses 1 and 3.   † *Songs of Praise*, 54.

to be heard, though it is probably in its dotage ; but " Lead us, heavenly Father, lead us " * is one of our classics, and we shall find a number of references to it in our section on weddings.   Its only notable defect, possibly an accident of the changing meanings of words, is the intolerable reference in it to our Lord as " dreary ".

The medical profession provides us with two names, that of the Cornish doctor, Edwin Osler, who wrote the Communion hymn, " O God, unseen, yet ever near " † and the doxology, " Worship, honour, glory, blessing " ‡ as well as the revised version of a Doddridge hymn which appears in some books as " Fountain of good to own thy love ".§   The other doctor is Sir Ronald Ross, the hero of Panama and the discoverer of the cure for malaria, who at the height of his achievement wrote lines which one hymn-book has preserved, and which deserve quotation :

> Before thy feet I fall,
>   Lord, who made high my fate ;
> For in the mighty small,
>   Thou show'st the mighty great.
>
> Lo, while we ask the stars,
>   To learn the will of God,
> His answer unawares
>   Strikes sudden from the sod.
>
> He is the Lord of light ;
>   He is the thing that is ;
> He sends the seeing sight ;
>   And the right mind is his.
>
> Henceforth will I resound
>   But praises unto thee ;
> Though I was beat and bound,
>   Thou gav'st me victory.‖

As a celebration of a great scientist's thankfulness for the

---

* *E.H.*, 426.   † *Hymns Ancient and Modern*, 320/412.
‡ *E.H.*, 535, verse 3.   § *Congregational Hymnary*, 669.
‖ *Songs of Praise*, 452.   See also page 97.

successful conclusion of long, thankless, and dangerous researches this is outstanding, even if it is not really a hymn for public worship.

If we may once more admit a musical reference, we would observe that Sir Francis Champneys, the great obstetrician, was responsible for three tunes in the 1904 edition of *Hymns Ancient and Modern*, including one fine one which has survived, St. Jerome.*

The army has given us no hymn-writers of distinction ; the only contribution we have from a full-time army officer is Colonel Ewing's tune, Ewing, for " Jerusalem the golden ".† Ewing gained distinction in the Crimean War and afterwards served in Australia and China. It is believed that he never wrote a note of music besides this tune, but for it he deserves honour.

William Chatterton Dix, the author of " As with gladness men of old " ‡ and " Come unto me, ye weary ",§ was manager of a marine insurance company. William Vaughan Jenkins, author of " O God our Father, who dost make us one ",‖ was a chartered accountant, and George Rawson, author of " We limit not the truth of God " ¶ and " Father in high heaven dwelling " ** was a practising solicitor ; they are the only hymn-writers of distinction from their respective professions.

Finally we might mention two slight curiosities—hymns written by church musicians. It is not altogether uncommon for an author to write his own tune, though often that tune does not become the accepted one in later days. But perhaps it is not well known that J. B. Dykes, the great Victorian hymn-tune composer who wrote the tunes for " Holy, Holy, Holy ", " Eternal Father, strong to save ", and " The King of love " among many others, wrote the last four lines of " Lord of glory, who hast bought us " †† as well

* *C.P.*, 606.   † *E.H.*, 412.   ‡ *E.H.*, 39.
§ *E.H.*, 379.   ‖ *Methodist Hymn Book*, 688.
¶ *C.P.*, 230.   ** *C.P.*, 624.
†† *Hymns Ancient and Modern* (standard edn.), 367.

as its tune.   More remarkable still is a complete hymn for
choir festivals * by the late Sir Sydney Nicholson, Organist
of Westminster Abbey and founder of the Royal School of
Church Music, and published in the latest *Hymns Ancient
and Modern.*

As a closing section to this chapter we might mention
some other interesting people who have a place in this story,
and who fall into some of the categories we have already
enumerated.

Many of us know, and have profited from, a rather
strange hymn beginning " O the bitter shame and sorrow "
which has in each verse a developing refrain :

> All of self and none of thee ;
> Some of self and some of thee ;
> Less of self and more of thee ;
> None of self and all of thee.†

Its author was Theodore Monod, a French Protestant
clergyman in Paris, who wrote it in English during a series
of Consecration meetings at Broadlands, Hampshire, in 1874.
Those who know both the hymn and Rachel Field's best-
selling novel, *All This and Heaven Too* (1939), will perhaps
have noted that Theodore's father, the Rev. Frédéric Monod,
plays a large part in that tale as the clergyman who be-
friended Mademoiselle Desportes (" Mademoiselle Deluzy ")
at the time of her trial in Paris ;   Theodore himself appears
at one point as a ten-year-old boy.‡   The book is, its author
claims, largely historical, and enough is there written of the
Monod family to give us some idea of the background of
Theodore's life.

One of the great social services which found its inspiration
in the nineteenth century was that group dealing with
children's welfare.   The greatest name in this field is no

---

* *Hymns Ancient and Modern* (1950), 493.
† *Methodist Hymn Book*, 170.   ‡ Page 245 (chapter 23).

doubt that of Doctor Barnardo, who founded his " family "
in 1866. Benjamin Waugh's must be one of the nearest to
his in honour, inasmuch as he founded the London Society
for Prevention of Cruelty to Children in 1884 ; this became
the National Society in 1888. Waugh wrote a few hymns,
all for children, of which one has had a good deal of currency.
Two of its verses run as follows :

> Now let us see thy beauty, Lord,
>   As we have seen before ;
> And by thy Spirit quicken us
>   To love thee and adore.

> Lord, it is coming to ourselves
>   When thus we come to thee ;
> The bondage of thy loveliness
>   Is perfect liberty : *

they express well the tenderness and love of children that
inspired the life-work of this Congregational minister.

Englishmen owe a great deal to the National Trust for
Places of Historic Interest and Natural Beauty, commonly
called simply the National Trust. Its founder and first
secretary was Canon H. D. Rawnsley. Rawnsley is the
author of a few hymns of which the best known is " Father
whose will is life and good ", published in 1922 (after his
death) and written for medical missions. But he wrote
another hymn which might well be the theme-song of the
National Trust, and especially of lovers of the Lake District,
where, at Crosthwaite near Keswick, Rawnsley was vicar
for thirty-four years. The hymn, " Lord God, our praise
we give ", has only appeared, so far as we know, in the
unsuccessful 1904 revision of *Hymns Ancient and Modern*, there
set, incidentally, to a youthful and charming tune by Mr.
(later Sir) Sydney Nicholson. Behind its romantic but
simple lines it is not difficult to see the outlines of Scafell,
Great Gable and Pillar Rock.

* *C.P.*, 278, verses 1 and 5.

Lord God, our praise we give
  For lake and sea, and mountain ;
The power by which we live
  Flows freely from thy fountain ;
Like dew at morn and eve,
  Thou enterest every heart
Of those who will receive,
  Thy blessing to impart.

On earth, in heaven above,
  One anthem life is singing ;
Thy creatures as they rove,
  The bird in beauty winging,
The wave with rhythmic call
  The music of the wind,
The lake, the waterfall,
  Praise one Creator's mind.*

Rawnsley is the nearest we have to a " hymn writer of lakeland ", and he will hardly stand up to Wordsworth's stature
in general letters.   His counterpart in hymn-tune composition was Sir Arthur Somervell, who was a lover of that
country and gave most of his hymn-tunes lakeland names,
such as WINDERMERE, STONETHWAITE, BLENCATHRA, and
KENDAL.†

Another institution to which many Englishmen owe a debt
of gratitude is Mudie's Library.   The founder of this admirable institution was Charles Edward Mudie, a Congregationalist bookseller who started it when he was 24 years
old in 1842.   Mudie was a keen lay-preacher and a well-
known figure in the neighbourhood of the Vauxhall Bridge
Road.   He left us the familiar lines beginning

I lift my heart to thee,
Saviour divine.‡

Nor must we forget the immortal work of G. A. Studdert
Kennedy, loved by the forces in the First World War as

* *Hymns Ancient and Modern* (1904 edn.), 329, verses 1 and 3.
† *Songs of Praise*, 332, 399, 394, and 315.   ‡ *C.P.*, 481.

one of the outstanding military chaplains, and known generally as "Woodbine Willie". His *Rough Rhymes of a Padre* and *The Unutterable Beauty* contain poetry which leaves the reader with a deep impression of the beauty of holiness striking through the harshness of post-Christian Europe. His most famous lines are those which we have before referred to, "When through the whirl of wheels and engines humming"; * but although they are known for their striking imagery, probably "Awake, awake to love and work" † is more often sung, thanks to a happy tune in the Methodist Hymn Book. "Woodbine Willie" was too much a man of a single message to be a prolific hymn-writer; but the message, that the Feet could walk not only on the mountains green but also in the satanic mills, was one which men heard with gratitude. It is well proclaimed in the following lines :

> Close by the heedless worker's side
>   Still patient stands
> The carpenter of Nazareth
>   With piercèd hands
> Outstretched to plead unceasingly
>   His love's demands.
>
> Longing to pick a hammer up
>   And strike a blow ;
> Longing to feel his plane swing out,
>   Steady and slow,
> The fragrant shavings falling down
>   Silent as snow.
>
> Because this is my work, O Lord,
>   It must be thine ;
> Because it is a human task
>   It is divine.
> Take me, and brand me with thy cross,
>   Thy slave's proud sign.‡

* *Songs of Praise*, 698.   † *C.P.*, 562.
‡ *Songs of Praise*, 469.

Another great figure in the First World War was the founder
of Toc H, Canon P. B. Clayton, who has already been
mentioned as the author of the hymn on the *Pilgrim's
Progress*.   He does not reckon himself a poet, but he has
written another hymn, a typical " padre's hymn " which
breathes the honest and simple spirit of his excellent organization.   (Oddly enough it stands, in the only hymn-book
which prints either of them, next to the Studdert Kennedy
hymn we have just quoted.)   It begins :

> Come, kindred, upstand in the valour of Jesus,
>   And praise him and plight him the troth of true men.
> His yoke we are breasting together will ease us
>   When back at the pick and the lathe and the pen.
>
> How honest his harness ! O be ye then humble
>   To know that he gives us a thing to be done !
> Let us laugh at each setback, and learn from each stumble
>   With his hand to help us, his light leading on.*

   Finally we might refer to the fact that a title higher than
that of baronet very rarely appears in the authors' indexes
of our hymn-books.   English hymn-writing does not come
from the period of history when art, letters, and music were
recreations of the aristocracy.   Lord Tennyson scarcely
counts as a hymn-writer, although we sometimes sing from
In Memoriam " Ring out, wild bells " † and " Strong Son of
God ",‡ and " Crossing the Bar " § appears fairly regularly
in hymn-books.   Victoria, Lady Carbery may be mentioned
as the moving spirit and editor of the *Church Hymnal for the
Christian Year*, a hymn-book for the evangelical groups in the
Church of England still used fairly extensively in the north
of England ; we gather that her own contributions to that
book do not receive much attention now, however, and
few of them have been printed in other collections.   Pur-
suing the steeper slopes of hereditary honour we come to

---

* *Songs of Praise*, 470, verses 1 and 2.
† *Ib.*, 633.   ‡ *Ib.*, 648.   § *Ib.*, 649.

the ninth Duke of Argyll, a man of letters of some notability, whose paraphrase of the 121st Psalm is occasionally to be met with in current books. Its first verse runs :

> Unto the hills around do I lift up
>   My longing eyes ;
> O whence for me shall my salvation come,
>   From whence arise ?
> From God the Lord doth come my certain aid,
> From God the Lord who heaven and earth hath made.

This happens to be the only extant version of the psalm which brings out the sense of its opening verse upon which modern critics are now agreed—that the hills are regarded not as the source of help but as symbolizing a place from which no help will come : " I will lift up mine eyes unto the hills. From whence cometh my help? My help cometh even from the Lord . . ." [56]

But hymn-music, not hymn-writing, has the sole claim to the entertainment of royalty ; no king, queen, prince, or princess has, to our knowledge, written a published hymn (unless conceivably the ascription of a hymn in *Hymns Ancient and Modern* to King Alfred can be reliable ; * and unless we include the psalm-versions of King James I). But Albert, Prince Consort of England, has a tune in the 1904 *Methodist Hymn Book* † which indicates that he was by no means a negligible composer.

Finally, in a study such as this we ought not to overlook our duty to pay tribute to the prince of hymnologists, Dr. Julian, who compiled the monumental *Dictionary of Hymnology* in 1891, and presided over its revision in 1907. In the preparation of this work he estimated that he examined four hundred thousand hymns, and it remains the source-book for the subject. Julian wrote a few hymns himself, which he modestly omits to mention in his dictionary. The

---

* *Hymns Ancient and Modern* (standard edn.), 664, " O God, our Maker, throned on high ".   † No. 827.

only one which has achieved much recognition is that
beginning

> Father of all, to thee
> With loving hearts we pray
> Through him in mercy given,
> The Life, the Truth, the Way ;
> From heaven, thy throne, in mercy shed
> Thy blessings on each bended head.

This was first published in the 1889 edition of *Hymns Ancient
and Modern,* and has a place in the *English Hymnal.**

The other English hymnologists, Montgomery and Percy
Dearmer, we have already mentioned. The American
hymnologists, Louis Benson and Winfred Douglas, will
appear at a later stage.

* No. 386.

CHAPTER 16

Women Hymn-Writers

THE reader will not fail to observe in this and the three foregoing chapters a tacit acceptance of the ancient classification of human beings into men, women, and clergymen. It is possible, also, that the reader will feel less objection to the segregation of the clergy than to that of the women in this connection. It is one of the marks of the twentieth century that many attributes which had been regarded as feminine properties were found, or at least asserted, to be but accidents of the feminine state, and the separation of these accidents has brought with it a reaction against the sharp cleavage between the sexes which was one of the marks of Victorian England.

Now it happens that women have made a contribution to hymnody parallel to that which they have made to English letters. But there is one curious difference between the two contributions, which is that while the emancipation of women has produced a substantial increase in the number, and an enormous elevation of the literary standard, of women novelists, the coming of that age corresponds exactly with a virtual drying-up of the gift of hymn-writing in women. The only qualification of that generalization that we can admit is to say that women are still writing good things for children ; but nothing at all is coming from the women of the present generations in the way of universal hymnody. The course of the present chapter will prove this.

Another interesting fact, obvious as soon as one pays attention to the subject, is that the classical age of women hymn-writers falls somewhat earlier than that of women

novelists and poets. Jane Austen was born in 1775 ; she
has no women-contemporaries in novel-writing, but if we
allow women fifteen years her junior to be her contemporaries, she has two, not to mention one woman old
enough to be her mother and one old enough to be her
grandmother, who have written hymns that are still in
wide use.

But what makes it not only permissible, but even necessary
to segregate the women hymn-writers into a chapter such as
this is the fact that with very few exceptions they segregate
themselves by their subject-matter and style.   In the whole
field of hymns written by women and still current we find,
apart from children's hymns and translations, only a single
hymn of a theological, outward-looking kind, Caroline
Noel's " At the name of Jesus ", which, as " In the name of
Jesus ", appeared in 1870 in a little collection called *The
Name of Jesus, and other Verses for the Sick and Lonely.*   The
title of that book is important ; for in it Miss Noel falls into
line with the great majority of her sisters.   Our women
hymn-writers have specialized in hymns of personal devotion, and more particularly in hymns written for, and often
indeed by, people in frail health.   The fact that women in
the ages of their social segregation and economic dependence
often lived long lives in a precarious state of health—for
they were, if they came from the class from which hymn-
writers have normally come, both subject to maladies in
those days obscure and beyond the purview of the ordinary
physician, and also extremely carefully looked after—has
reflected itself in their hymns, and has been turned by the
best of them to a means of grace.

The preface to this chapter must, perhaps, include reference to two women who lived in the days before English
hymnody began.   One of these is a shadowy figure who
used to be called Bernard of Clairvaux ; indeed, it is only a
conjecture that the hymn, *Dulcis Jesu Memoria*, translated as
" Jesu, the very thought of thee ", is by an anonymous
religious of a French nunnery.[57]   But it may well be so, and

if it is so, and we may admit the lines as a hymn, then she becomes positively our earliest hymn-writer. The other name is that of Madame Guyon, that remarkable French Quietist of the seventeenth century of whom Monsignor Ronald Knox writes, " to tell the truth, I see her . . . as an anticipation of Mrs. Jellyby ".[58] Madame Guyon was a voluminous authoress as well as an insatiable talker, and she comes into our story because one or two selections from her poems were translated by William Cowper. This gives rise to speculations about the value which Cowper set on this strange half-Catholic, half-Protestant enthusiasm of seventeenth-century France into which we must not go here. The lady was an eccentric person even by the racy standards of the age of Louis XIV, but as interpreted by Cowper her lines have a sufficiently conventional ring of devotion. Two of her hymns have appeared in a book still in use, and one of them begins thus :

> 'Tis not the skill of human art
>   That gives me power my God to know ;
> The sacred lessons of the heart
>   Come not from instruments below.
>
> Love is my teacher. He can tell
>   The wonders that he learnt above ;
> No other master knows so well ;—
>   'Tis Love alone can tell of Love.*

The first woman writer of hymns in English, however, was Anne Steele,† a Baptist whose father and great-uncle were Baptist ministers at Broughton in Hampshire ; Bishop Burnet had replied to the local vicar who had complained that Steele, senior, was drawing off his congregation by his preaching, " Go away and preach better than Henry Steele." Her life was scarred by a great tragedy ; on the day on which she was to be married her betrothed was accidentally drowned in the river while bathing. She is,

---

* *Worship Song*, 335. (The other is no. 242 in that book.)
† 1716–78.

therefore, the mother not only of English women hymn-writers but also of all those who turned their own sorrow to the profit of the singing congregations. Her hymns were published in 1760, and one of them is still very well known, " Father of mercies, in thy word what endless glory shines ".* But more characteristic of her work, perhaps, is the following graciously restrained hymn of trust :

> Lord, teach me to hold fast thy hand,
> And when my griefs increase,
> To see beyond this lower land
> The hills of heavenly peace.
>
> And oh, whate'er of earthly bliss
> Thy sovereign hand denies,
> Accepted at thy throne of grace
> Let this petition rise :
>
> Give me a calm, a thankful heart,
> From every murmur free ;
> The blessings of thy grace impart,
> And let me live to thee.†

Anne Steele knew how to practise what here she preached.

The next woman hymn-writer whose work has survived is a generation younger, Anna Letitia Barbauld, the Unitarian, born in 1743. Her father was a Dr. Aikin, classical tutor at the dissenting academy at Warrington, and her husband a Unitarian minister of French descent, the Rev. Rochemont Barbauld. She wrote twenty-one hymns, all of which were preserved in Unitarian hymnals at the time (1891) of the first edition of Julian's *Dictionary*. The only hymn of hers which has wider currency at present is the harvest-hymn, " Praise to God immortal praise ".‡

Of the next generation again, but still older than Jane Austen by two years, is Harriet Auber, born in 1773,

---

* *C.P.*, 227.

† *Worship Song*, 272, verses 2–4. Compare *Hymns Ancient and Modern*, 515/180.

‡ *Hymns Ancient and Modern* (1950), 485.

authoress of " Our blest Redeemer ", perhaps the most
widely known of hymns on the Holy Spirit save only Cosin's
" Come, Holy Ghost ".   Miss Auber spent all her life in
the neighbourhood of Hoddesdon on the borders of Hertfordshire and Essex, and it was there that she wrote her
famous hymn along with a number of versions of the Psalms
which were much admired by Spurgeon but are now forgotten.   There is a story that she wrote " Our blest
Redeemer " * with her ring on a window-pane, having
neither pen nor paper by her when the inspiration came.
What enforced imprisonment brought about this odd cir-
cumstance has never been suggested, and although there is
no means of denying that somebody scratched the words on
glass (since the glass has long since disappeared), in the words
of one commentator, " there is no evidence that it was she
who scratched it." †   But the picturesque and unlikely
legend is less important than the exquisite words of the
hymn.

One other important woman hymn-writer was born in
the eighteenth century, Charlotte Elliott.   Perhaps she is
the most important : at all events, as Anne Steele set the
example, so Charlotte Elliott formed it into something of
a tradition.   She is the author of that most admirable of
evangelical hymns, " Just as I am, without one plea." ‡
In her youth she wrote humorous poems, but in 1821, at
the age of 32, she had a serious illness which made her a
permanent invalid through the remaining fifty years of her
life.   The impression made on her constitution by the illness was accompanied by a religious conversion in the
following year which she owed to the preaching of the Swiss
evangelist, César Malan. [59]   She remained in touch with
Malan by correspondence for many years after this, and her
literary talents were, as might be expected, wholly turned
after this to religious uses.   A glance at the titles of her

---

* E.H., 157.

† K. L. Parry (ed.), *Congregational Praise Discussed*, literary comment
on Hymn 209.   (Not yet published.)   ‡ E.H., 316.

H.H.L.

P

chief publications will show how her thoughts ran ; *Hours of Sorrow Cheered and Comforted* (1836) ; *The Invalid's Hymn Book* (1834) ; *Thoughts in Verse on Sacred Subjects* (1869).

Up to the time of her illness she lived at Clapham. Then she moved to Brighton, where her brother, the Rev. Henry Venn Elliott, had a charge. "Just as I am" was written one day while the rest of the family had gone out to help with a church bazaar, leaving Charlotte at home ; the thoughts that inspired the hymn began with reflections on her own loneliness, her frail health, and above all, as it seemed, her uselessness. Such depression is the cross which many people have to bear, and the hymn is for all these. It is a brave hymn, frank without introversion or sentimentality, with a magnificent last verse :

> Just as I am, of that free love
> The breadth, length, depth, and height to prove,
> Here for a season, then above,
> O Lamb of God, I come.

The hymn was made the basis of another hymn by " Marianne Farningham " (the pen name of Mrs. Hearn of Farningham, Kent) beginning "Just as I am, thine own to be ",* and intended for young people of sound health. The intention of the earlier hymn was thus precisely reversed in the later, and while the naïve confidence of Marianne Farningham's lines has made them justly popular, it has tended to make people look on the older hymn with the thoughtless patronage which the young and healthy sometimes extend to the old and ailing. Therefore the older "Just as I am" is much less sung now than it used to be ; but it is the finer hymn, and speaks of the deeper experience.

Miss Elliott's other well-known hymns are the upstanding lines beginning " Christian, seek not yet repose " †— another fine utterance from a woman who hated the idleness to which she was forced—and " My God, my Father, while I stray ".‡ The former has the refrain, " Watch and

---

* *C.P.*, 457.   † *E.H.*, 374.   ‡ *E.H.*, 440.

pray ", the latter, " Thy will be done ".   Curiously enough
" My God, my Father ", like " Just as I am ", has been
rewritten by a later hand ; this time it is that of Frederick
Mann, who also knew the acuteness of suffering, and who
produced the manly lines beginning " My God, my Father,
make me strong ",* using the same refrain.   Where the
older hymn was resigned, the later one is bold ; but although
Dr. Dearmer alluded rather pointedly to the resigned spirit
of Miss Elliott's lines as being not to our more upstanding
taste, let it not be forgotten that, as in " Christian, seek
not yet repose ", Miss Elliott could be bold.

But it is possible to say that Miss Elliott's preference for
metres which use a short final line, as in all three of the
hymns here mentioned and many others, gives an impression
of softness and resignation to her hymns which, if it is not
to be overdone, requires careful musical treatment.

Out of her turn, but appropriately because of her relation-
ship, we may mention here Emily Elliott, niece of Charlotte, who is known for a popular hymn of the nativity,
" Thou didst leave thy throne and thy kingly crown ".†
Emily was an energetic worker at the mission at Mildmay
Park, and by no means an invalid or a lady of retired life
like her aunt.

Mrs. Felicia Hemans, one of the archetypal " Gothic-
romantic " poetesses of the early nineteenth century, made
a few contributions to hymnody which are little remembered now, nor need they be resurrected from a decent
burial in *Worship Song.*‡

But as soon as we enter the nineteenth century we come,
in the year of Trafalgar, to the birth of Sarah Flower Adams,
authoress of one of our universal classics, " Nearer, my God,
to thee ".§   Mrs. Adams was the wife of a civil engineer,
and lived in London.   There is no romantic story of the
birth of " Nearer, my God, to thee ", but everybody knows
that it was played—to what tune remains in doubt—by the

* *C.P.*, 530.   † *E.H.*, 585.
‡ Nos. 87 and 734.   § *C.P.*, 480 for full version.

ship's band when the *Titanic* sank in 1912. By that date it was, of course, already established in the minds of English and American Christians, a popularity amply justified by its picturesque and intimate application of the old story of Jacob's ladder.

Jane Eliza Leeson (1807–82) is the only hymn-writer in general currency who comes from the Catholic Apostolic Church, founded in 1832 by Edward Irving. She is well known for two children's hymns, " Loving Shepherd of thy sheep " * and " Saviour, teach me day by day ",† both of which are among the real classics of children's hymnody. Some of her other hymns were improvised after the technique, cultivated in the Irvingite sect, of " prophetical utterance ", a revival, as was supposed, in the " enthusiastic " tradition, of the ancient " gift of prophecy " of which St. Paul writes in *I Corinthians* xiv. These have not survived.

Jane Crewdson, wife of a Manchester manufacturer, was another confirmed invalid who has given us two hymns in the style of Charlotte Elliott, one of which is brief and beautiful enough to be quoted here in full ;

> O Saviour, I have nought to plead,
>   In earth beneath or heaven above,
> But just my own exceeding need,
>   And thy exceeding love.
>
> The need will soon be past and gone,
>   Exceeding great, but quickly o'er ;
> The love unbought is all thine own,
>   And lasts for evermore.‡

The minute compass and painstaking symmetry of this reminds one of the eminently Victorian accomplishment of sewing samplers. It is a quality which we shall see again more highly developed in Elisabeth Rundle Charles. Mrs. Crewdson's other hymn in currency is " There is no sorrow, Lord ".§

---

* *Hymns Ancient and Modern*, 334/444.   † *C.P.*, 448.
‡ *C.P.*, 771.   § *Songs of Praise*, 665.

The generation born about 1820 is the most fertile in women hymn-writers, and it is heralded by that strange trio, the sisters Brontë. All short lived, all brilliant in letters, two of them, Emily (1818–48) and Anne (1819–49), wrote poems which have come into use as hymns. Charlotte alone made no excursions into religious poetry. Both Emily and Anne are known for hymns of surpassing courage —" Believe not those who say " and " No coward soul is mine " * which have lately found some acceptance. Emily's lines are perhaps beyond the border of hymnody and even of Christian orthodoxy ; but they are highly characteristic of that emotional fervour which took hold on the lettered Victorians of her day :

> Vain are the thousand creeds
> That move men's hearts—unutterably vain,
> Worthless as withered weeds
> Or idlest froth amid the boundless main,
>
> To waken doubt in one
> Holding so fast by thine infinity ;
> So surely anchored on
> The steadfast rock of immortality.†

Anne is perhaps a little less turgid, in " Believe not those who say " :

> Be this thy constant aim,
> Thy hope, thy chief delight ;
> What matter who should whisper blame,
> Or who should scorn or slight,
>
> If but thy God approve,
> And if, within thy breast,
> Thou feel the comfort of his love,
> The earnest of his rest.‡

Anne has also a penitential hymn in the same metre

---

* *Songs of Praise*, 588 and 453.
† *Ib.*, 588, verses 3 and 7.   ‡ *Ib.*, 453, verses 5 and 6.

beginning " Oppressed with sin and woe ", and containing
the lines

> I need not fear my foes,
> I need not yield to care,
> I need not sink beneath my woes,
> For thou wilt answer prayer.*

There was always something slightly hag-ridden about the
household at Haworth, and the fury of Emily and the
stoicism of Anne in these lines come from this experience.
One can see the author of *Wuthering Heights* in some of
those strange utterances in " No coward soul ".

An antidote to these troubled musings is the great hymn
of praise to the exalted Christ, " At the name of Jesus ",
by Caroline Noel ; this, though you would not guess it
from internal evidence, is the result of sickness ; a serious
illness in her fortieth year revived in this daughter of the
vicarage a poetic talent which had lain dormant, after an
early and abundant bloom, for twenty years.

1823 was the year in which Anna Letitia Waring was
born. We have not yet commented on the longevity of our
women hymn-writers ; but it has been, with some notable
exceptions, well maintained. Anne Steele lived to be 61,
Mrs. Barbauld 81, Harriet Auber 89, Charlotte Elliott 82.
The Brontës and Sarah Adams are the great exceptions ;
but Miss Waring achieved the ripe age of 87. She lived
all her life at Neath, Glamorganshire, and has left us some
hymns which combine great lyric virtues with an emphasis
on Christian resignation that almost amounts to fatalism.

> Father, I know that all my life
> Is portioned out for me.†

This is the opening of one of her well-known hymns, and
as a corrective to impious pride and perverse stoicism it
and her other hymns have much to say. But it is a world
away from the courage of Charlotte Elliott, who did suc-

---

* *C.P.*, 777, verse 5.   † *C.P.*, 410.

ceed in making something positive out of the act of resignation ; and Anna Letitia Waring's most famous hymn, " In heavenly love abiding ",* when sung to that most yielding of Welsh tunes, PENLAN, is the kind of hymn that causes misjudgments about Charlotte Elliott, and, more generally, a contempt for hymn-singing as the refuge of non-combatant Christians.

1821 is the " peak year " for women hymn-writers, for in it were born Eliza Scudder, Jeannette Threlfall, and Dora Greenwell. Not much need be said about the first two, but Dora Greenwell is worth noting as one who raised the purely imaginative virtues of hymn-writing among women higher than they had yet come. Two of her hymns are still sung ; one of them is along the usual line of " trust and resignation ", beginning

> I am not skilled to understand
> What God hath willed, what God hath planned ;
> I only know at his right hand
> Stands one who is my Saviour.†

In her other hymn, however, " And art thou come with us to dwell ", Miss Greenwell rose to at least one really moving verse. Her eschatology is not what a modern theologian would require, and in this hymn there is more poetry than sound doctrine : but its two opening verses are worth quoting for their final couplet :

> And art thou come with us to dwell,
>   Our Prince, our Guide, our Love, our Lord ?
> And is thy name Immanuel,
>   God present with his world restored ?
>
> The heart is glad for thee ! it knows
>   None now shall bid it err or mourn,
> And o'er its desert breaks the rose
>   In triumph o'er the grieving thorn.‡

* C.P., 412.   † Methodist Hymn Book, 381.
‡ C.P., 169, verses 1 and 2.

This was written as a Christmas poem, but it is really a
romantic poem on the Second Advent, and it shows excellently the new approach to this doctrine which advancing
Christian social thinking was producing in the middle of the
nineteenth century ; it was published in 1869. If you try
to disentangle time from eternity in it you will be in trouble ;
but there are fine thoughts in it. Miss Greenwell was a
native of County Durham and lived there most of her life.

This brings us to the greatest of women hymn-writers in
English, Mrs. Alexander, who when she wrote her famous
series on the Catechism for children was still Miss Hum-
phreys. She was an Irishwoman, and became the wife of
the Rev. W. Alexander who became Primate of all Ireland.
She was not, as has been sometimes claimed, the first writer
of children's hymns ; we shall mention a group of women
who wrote them earlier than 1848, in which year her series
appeared. But she was to her forebears what Charlotte
Elliott was to Anne Steele—she established a respectable
tradition, and several of the hymns which she wrote in order
to expound the articles of the Creed to children are among
our imperishable treasures. " Once in royal David's city ",*
" There is a green hill ",† and " All things bright and
beautiful " ‡ are unassailably in the front rank, and " Jesus
calls us " § and her magnificent translation of " St. Patrick's
Breastplate " ‖ are not far behind in popular affection. In
" We are but little children weak " ¶ she set a fashion of
hymn-writing for children which was less lasting and less
admirable—in making the children refer to themselves as
" little ", which nowadays is thought to be a psychological
miscalculation ; and while in that hymn Mrs. Alexander
has something not unimportant to say, the fashion was
taken up by lesser writers with somewhat mawkish results.
The greatness of Mrs. Alexander's children's hymns lies in
the fact that the three best known of them have been firmly
appropriated by the adults. They have the simplicity that

* *E.H.*, 605.   † *E.H.*, 106.   ‡ *E.H.*, 587.
§ *E.H.*, 205.   ‖ *E.H.*, 212.   ¶ *E.H.*, 610.

a Christian person need never grow out of. Perhaps we ought not to try to disguise the fact that Mrs. Alexander is the author of what is perhaps the most-laughed-at hymn in *Hymns Ancient and Modern* :

> Within the churchyard, side by side
>   Are many long, low graves ;
> And some have stones set over them ;
>   On some the green grass waves.
>
> Full many a little Christian child,
>   Woman, and man lies there ;
> And we pass near them every time
>   When we go in to prayer. . . .
>
> They do not hear when the great bell
>   Is ringing overhead ;
> They cannot rise and come to church
>   With us, for they are dead.*

But although this must be called material which does not come naturally to the singing congregation, those of us who in our time have had a good laugh at the *naïveté* of the last line quoted may expect a later modification of our ribaldry. Mrs. Alexander was doing her best to answer the children's questions about eternal things. " How was Jesus born ? "—" Once in royal David's city." " Why did he die ? "—" He died that we might be forgiven." " Who made the birds and the flowers ? "—" The Lord God made them all." Well, what do you do when your child points to a gravestone and asks, " What is that, Daddy ? " It might well be contended that the truth thus frankly, if baldly, stated is better than " Sh, dear ! it's not very nice."

Mrs. Alexander stands with Caroline Noel, then, as a great woman writer of credal hymns—hymns that answer the questions rather than declare experiences. She stands at a higher level because she succeeded so remarkably often in compelling the older folk to join the children's circle.

* *Hymns Ancient and Modern* (standard edition), 575, verses 1, 2, and 5.

Elisabeth Rundle Charles (Miss Rundle, Mrs. Charles, and often misspelt in her Christian name) became the wife of a barrister, and, like Charlotte Elliott, nearly forty years her senior, was led to Christ by César Malan in her early youth. She left a number of hymns, but only one is both meritable and popular. We anticipated our reference to her a few pages back by likening her work to the sewing of a sampler. Look at a few verses of her " Never further than thy cross ", and the simile will explain itself.

> Never further than thy cross,
>   Never higher than thy feet ;
> Here earth's precious things seem dross,
>   Here earth's bitter things grow sweet.
>
> Gazing thus, our sin we see,
>   Learn thy love while gazing thus—
> Sin, which laid the cross on thee ;
>   Love, which bore the cross for us.
>
> Here we learn to serve and give,
>   And, rejoicing, self deny ;
> Here we gather love to live,
>   Here we gather faith to die.
>
> Symbols of our liberty
>   And our service here unite ;
> Captives, by thy cross set free,
>   Soldiers of thy cross, we fight.*

The pattern of repetition and antithesis in these verses is, if you look at them carefully, intricate and neat in just the way that a Victorian fire-screen might be intricate and neat. It is almost too neat to be genuine, too tidy, too symmetrical ; the hymn would be intolerable if in the last two verses Mrs. Charles did not find her pattern at last broken through by the urgency of her message, so that not only does she abandon static symmetry for energetic movement, but she actually finishes a verse with a comma :

* C.P., 453, verses 1–4.

Pressing onwards as we can,
    Still to this our hearts must tend—
Where our earliest thoughts began,
    There our last aspirings end,

Till amid the hosts of light,
    We in thee redeemed, complete,
Through thy cross made pure and white,
    Cast our crowns before thy feet.

Adelaide Anne Procter was a contemporary of Mrs. Charles. She was born in 1825 and lived to be only 39. In 1851 she became a member of the Roman Catholic Church. She wrote a good deal of verse from an early age ; some of it was contributed under the pseudonym " Mary Berwick " to Charles Dickens's periodical, *Household Words*. Her best-known hymn is " My God, I thank thee, who hast made the earth so bright ",* which is a fairly freely altered version of her poem, " I thank thee, O my God, who made ". " The shadows of the evening hours ",† an evening hymn, had considerable vogue in the past but seems now to be passing out of use. Her work is always of the intimate and devotional kind with no great emotional pressure.

I shall have a little to say later about mission-hymns of the " Sankey " type ; I have elsewhere ‡ recorded my conviction that " There were ninety and nine " § is one of the really fine hymns to be found among the luxuriant vegetation of the Gospel Songs. Its authoress was Elizabeth Clephane, who was born five years later than Miss Procter, and like her died when she was 39. Her life was entirely passed in Scotland. She wrote the verses, it is believed, in a very short time, and they were published in the year before her death. They attracted no attention until Ira D. Sankey at a mission meeting some time between then and 1874 improvised his tune for them. The composition of

* *C.P.*, 62.   † *Congregational Hymnary*, 608.
‡ *The Church and Music*, p. 187.   § *E.H.*, 584.

this tune is one of the very few examples in music of an improvisation being " caught " by its composer and encaged in music-symbols.

Christina Rossetti, one of the more considerable poetesses of the nineteenth century, was born in the same year, 1830, as Miss Clephane, and lived to 1894. She did not, strictly speaking, write hymns ; her metres are too wayward and irregular for perfection in the hymn-form. But some of her poems have found their way into hymn-books, the best known of them being the carols " In the bleak midwinter " and " The shepherds had an angel ".* Christina Rossetti is outstanding among her contemporaries in being a passionate evangelical in conviction and in language. There is nothing of the sampler about this :

> None other Lamb, none other name,
> None other hope in heaven or earth or sea,
> None other hiding place from guilt or shame,
> 　None beside thee !

> My faith burns low, my hope burns low ;
> Only my heart's desire cries out in me
> By the deep thunder of its want and woe,
> 　Cries out to thee.†

Conventional nineteenth-century platitudes were not for Christina Rossetti, and she is utterly unlike any of her women contemporaries in this respect. " Love is the key of all unknown " is another poem of hers to be found in one hymn-book.‡ She is one of the few woman hymn-writers who are open to criticism for giving expression to an undue richness of evangelical devotion.

The last of our great women-writers was Frances Ridley Havergal, another short-lived author. She was the daughter of the Rev. W. H. Havergal, one of the more distinguished amateurs of church music of the early nineteenth century, and she outlived him by only nine years. She wrote a

* *C.P.*, 90 and 91.　　　　　　　　† *C.P.*, 308, verses 1 and 2.
‡ *Methodist Hymn Book*, 435.

very large number of hymns of an evangelical turn, and a few tunes also. Of her hymns the best known are " Take my life, and let it be ",* " Who is on the Lord's side ? " † and " Lord, speak to me, that I may speak ".‡ She was a woman of great saintliness, and one gathers that she had the rare and happy gift of being able to influence everybody whom she met for the better without leaving them with a sense of patronage. She was no great poetess, but if she erred in the direction of facility, in one hymn, less well known than those we have mentioned, she struck the authentic note :

> Thy life was given for me,
>   Thy blood, O Lord, was shed,
> That I might ransomed be,
>   And quickened from the dead :
> Thy life was given for me ;
> What have I given for thee ? §

Perhaps her life is best summed up in the lines :

> Lord, speak to me, that I may speak
>   In living echoes of thy tone ;
> As thou hast sought, so let me seek
>   Thy erring children, lost and lone.

That is undeniably what she spent her time doing. She herself told how " Take my life " came to her.

> There were ten persons in the house, some unconverted and long prayed for, some converted but not rejoicing Christians. He gave me the prayer, " Lord, give me ALL in this house." And he just did. Before I left the house every one had got a blessing.[60]

This is not the introverted evangelicalism of Christina Rossetti but a supremely unself-conscious and extroverted frame of mind. Miss Havergal's methods might have been alarming to a twentieth-century household ; but nobody is

---

* C.P., 458.   † C.P., 528.   ‡ C.P., 552.
§ Methodist Hymn Book, 391.

recorded as having thought otherwise in her own generation than that she was a saint.

After Miss Havergal the line begins to grow thinner. We ought to mention three women of this generation to whom hymnody owes a debt. There is first Isabella Stevenson, born in 1843, who had placed two generations in her debt by her lines beginning

> Holy Father, in thy mercy
>   Hear our anxious prayer ;
> Keep our loved ones, now far distant,
>   'Neath thy care ; *

these lines were frequently sung in churches of all denominations during both World Wars.

Ella Sophia Armitage (1841–1931) was the wife of a Congregational minister, and contributed a few hymns to the *Congregational Church Hymnal* of 1887. They were chiefly children's hymns, and they show a singular gift of lyric poetry. The most widely circulated was " O Lord of life and love and power ",† the most used in her denomination was " In our dear Lord's garden " ; ‡ but probably the happiest, showing at its best the delicate work of which she was a master—lacework rather than sampler work—is the hymn whose first two verses are :

> Not only for the goodly fruit trees tall
> The Master cares, whose love is over all ;
> The tiny herbs which blossom everywhere
> No less his watchful toil and patience share.
>
> And all small flowers of fair humility,
> Sweet temper, daily patience, charity,
> Kind words and cheerfulness to him are dear,
> More than most deeds whose praise men tell and hear.§

Then we must not forget the authoress of the most famous of wedding hymns, " O perfect Love ",‖ of which we shall

---

* *E.H.*, 520.   † *Congregational Hymnary*, 646.
‡ *C.P.*, 698.   § *C.P.*, 40.   ‖ *E.H.*, 346.

have more to say later. Mrs. Gurney was still Dorothy Blomfield when she wrote this for her sister's wedding in 1883, and after it was published in *Hymns Ancient and Modern* it achieved enormous popularity.

Mary Fawler Maude, wife of the Rev. Joseph Maude, vicar of St. Thomas's, Newport, Isle of Wight, has earned wide fame with " Thine for ever, God of love ".*   She was born in 1819 and lived to be 94 ; she wrote the hymn in 1847 for her Sunday-school class, but it was by no means her first literary effort, since it is recorded that while still in her teens she wrote three textbooks on *Scripture Manners and Customs, Scripture Topography*, and *Scripture Natural History*, based on the findings of Eastern travellers of the early nineteenth century.

Women have not, until recently, and then chiefly in hymns for children, contributed much to our hymn-tune treasury. But we must not neglect the daughter of a Scottish manse, Jessie Seymour Irvine, who is the composer of the now celebrated tune, CRIMOND.† The tune first appeared in the 1872 *Northern Psalter* attributed to David Grant ; Grant was the local tobacconist and musician who harmonized the tune. He may have modified its melody, —we cannot tell how far, since the manuscript no longer exists. But careful enquiries have placed Miss Irvine's original claim beyond question. The tune had not a great vogue until, along with some other Scottish psalm-tunes, it was made a frequent feature in the broadcasts of the Glasgow Orpheus Choir under Sir Hugh Roberton ; in his arrangement it has become widely known in this country, and although no English hymn-book printed it until the *Methodist School Hymn Book* was issued in 1950, almost every congregation in the country knew it by that time. Its popularity was finally established by its use at the marriage of the Queen to Philip, Duke of Edinburgh in November, 1947.

This is enough to show the general lines along which our women hymn-writers have worked. Their hymns have,

* *E.H.*, 344.   † *C.P.*, 729.

with a few famous exceptions, always been of the reflective rather than the objective sort ; but in this field they have led the way of Christian personal devotion throughout the nineteenth century.

We end this chapter by noticing some of the women who have enriched our hymnody by translations from the German.

The earliest in date is Frances Elizabeth Cox, born in 1812 at Oxford, who is remembered for " Who are these, like stars appearing ? " * and " Jesus lives ! " † among the many German hymns she translated.   Only a year younger than she was Jane Laurie Borthwick, who published in four volumes *Hymns from the Land of Luther*, and who during her lifetime directed that her hymns should simply be signed " H. L. L."   The best known of these is " Jesus, still lead on ".‡   Of her original hymns one, " Come, labour on ",§ is still widely known.

Then there is Jane Montgomery Campbell, another good linguist, who translated " We plough the fields, and scatter " ‖ for the Rev. C. S. Bere's *Garland of Songs* (1861).

Finally, and greatest of them all, we have Catherine Winkworth, who lived all her life of less than fifty years at Alderley Edge, near Manchester, and who published several series of translations including *Lyra Germanica* in two parts and *The Chorale Book for England*.   The first of these appeared when she was 26 years old, in 1855.   Many of Miss Winkworth's translations are excellent and a good company of them will be found in most hymn-books.   The most celebrated has become a national possession—" Now thank we all our God ",¶ and " Praise to the Lord, the Almighty " ** is not far behind it, though we do not usually sing it exactly as she wrote it.   " O Love, who formedst me to wear " †† and " Christ the Lord is risen again " ‡‡ are universally

* *E.H.*, 204.	† *E.H.*, 134.
‡ *C.P.*, 490.	§ *C.P.*, 542.
‖ *E.H.*, 293.	¶ *E.H.*, 533.
** *E.H.*, 536. †† *E.H.*, 460.	‡‡ *E.H.*, 129.

loved, and " Deck thyself, my soul, with gladness ",* perhaps the most beautiful of them all, is being brought into
frequent use at Choral Eucharist in the Church of England,
and is just beginning to find favour in non-Anglican communions.   The judgment of Percy Dearmer was that her
Lyra Germanica ranks with the devotional classics of the
nineteenth century.†

NOTE : Women writers of children's hymns are noticed
in Chapter 18 and American women hymn-writers in
Chapter 17.

* *E.H.*, 306.
† *Songs of Praise Discussed*, biographical note, page 528.

American Hymn-Writers

IN an earlier chapter we referred to certain hymns which have come from America, and we said there that the great contribution of America has come from the religious and social controversies of the nineteenth century. We owe so much to America in modern English hymnody that it is proper to enlarge here on this and add something to it.

American hymnody must be divided into four clear sections, namely, the hymns which came from America before the characteristically American tradition of civilization was begun, the hymns of the negro revival, the hymns of mature American culture, and the hymns of the later revivals of Sankey and Moody, and Torrey and Alexander.

The first two groups can soon be disposed of. American hymns of the eighteenth century are indistinguishable from English hymns of the same period. Until 1776 America was a colony, and the hymns we have from the America of that time are in the Wesleyan or Calvinist idiom. Only two authors survive in common English use—Samuel Davies, President of the New Jersey Presbyterian College, Princeton (1724-61), who wrote " Great God of wonders ",* and Timothy Dwight, President of Yale, to whom we have already referred as the author of " I love thy kingdom, Lord ".†

Neither of these authors is sung in England except by the dissenting bodies.

* *C.P.*, 67.   † *C.P.*, 246.

The " negro spirituals " which took such a hold on the oppressed negro population in the Kentucky Revivals of 1797–1805 are familiar to most people. Their moving words and haunting airs have captured the imagination of many distinguished European musicians ; some of the characteristic tunes of these songs are either quoted or echoed in the " New World Symphony " and the " Nigger Quartet " of Anton Dvořak (1841–1904), and many have been arranged as part songs for English singers. Although they are not usually sung in English churches, these are the real American hymns in the sense that they are songs of Christian experience from indigenous Americans. The experience was communicated to the negroes by white missionaries, but the songs are their own, set to their own music. It is one of the tragedies of Church History that the Christian Faith which took so firm a hold on the negro population of the South, and which upheld them so long in the suffering which slavery brought to them, never became a living force among those other native Americans, the Indians.[61] The white missionary did succeed in repairing in some measure the damage the white trader did to the negroes ; but he failed with the Indians, and we have no American hymnody from that quarter.

But perhaps the service done by the oppressed negroes to the Christian cause went beyond their own " spirituals " inasmuch as it was the great issue of slavery which led American Christianity to develop what has always been its distinctive virtue—a lively social conscience. American Christians have not, until the last seventy-five years or so, been pre-eminent in theological scholarship, but for a far longer time than that they have stirred the consciences of men in the matter of their duty to their neighbours.

We have mentioned in Chapter 9 some of the most famous hymns that have come out of this social teaching of the American Christians of the years 1825 to 1860. The main stream of American hymnody has always run in the direction of the liberal and social Gospel and has never returned to

Calvinism. When the emancipation of slaves was achieved, American Christianity remained essentially liberal and un-dogmatic, and the emphasis in American hymns is always, except in those of the Revivals, on social duty and on the necessity of building the Kingdom of God here on earth. We saw in " City of God " and one or two other hymns the lengths to which a militantly anti-dogmatic attitude would go ; nor was this in any way to be wondered at in a civiliza-tion which had so swiftly been transformed. American Christianity came alive in the years when the Industrial Revolution had made it possible for such changes to be made with almost miraculous speed, and emancipation was to the American Christian a symbol of the moral progress and achievement of man corresponding closely to the material progress that was going hand in hand with it. When Samuel Johnson and Samuel Longfellow said in their preface that they would admit nothing to their book that would offend a liberal literary culture, they were celebrating (this was in 1864, the crucial year of emancipation) the achievement of man, and in such an atmosphere the emphasis laid by traditional Calvinism on human sin and divine grace was obviously at a discount.

We have referred to enough American hymns already to make it unnecessary to quote many more here. Recall " City of God ", " Mine eyes have seen the glory " and " Eternal ruler of the ceaseless round ", and you will see at its best the youthful pride of American Christianity in the nineteenth century. We can now reinforce this by quoting a few of the famous hymns that came from this liberal culture.

One of the eldest of these American prophets of emancipa-tion was John Pierpont (1785–1866) ; he became pastor of a famous Unitarian church in New York, and resigned the pastorate in 1840 over the question of emancipation. He has left us one fine hymn of the universal church which deserves to be remembered :

O thou to whom in ancient time
  The lyre of Hebrew bards was strung ;
Whom kings adored in songs sublime,
  And prophets praised with glowing tongue ;

Not now on Zion's height alone
  Thy favoured worshippers may dwell,
Nor where at sultry noon thy Son
  Sat weary by the patriarch's well ;

From every place below the skies
  The grateful song, the fervent prayer,
The incense of the heart may rise
  To heaven, and find acceptance there.*

Notice the high literary standard which American hymnody
has already reached. Except in a few eighteenth-century
authors it is not infected with the language of Calvinism,
or the ecstasies of Wesleyanism ; nor indeed did it ever
suffer from the tradition of hack writing which disfigured
English hymnody after the Anglican liturgical revival. In
this early American hymn you have a pure and cultivated
style already flourishing—a style one or two stages ahead,
in literary quality, of James Montgomery. Indeed, the
scriptural references are incorporated with a good deal of
artistry—the Psalms, the prophets, the Deuteronomic Reformation which compelled everybody to worship at Jerusalem (621 B.C.), and the fourth chapter of St. John. This is
as near as American hymnody of the new kind ever came
to being scriptural in the ancient sense.

Bishop G. W. Doane of New York was the author of
" Thou art the Way " ; † his " Fling out the banner ! " ‡
is a more militantly evangelical mission hymn which has
had great success ; but Bishop Doane's hymns do not
bear the marks of the current controversy ; he died in
1859 before the Civil War broke out.

But William Cullen Bryant [62] (1794–1878) was right in
the movement for reform, and what he thought about the

* C.P., 273.   † C.P., 102   ‡ E.H., 546.

condition of American Christendom is sufficiently to be seen in these lines :

> Look from thy sphere of endless day,
>   O God of mercy and of might ;
> In pity look on those who stray
>   Benighted, in this land of light.*

He was founder of the *New York Review* and editor of the *New York Evening Post.*

Edward Hamilton Sears, born in 1810, is well known to us for " It came upon the midnight clear ", a hymn which characteristically links the Christmas message with the social and international needs of the world :

> And ye, beneath life's crushing load,
>   Whose forms are bending low,
> Who toil along the climbing way
>   With painful steps and slow—
> Look up ! . . .†

This was first published in 1850, in the heat of the controversy : Sears was, like most of these authors, a Unitarian minister.

Then look at these lines of Theodore Parker, another Unitarian minister :

> O thou great Friend to all the sons of men,
>   Who once didst come in humblest guise below
> Sin to rebuke, to break the captive's chain,
>   And call thy brethren forth from want and woe—
>
> We look to thee ; thy Truth is still the light
>   Which guides the nations, groping on their way,
> Stumbling and falling in disastrous night,
>   Yet ever hoping for the perfect day ; ‡ [63]

and these by W. H. Burleigh, editor of the abolitionist journal, *The Christian Freeman* :

---

* *Church Hymnary*, 340.   † *E.H.*, 26, verse 4.
‡ *C.P.*, 103, verses 1 and 2.

Lead us, O Father, in the paths of truth ;
Unhelped by thee, in error's maze we grope,
While passion stains and folly dims our youth,
And age comes on uncheered by faith or hope.

Lead us, O Father, in the paths of right ;
Blindly we stumble when we walk alone,
Involved in shadows of a darkening night ;
Only with thee we journey safely on.*

Both of these were written in the 'forties ; neither was intended for use as a hymn, but they found favour as poems and later editors of hymn-books have been glad to use them at further stages of the crusade against social evil and oppression.

The liberal faith in its missionary aspect is well reflected in George Duffield's " Stand up, stand up for Jesus ",† and in Samuel Wolcott's " Christ for the world we sing ".‡ Duffield was a Presbyterian minister, Wolcott a Congregationalist minister and missionary. Duffield's hymn is based on the dying words of the Rev. Dudley Atkins Tyng, " Tell them to stand up for Jesus " ; Tyng was another leader of anti-slavery agitation up to his death in 1858.

The same thought is memorably expressed in a hymn by a later author, Dr. W. Pierson Merrill. His " Rise up, O men of God " § has the same note of courage and pride of achievement in it, especially in his original version of the third verse :

Rise up, O men of God,
The Church for you doth wait ;
Her strength unequal to her task ;
Rise up, and make her great.

It is of the genius of American Protestantism that an author should write of men making the Church great ; Englishmen have come to prefer in these latter days the last two lines as their author altered them :

* C.P., 514, verses 2 and 3. Cf. E.H., 482.
† E.H., 581.   ‡ C.P., 333.   § C.P., 561.

> Her strength shall make your spirit strong ;
> Her service make you great,

which implies that the church makes men great.   But the author does not like the alteration, and it is the original, written in 1897, that follows the genuine American tradition.

More reflective, but still in the liberal climate, is a hymn of Oliver Wendell Holmes (1809–94), Professor of Anatomy and Physiology at Dartmouth College and (from 1847) at Harvard, son of Abiel Holmes the famous divine, and father of an equally famous judge.   It begins " Lord of all being, throned afar ", and its last verse contains an aspiration that shows the American tradition at its most gracious :

> Grant us thy truth to make us free,
> And kindling hearts that burn for thee,
> Till all thy living altars claim
> One holy light, one heavenly flame.*

Another well-known hymn of his expresses the liberal and undogmatic faith in which a great scientist found his home :

> Our Father, while our hearts unlearn
> The creeds that wrong thy name,
> Still let our hallowed altars burn
> With faith's undying flame.†

But perhaps the most influential of American hymn-writers was John Greenleaf Whittier, the Quaker poet, who never to his own knowledge wrote a hymn, but from whose works two or three familiar hymns were taken.   The most beautiful is that selection from his poem, " Our Master ", beginning

> Immortal love, for ever full,
> For ever flowing free,
> For ever shared, for ever whole,
> A never ebbing sea,

and containing the unforgettable verse :

* E.H., 434, verse 5. † C.P., 482, verse 1.

> But warm, sweet, tender, even yet
>   A present help is he ;
> And faith has still its Olivet,
>   And love its Galilee.*

The poem, written in 1856, has thirty-five verses, and other selections have been made. One of these which shows the anti-dogmatic strain fairly strongly, was quoted in an earlier chapter.† " Dear Lord and Father of mankind " is the other famous hymn of Whittier. It is taken from a poem whose subject is the contrast between the mesmeric ecstasies produced in certain heathen religions among the Indians by the brewing of a herb called Soma and the peace and sanity of the Christian Gospel. The poem gains all its force from the presentation of the Gospel as a source of almost platonic repose, not as a judgment or a challenge ; the hymn therefore emphasizes the peaceful aspects of the Gospel in such lines as these :

> Drop thy still dews of quietness,
>   Till all our strivings cease ;
> Take from our souls the strain and stress,
> And let our ordered lives confess
>   The beauty of thy peace.‡

The one thing that a Quaker will fight for is peace ; it is an interesting reflection, indeed, that a follower of that body which was founded by the enthusiastic and turbulent George Fox should find the only thing in anybody else's religion that he ever wanted to criticize to be excess of religious ecstasy.

This hymn is one of those that have built themselves into English national life ; I am able to say this because many of us will remember a broadcast by some senior officer of the British Government during the late war ending with a quotation of the verse I have just quoted. The broadcast

---

* *E.H.*, 408, verses 1 and 4.
† Page 116.   ‡ *E.H.*, 383, verse 4.

was not a religious address but an exhortation to the population to submit to the discipline of thrift and to see to it
that the waste paper and bones were put out for the salvage
collector.   It was, one may guess, " ordered lives " rather
than " peace " that was here being preached.

The " social Gospel " of American hymn-writing is
admirably summed up in the hymns of Frederick Lucian
Hosmer, yet another Unitarian minister, who lived from
1840 to 1929 and wrote a large number of hymns.   One of
these is now extremely popular,

> Thy kingdom come ! on bended knee
> The passing ages pray.*

Two others are in frequent use, " We pray no more, made
lowly wise ",† and " O beautiful our country ", ‡ and his
funeral hymn " O Lord of life, where'er they be " § has,
found favour because of its courageous avoidance of the
lugubrious note sounded by most hymns written for these
occasions.   But Hosmer shows American hymnody in de-
cline, inasmuch as all his hymns have a strangely nebulous
quality.   They face the future with confidence because their
description of the future is in remote imagery.   But there
is not in these hymns the wrath of the hymns of fighting
American puritanism ; he does not deal so starkly as do the
earlier authors with social evils ; when writing of death he
does not mention death if he can help it : indeed, one hymn
of his begins

> We cannot think of them as dead.

There is an optimism here that can run to shallowness and
evasiveness ; and in Hosmer you can see the dangers towards which American hymnody tended to be drawn.

America has been the home of liberalism in theology and
politics, and the hymn-writers of America have been at their
best when they were fighting oppression, ecclesiastical or

* *E.H.*, 504.   † *C.P.*, 459.
‡ *C.P.*, 570.   § *C.P.*, 677.

political. American hymnody always reached a high standard of literacy. All that tradition in our own hymnody which demands a suspension of the conventions of lyric poetry for the sake of a moving presentation of the Gospel is in America packed into the negro spirituals and the hymns of revival. The hymns of the church at large are always neat, always polished, never written at high devotional pressure. The thought is never, as it so often is in Watts and Wesley and even Montgomery, too big for the metre and the form. American hymns have the stamp of Boston, Massachusetts, on them—serene culture, settled prosperity, and a strong Puritan conscience that is " a devil when roused ".

But there is one American who English readers often find it difficult to remember was an American ; he is the one American of his age whose work is indistinguishable from contemporary English work, and his name is Ray Palmer. Palmer was a Congregationalist minister who wrote most of his hymns at Bath, Maine, where he was minister in the 'forties. His first and most famous hymn was " My faith looks up to thee ",* but it is probable that " Jesu, thou joy of loving hearts " † and " Jesus, these eyes have never seen " ‡ are now more frequently sung. He has all the American polish, but is unique in the warmth of his devotion to the person of Christ. He is outstanding, also, in the variety of subjects which he treated. If we quote two verses from his hymns we shall show how remarkable, for the American tradition, was his capacity for meeting many moods. Here is a verse from " Eternal Father, thou hast said " :

> Thy hosts are mustered to the field,
>   " The Cross ! the Cross ! " their battle-call ;
> The old grim towers of darkness yield,
>   And soon shall totter to their fall.§

* *E.H.*, 439.   † *C.P.*, 291.
‡ *E.H.*, 421.   § *C.P.*, 335, verse 3.

And here is a verse from the meditation beginning, " Lord, my weak thought in vain would climb " :

> When doubts disturb my troubled breast,
>   And all is dark as night to me,
> Here, as on solid rock, I rest—
>   That so it seemeth good to thee.*

Palmer does not show any sign of being disturbed by the controversies of his lifetime (1808–87) ; but he is the nearest the Americans have ever had to a mystical hymn-writer, and he is the senior American, except Presidents Davies and Dwight, to find wide currency in this country.

So much for the main line of American hymnody. We ought to mention the leading American women hymn-writers. There is Harriet Beecher Stowe, wife of Calvin Stowe, sister of Henry Ward Beecher, authoress of *Uncle Tom's Cabin,* and prominent abolitionist, who wrote a few hymns in a rather fulsome style, of which " Still, still with thee " † is probably the best known. Then there is Love Maria Willis, whose hymn " Father, hear the prayer we offer " is now so popular, although it contains as rude a rejoinder as the psalmist has probably ever received :

> Not for ever in green pastures
>   Do we ask our way to be ;
> But the steep and rugged pathway
>   May we tread rejoicingly.
>
> Not for ever by still waters
>   Would we idly rest and stay ;
> But would smite the living fountains
>   From the rocks along our way.‡

Admirable sentiments, you might say, but here they are expressed with singular lack of tact.

Mrs. Willis, however, is the only woman writer from

* *Songs of Praise,* 563, verse 4.
† *Congregational Hymnary,* 597. Cf. *Methodist Hymn Book,* 469.
‡ *E.H.,* 385, verses 2 and 3.

America who has given us a famous hymn, apart from those revivalist writers whom we shall turn to in a moment.

But before we do that, we must mention with gratitude two translators from America who have enriched our store, James Waddell Alexander, who has translated " O sacred head " * in a manner that avoids the pietism of both Robert Bridges and the *Hymns Ancient and Modern* translation : and Elizabeth Lee Smith, who has so happily translated a hymn of J. C. Lavater to begin " O Jesus Christ, grow thou in me ".†

Modern American hymnody is carrying on the tradition of liberal culture and theology. We have not space to quote in full from many modern authors here ; we may refer, however, to Frank Mason North's " Where cross the crowded ways of life ",‡ which has made so deep an impression in America, and F. J. Moore's " Father of mercy, lover of all children ",§ written in 1935, which has just appeared for the first time in England. Three quotations from the *Hymnal* of the Episcopal Church of the U.S.A., published in 1943, will serve to show that American hymn-writing has not in these later days lost its literary grace or its spirit of adventure.

> And have the bright immensities
>   Received our risen Lord ?
> Where light years frame the Pleiades
>   And point Orion's sword ?
> Do flaming suns his footsteps trace
>   Through corridors sublime,
> The Lord of interstellar space
>   And Conqueror of time ?
>
> The heaven that hides him from our sight
>   Knows neither near nor far :
> An altar candle sheds its light
>   As surely as a star ;

* *C.P.*, 127.   † *C.P.*, 443.
‡ *Hymnal* (1940), U.S.A., 498.   § *C.P.*, 682.

And where his loving people meet
To share the gift divine,
There stands he with unhurrying feet ;
There heavenly splendours shine.*
                    HOWARD CHANDLER ROBBINS, 1932.

God of grace and God of glory,
On thy people pour thy power,
Crown thine ancient church's story ;
Bring her bud to glorious flower.
Grant us wisdom, grant us courage,
For the facing of this hour.

Lo, the hosts of evil round us
Scorn thy Christ, assail his ways !
From the fears that long have bound us
Free our hearts to faith and praise :
Grant us wisdom, grant us courage,
For the living of these days.†
                    HARRY EMERSON FOSDICK, 1930.

All praise to thee, for thou, O king divine,
Didst yield the glory that of right was thine,
That in our darkened hearts thy grace might shine,
                                        Alleluia !

Let this mind be in us which was in thee,
Who wast a servant that we might be free,
Humbling thyself to death on Calvary,
                                        Alleluia ! ‡
                    F. BLAND TUCKER, 1938.

The first of these is a striking attempt to write a hymn
embodying modern scientific language : the second is a
hymn of social service in the classic American tradition,
written by America's most famous preacher ; and the
third and latest is a simple and faithful exegesis of
Philippians ii. 5–12, in a scriptural tradition which has been

* *Hymnal* (1940), U.S.A., 354.
† *C.P.*, 563, verses 1 and 2.   ‡ *C.P.*, 197, verses 1 and 3.

for a century and more foreign to the American genius of hymn-writing, and which indicates, as do other hymns which we could quote if we had room, a turning to traditional theology in America's hymnody. H. C. Robbins was Dean of the Cathedral of St. John the Divine, New York, from 1917 to 1929, and then became Professor of Pastoral Theology at General Theological Seminary until he retired in 1941. F. Bland Tucker is an Episcopal clergyman, Rector of Old Christ Church, Savannah, Georgia, since 1942. We must not forget, either, the hymns of Louis F. Benson, author of that classic book *The English Hymn* (1915) ; his hymns are sung in America and not in this country, but even in his own land he has less recognition than he deserves.

The excellent tradition that American hymnody is sustaining is largely due to the great work of the late Winfred Douglas (1867–1944), a large number of whose translations appear in the *Hymnal* (*1940*) of the American Episcopal Church, and who directed the research which issued in the excellent historical *Companion* to that hymn-book which appeared in 1949. He is without doubt one of the greatest figures in American hymnology.

American hymns, then, faithfully reflect American civilization and life, and they are at their most effective when they are celebrating the progress of mankind in that continent in moral and spiritual things. America has long left it to Watts and Wesley to supply her with credal songs ; but it may be that the arising of theologians in these latter days of the standing of Niebuhr and van Dusen in the U.S.A. will be answered in another generation by a new credal hymnody.

And now we must say a word about the hymns and tunes of American revival which we associate primarily with the names of Dwight L. Moody and Ira D. Sankey. I have written elsewhere about the spiritual value of these hymns, and their historical and social background.* Here I think

* *The Church and Music* (Duckworth, 1950), pp. 187 ff.

it is only necessary to remind the reader what is their connection with the human life of Americans and Englishmen. I said, in the place to which I have just referred, that the revivalist hymn and tune was the refuge of the dispossessed people of industrial America and England. The whole movement originated in America ; but it was because there were in England large masses of people in just the same condition of dejection and homelessness that Moody and Sankey had met in America that the movement took such fire in this country. The music is the folk-music of the music-hall, the words have almost always the same nostalgia and yearning for heaven which is to be heard in the negro spirituals ; it is only a step from " Swing low, sweet chariot " to " Safe in the arms of Jesus ".

I once heard these songs called by a capital generic name. The lady who was contributing to a discussion in the making of a recent hymn-book called them " Tipperaries " ; this was not an abusive or derisive nickname ; it was uttered almost in tones of affection. And it does tell the truth about these hymns ; for what " Tipperary " did for soldiers who were involved in nameless and unimagined horrors in the France of 1916, " Safe in the arms of Jesus " and " There were ninety and nine " did for the industrialized peasantry of England and America. " Tipperary " and all those songs have the nostalgia and the cheerful courage which is spiritualized in the heavenward vision and the jaunty tunes of the " Sankeys ".

Perhaps you could say that the existence of Sankey's music and its imitators is an indictment of American and English nineteenth-century Christianity. You can say that if you believe that there is something essentially imperfect, immature, or even pernicious about them. The defence of the " Sankeys " is always that they brought religion to people who were untouched by the established forms of churchmanship ; that they brought faith to a generation for which the church at large had found itself totally unprepared. And if the " Sankeys " are seen against the background of their contemporary American and English hymnody, the indictment will be well reinforced. We have just pointed out the very high level of culture and literacy in American hymns from their very beginning. The anti-abolitionists of the 'fifties sang with passion and anger, but they sang in uncommonly good English. F. L. Hosmer, the contemporary of the Sankey movement, we have judged to be a trifle fugitive and decadent.

> But the slow watches of the night
> No less to God belong,
> And for the everlasting right
> The silent stars are strong.

This is well turned and appeals to the imagination. But there were people in America and England when those words were written who were full of bitterness and who would have said with one indignant voice, had they had any of the gift of repartee which made the later Labour leaders what they were, that the silent stars were not helping them just at present.

> And lo, already on the hills
> The flags of dawn appear ;
> Gird up your loins, ye prophet souls,
> Proclaim the day is near.

" Speak for yourself ! " would have been the sneer that arose from Pittsburgh and Birmingham and Chicago and Manchester in the 'eighties. We have given sufficient credit to the hymn-writers of social service to be able to say now that the celebration of man's material progress and moral stature was wormwood of the bitterest sort to those for whom that progress meant new techniques of industrial oppression, and the increase of cruel self-righteousness in those who were best convinced of their own moral advance.

We have, indeed, as it were in a game of snakes and ladders, slithered right back to our first page. " The Holy

H.H.L.

R

Humbug "—that sums up the betrayal of Christendom by the Christians of a certain kind in the nineteenth century.

Now Sankey and Moody had a reply of a kind to offer. They gathered people together and made them sing songs of spiritual security ; they preached conversion and salvation, they made much of the lost sheep and the prodigal son, and they brought thousands to a peace of mind which saved them from despair and even suicide.

And so we come back to Howard Spring and his Methodists. For Moody and Sankey answered one need, but they left another as wide open as ever. What was to prevent those saved by the revival from becoming in their own way as much " holy humbugs " as those whom they accused of having shut the doors of the church on them ? It may have been the mill-owners and speculators who disgusted other people with the established church ; it was in a later age the hymn-singers of revival who disgusted their own children with revivalist religion and inoculated them against it. The mill-owner may have been a snob ; but his servant, when she was converted at the chapel, became sometimes a worse snob. The millionaire may have been a crusty Puritan who frowned and trampled on a small selection of vices and condoned others ; his Puritanism was nothing to that ugly complacency which laid hold on some of his tenants in about 1900. Not Moody and Sankey nor General Booth and his army could avert the tragedy which has now fallen on Western civilization—the tragedy of secularism and lost faith. And that tragedy is the last act of a greater tragedy of which we are, in this study, witnessing one small scene in the corner of the stage. It was the very beauty and serenity of English and American hymnody in the nineteenth century that produced by reaction the rantings of the salvationist songs ; and the ranters have accomplished little more than did the poets. We stand now, therefore, at the opening of an age in which the *Internationale* clamours for a hearing and gets it.

Our judgment of the Sankey songs, and all hymns of that

kind, must rest on the ground that they were designed for a special purpose ; whether we continue to use them depends on whether we think they are the best instruments for achieving the same purpose today. In practice the singing of these songs is now confined to a limited section of the Christian population of the country. A few of them have found a place in our standard hymnals, such as Philipp Bliss's " Man of Sorrows ", Katharine Hankey's " Tell me the old, old story ", E. Clephane's " There were ninety and nine ", Midlane's " Revive thy Work ", Joseph Scriven's " What a friend we have in Jesus " and Francis Rowley's " I will sing the wondrous story ". The more song-like and dramatic of the hymns, like " Shall we gather at the river ? " and " Christ is the answer " are confined to those meetings which specialize in such songs. But enquiries have shown that nowadays these hymns are less used than they were in the Sunday worship even of the nonconformist missions in industrial areas.[64]   Their home is in the rallies of the Salvation Army and in the women's and men's meetings, Pleasant Sunday afternoons, and weeknight missions of the churches. The most advanced (in its day) of standard English hymn-books, the *English Hymnal*, included a section of these hymns under the heading " For Mission Services " ; but that section, in the later edition of that book, is discreetly subheaded " Not suitable for general use ". They are not, in fact, by common consent, vehicles of the worship of the Church as a whole, though their use as devotional songs is still strongly supported in some places, and books containing a thousand at a time of such pieces are still printed in large numbers.

A list of the authors of these hymns would occupy too much space here to be worth attempting, but we must mention here the heroic American lady, Frances van Alstyne, commonly known as Fanny Crosby, who, blind from birth, lived to be 84, and composed, as it is believed, over eight thousand of these songs. With typical American enterprise and efficiency, one firm commissioned her to write three songs a week through all the year, and for two firms alone she wrote over five thousand hymns. She used, it is said, 216 different pen-names for her writing. She has the distinction of being one of the very few " Sankey " type authors to appear in *Hymns Ancient and Modern,* in whose 1916 edition her " Rescue the perishing " * was given a place.

The fact that everybody now claims to be educated has much to do with the passing of these hymns into disuse as agents of revivals. It is probably true to say that in modern revivals you are more likely to hear " City of God " than anything by this school of writers. And although many stories are told of souls saved by Sankey's hymns, the hymns of Charles Wesley have a yet longer score, and are still as warmly alive as ever.†

* *Hymns Ancient and Modern* (standard edn.), 764.

† An interesting development of the " Sankey " technique is in the modern American " choruses ", used in revivals whose most distinguished English exponent is Mr. Tom Rees of Hildenborough Hall, Tonbridge.

CHAPTER 18

Youth and Hymns

I. HYMNS WRITTEN BY YOUNG PEOPLE

ONE of the facts to which I do not recall seeing my attention drawn anywhere is that our hymns are so frequently the work of young people. The number of hymns written by people under thirty is enormously greater than the number written by people over sixty. If we are concerned to draw out the connection between hymns and human life, and to see what sort of people wrote our hymns, we cannot altogether overlook this fact of history. The inspiration that leads to hymn-writing seems to come to people, on an average, at the age of thirty-five or before ; that is natural enough. It would be much odder if we found that a large number of people reached maturity before they discovered in themselves this talent. But what is more interesting is the number of hymns of real value that turn out to be the work of quite young people. Some of these have already come our way, but here are some others.

I suppose that the youngest hymn-writer who has any currency now is Joseph Grigg, who wrote a hymn at the age of 10 which, not much altered, still appears in some books as " Jesus, and shall it ever be ? " It is really not very good, even as altered by John Francis, but it is something of a curiosity. It begins—

> Jesus ! and shall it ever be,
> A mortal man ashamed of thee,
> Ashamed of thee, whom angels praise,
> Whose glories shine through endless days ?

Thus it continues on a repetitive and rather platitudinous journey. The evidence for its very early composition is not very safe, because we are not sure whether Grigg was born in 1728 or 1720, and there is in any case no dated manuscript to judge from ; so perhaps on the whole this is a false start.

Isaac Watts's sixteen-year-old effort, " Behold the glories of the Lamb ", has had sufficient attention already, so has Milton's " Let us with a gladsome mind ",* written in his sixteenth year, 1623.

Three well-known hymns come from authors who were under 21 when they wrote them. Charles William Everest, who became an American Episcopal clergyman, wrote " Take up thy cross, the Saviour said " † when he was nineteen. In all the versions which we sing it has been substantially altered, but the idea and form of the hymn is his.

" Oft in danger, oft in woe " is a revised version of an incomplete hymn left by Henry Kirke White, who was born in 1785 and died in his twenty-first year. He was the son of a Nottingham butcher, but after being apprenticed to a stocking-maker and then for a short time articled to a solicitor, he felt a call to the ministry and became a student at St. John's, Cambridge. He published his first book of poems at 17, and was thought to be a young man of great promise, and when he died at 21 his *Remains* were published by Southey, and among the many eminent men of letters who wrote commemorative verses for him were Josiah Conder and Lord Byron. The ten-line fragment beginning " Much in sorrow, oft in woe ",‡ which was completed by Sarah Fuller Maitland to form a six-verse hymn, and further slightly altered to make the hymn as it is now usually sung, is symbolic of the fragment of life thus cut short.

Another young man who rose to eminence and died young was Michael Bruce, whose work is probably to be found in some of the Scottish Paraphrases. Bruce was the son of a Scottish weaver and studied for the ministry of the Church

---

* *E.H.*, 532.   † *E.H.*, 484.   ‡ *E.H.*, 467.

of Scotland. Before he completed his studies he was accidentally drowned in 1767, aged not yet 21. Unfortunately it is not possible to quote anything as being certainly his work, because of an unpleasant controversy which arose between Bruce's parents and John Logan, one of the editors of the 1781 *Scottish Paraphrases*, over the authorship of some verses published by Logan. It looks as if Logan did indeed " pirate " some of Bruce's work and publish it as his own.* The result of the controversy was to make the authorship of certain Paraphrases irretrievably obscure ; but it is possible to say with fair certainty that Bruce wrote the eighteenth, " Behold the mountain of the Lord " † and the fifty-eighth, " Where high the heavenly temple stands ", both of them faithful renderings of Scripture passages and full of Scottish ruggedness and strength. " Where high the heavenly temple " is now one of our universally accepted hymns of the Exalted Christ, and one of the very few in our language which deal with his High Priesthood. Without it, the celebration of the Ascension lacks an indispensable note of solemnity :

> Though now ascended up on high
> He bends on earth a brother's eye ;
> Partaker of the human name
> He knows the frailty of our frame.‡

Ray Palmer, whom we have already shown to be one of America's greatest hymn-writers, wrote his most celebrated hymn, " My faith looks up to thee ",§ when he was 21, and W. Chatterton Dix wrote the best and most famous of his hymns, " As with gladness men of old " ‖ at the same age. Dix's other well-known lines, " To thee, O Lord, our hearts we raise " ¶ were written when he was 27.

Gerald Massey, Chartist and Christian Socialist, published at 20 a volume called *Poems and Chansons* (1848) from which

* See *The Life and Works of Michael Bruce*, Bicentenary Edition, Perth, 1951.

† *C.P.*, 322.   ‡ *C.P.*, 184, verse 3.
§ *C.P.*, 479.   ‖ *E.H.*, 39.   ¶ *E.H.*, 292.

some lines were taken to make a hymn of social intention in *Songs of Praise*. It stands worthily next to Ebenezer Elliott's " When wilt thou save the people ? " Its third verse contains the lines :

> Build up heroic lives, and all
> Be like a sheathen sabre,
> Ready to flash out at God's call,
> O chivalry of labour ! *

This is, of course, one of the English " hymns of wrath " of which we wrote in Chapter 5.

Dean Alford (see page 139) wrote his last hymn a few months before his death ; his earliest, written at 22, is " In token that thou shalt not fear ",† the Baptismal hymn. At the same age Henry Downton wrote " For thy mercy and thy grace " ‡ and Sherman Oakeley, the missionary, wrote " Enduring soul of all our life ".§ John Cennick (page 15) published his hymns at 24, including " Children of the heavenly King ", ‖ and we have also noted the circumstances in which J. W. Chadwick, at the same age, wrote " Eternal ruler of the ceaseless round " ¶ (page 101). " O perfect love " was written by Miss Blomfield (later Mrs. Gurney) when she was 25, and James Russell Lowell, one of America's leading writers in the forceful style of the abolitionists, wrote " Men, whose boast it is that ye " ** and " Once to every man and nation " †† at about the same age. Mrs. Alexander (page 214) was 25 when she published her famous series of children's hymns, and John Sterling wrote " O source divine and life of all " ‡‡ in his early twenties. Two of the hymns referred to in note 38§§ were written by students under 25. Mary Duncan, who wrote the well-known children's verses, " Jesu, tender shepherd ", ¶¶ lived to be only 26. Henry Mayo Gunn, Con-

---

* *Songs of Praise*, 313.   † *E.H.*, 337.   ‡ *E.H.*, 286.
§ *Songs of Praise*, 482.   ‖ *E.H.*, 373.   ¶ *E.H.*, 346.
** *Songs of Praise*, 306.   †† *Ib.*, 309.
‡‡ *Ib.*, 612.   §§ page 323.   ¶¶ *E.H.*, 599.

gregational Minister at Basingstoke, was in his 26th year
moved by the disruption of the Church of Scotland (1843)
to write a hymn much loved by Congregationalists beginning
" Our fathers were high-minded men ".*

Samuel John Stone wrote " The Church's one foundation " † (page 114) when he was 27, Bishop Heber wrote
" Brightest and best " ‡ at 28, and William Williams wrote
" Guide me, O thou great Jehovah ", § in Welsh at the
same age. James Edmeston was 29 when he wrote
" Saviour, breathe an evening blessing " ‖ and a year older
when he published " Lead us, heavenly Father, lead us " ¶
(page 193). Jan Struther (page 181) came to notice as a
hymn-writer when her hymns were published in *Songs of
Praise* in her thirtieth year. Nor must we forget that Isaac
Watts's *Horae Lyricae* were published in his thirty-first year,
and his *Hymns and Spiritual Songs* in his thirty-third, nor that
Charles Wesley's first great collection of 1739 was published
in his thirty-second.

Most of these authors published hymns early but did not
die young. If we look at those whose lives were so short
that their works had to be published posthumously, we shall
find the list to include Joachim Neander, who died at 30
(page 47), both the Brontës, who died at 30 (page 211),
Charles Oakley, Rector of St. Paul's, Covent Garden,
who died at 33, having written " Hills of the north,
rejoice ",** and Donald Hankey, who was killed in the First
World War at 32, and is remembered for " Lord of the
strong ".††

Sidney Godolphin, the brilliant young cavalier, who was
killed in the Civil War in 1643 while fighting in the cause of
King Charles I, left a poem from which a hymn has been
fashioned, beginning " Lord, when the wise men came from
far ". Of Godolphin's original thirty lines, sixteen were
taken by the editor of *Songs of Praise* to form the only hymn

---

* *C.P.*, 516.   † *E.H.*, 489.   ‡ *E.H.*, 41.
§ *E.H.*, 397.   ‖ *Songs of Praise*, 54.   ¶ *E.H.*, 426.
** *C.P.*, 337.   †† *Songs of Praise*, 568.

in common use that has something especially to say to men of artistic and learned callings.

> Lord, when the wise men came from far,
> Led to thy cradle by a star,
> Shepherds in humble fearfulness
> Walked safely, though their light was less.

> There is no merit in the wise
> But love, the shepherds' sacrifice :
> Wise men, all ways of knowledge past,
> To the shepherds' wonder come at last.*

To nobody is that better suited than to the student or professor of theology, to whom the thought often comes that learning and obscurity go together, and that the achievements of scholarship are often in danger of robbing the simple of their faith.

We have mentioned Robert Murray McCheyne, who lived to be only 30 (page 165), and who wrote " When this passing world is done ",† a moving meditation on the Beatific Vision showing insight in a direction in which Scotsmen of the earlier nineteenth century did not usually travel far.

It will be noticed that hymns by young people, even hymns by people who died young, have nothing in common with each other. They seldom bear evidence of immaturity or premonition of early death. There are two authors, however, who wrote all their hymns actually on their deathbeds. Strangely enough, each lived to be only 28, and the dates of each are separated by only a year. One of them was Thomas Rawson Taylor (1807–35), who wrote " I'm but a stranger here " while he was dying of a painful disease. His hymn does not find much favour now in congregational worship, but its lines come poignantly from the young sufferer :

---

* *C.P.*, 434, taken from *Songs of Praise*. The longer version is at no. 138 in the *Oxford Book of Christian Verse*.

† *C.P.*, 772.

> What though the tempest rage,
>   Heaven is my home :
> Short is my pilgrimage,
>   Heaven is my home.*

More tragic, because more brilliant, is the name of Joseph
Anstice (1808–36), who at Oxford was Gladstone's greatest
friend and who became Professor of Classical Literature at
King's, London, at the age of 22.   During his last illness he
dictated a number of hymns to his wife, the best known of
which is still a classic—" O Lord, how happy should we
be ".   Its last verse comes bravely as a message of confidence
to many who are twice the age of its author :

> Lord, make these faithless hearts of ours
> Such lessons learn from birds and flowers ;
>   Make them from self to cease ;
> Leave all things to a Father's will,
> And taste, before him lying still,
>   Ev'n in affliction, peace.†

The only other hymn of Anstice's that is at all well known
is his beautiful Advent hymn, " When came in flesh the
Incarnate Word ".‡

Perhaps we may in conclusion refer to some famous hymn-
tunes which are known to have been composed by young
people.   Pre-eminent is MILES LANE, for " All hail the
power of Jesu's name ",§ written by William Shrubsole and
published in 1779 when he was 19 ; it is not known that he
wrote any other music.   The Welsh tune HYFRYDOL ‖ is
confidently supposed to have been written by R. H. Prichard,
a loom-tender's assistant in North Wales, when he was 20.
WILTSHIRE ¶ (" Through all the changing scenes of life ")
was written by George Smart when he was 19, in 1795, and
slightly revised by him when he was Sir George and an
octogenarian sixty-eight years later (1863).   The new

---

* *Congregational Hymnary*, 462, verse 2.
† *E.H.*, 457, verse 3.   ‡ *E.H.*, 13.
§ *E.H.*, 364.   ‖ *E.H.*, 301.   ¶ *E.H.*, 502.

Hymns Ancient and Modern has a tune by R. H. Jesson, BARNET, written when he was a fifteen-year old choirboy at Barnet, and another, MERNLE, by D. P. Symonds, who was 21 when the book was published. *Congregational Praise* (1951) contains tunes by J. P. B. Dobbs (1922–) and T. C. Micklem (1925–) and a chant by J. D. Wellingham (1930–). Those who like research into these matters will find in *Songs of Praise* a tune by Morfydd Owen,* who died aged only 25, and in the earlier edition of that book two tunes by Imogen Holst, who was 18 when that edition appeared.

II. HYMNS WRITTEN FOR YOUNG PEOPLE

So much for hymns written by young people principally for older people. I ought now to say something about hymns written by older folk for young people and children. Enough has been written already on this subject to make unnecessary any lengthy treatment here ; I can probably tell the story most briefly in a series of quotations.

We may begin with Isaac Watts's *Divine Songs for Children.* This slim volume contains twenty-eight hymns called " Divine songs " and eight called " moral songs " with a few interpolated hymns and doxologies. Look at some of the titles of the " Divine songs " and you will see what Watts wanted his children to sing about.

    I.   A general song of praise to God.
    II.   Praise for creation and providence.
   III.   Praise to God for our Redemption.
   IV.   Praise for mercies spiritual and temporal.
   V.   Praise for birth and education in a Christian land.
   VI.   Praise for the Gospel.
  VII.   The excellency of the Bible.

It is only when the exercise of praise is well gone through that Watts turns to such subjects as " Against idleness and

* Several other tunes by this composer are well known in Wales.

mischief " and " Against pride in clothes ". We may smile
broadly at " How doth the little busy bee " (no. XX), but
Hymns Ancient and Modern finds room for no. XXVI, " And
now another day is gone ",* and no. II is as fine a children's
hymn as has ever been uttered :

> I sing the almighty power of God
> That made the mountains rise ;
> That spread the flowing seas abroad,
> And built the lofty skies.
>
> His hand is my perpetual guard,
> He keeps me with his eye :
> Why should I then forget the Lord,
> Who is for ever nigh ? †

The " moral songs ", which were not meant to be
hymns, include the carol, " Hush, my dear, lie still and
slumber ".

Charles Wesley was not, on the whole, in touch with the
child's mind as closely as Watts. Watts's hymns for children are redeemed from unrelieved moralism by the note of
praise which so often breaks in, and which was so notable
a characteristic of his other hymns. Wesley's, as we have
said, were rather hymns of experience, and of his hymns for
children we now have only " Gentle Jesus, meek and mild ",
whose first line was referred to by the late Bernard Shaw as
a " snivelling travesty ", but which contains none the less
some fine thoughts. This and his other children's hymns
chiefly appeared in one of his latest works, *Hymns for Children*
(1763), which was published again four years later with the
cautious addition to the title of the words, *And Others of
Riper Years*. What John Wesley wrote in a preface, dated
1790, to a later edition, makes interesting reading. Charles
was now two years dead, and John himself was in his eighty-
seventh year. " There are two ways ", he says, " of writing

---

* *Hymns Ancient and Modern* (1950), 36.
† *C.P.*, 33, verses 1 and 6.

or speaking to children ; the one is, to let ourselves down to them ; the other, to lift them up to us. Dr. Watts has wrote in the former way, and has succeeded admirably well, speaking to children as children, and leaving them as he found them. The following hymns are written on the other plan ; they contain strong and manly sense, yet expressed in such plain and easy language, as even children may understand. But when they do understand them, they will be children no longer, only in years and stature."

That was all very well, and although only one of Wesley's many children's hymns has become popular against the three out of Watts's forty-odd, modern Sunday-school leaders would probably incline to agree with Wesley rather than with Watts.

The real difficulty, however, is now thought to have been over-simplified by John Wesley, and it is perhaps best stated like this. Is it a sin, a disadvantage, an advantage, or a virtue to be young? Some of the eighteenth-century Calvinists seem to have thought it was something rather like a sin. At the least, they wrote so menacingly that they must be thought to have held that to be a child was to be in a special degree open to the assaults of the devil. Dr. Percy Dearmer * accuses Watts of gross Calvinism by claiming, quite wrongly, that he wrote for children a hymn beginning " My thoughts on awful subjects roll ". He did not write that for children at all ; and although there are some rather displeasing moralizings in his hymns, what is remarkable about Watts is that he *did* write " I sing the almighty power " for children. Others are much more fierce with the young than he was. Cowper, for example, could write this for young people :

> We feel for your unhappy state
> (May you regard it too),
> And would a while ourselves forget,
> To pour our prayer for you.

* *Songs of Praise Discussed*, pp. 197 f.

> We see, though you perceive it not,
> Th' approaching, awful doom ;
> O tremble at the solemn thought,
> And flee the wrath to come *

But we are not concerned in this book to give examples of hymnody at its worst. Those who want to see to what lengths religious folk would go to frighten children into being good had better read Dr. Dearmer's article for a start and then take a course of *Gadsby's Hymns*.

Dr. Dearmer said it was William Blake who first thought of treating children as human beings who could achieve some degree of natural goodness in their condition of imperfect physical development ; he also says that it was a hundred years before this notion gained acceptance ; but this is far from being true. The development of Sunday schools between about 1770 and 1870, more especially during the second half of that period, gave a considerable impetus to the writing of children's hymns by creating a demand for hymns that taught, and hymns that children could enjoy. Of the writers of these hymns by far the greater number were women, and their leaders were Ann and Jane Taylor, who published *Original Hymns for Sunday Schools* in 1810. Ann Taylor (born in 1782) became Ann Gilbert, and under that name she is still remembered for a children's hymn of surpassing excellence beginning

> Great God, and wilt thou condescend
> To be my Father and my Friend—
> I a poor child, and thou so high,
> The Lord of earth and air and sky.†

This was one of the hymns published in 1810, and if it emphasizes the special condition of children by a reiteration of the word " little " which modern ears find perhaps a trifle precious, it is none the less a hymn well in advance of its contemporaries in dealing with children's thoughts. The

* *Olney Hymns*, II, xi, verses 4 and 5.
† *Church Hymnary*, 550, verse 1.

best known of her sister's (Jane Taylor) hymns for children
is " Lord, I would own thy tender care ".*

It would be unprofitable to give too extended a catalogue
of nineteenth-century children's hymns.   The vigour of the
Sunday-school movement ensured a market for new hymns
for children, and while many had a short life, some became
extremely well known.   John King's " When, his salvation
bringing " † and Jemima Luke's " I think, when I read
that sweet story of old " ‡ were especially successful among
the earlier hymns, shortly to be followed by Mary Duncan's
" Jesus, tender Shepherd, hear me ".§

Mrs. Alexander we have already mentioned as the queen
of children's hymn-writers.   Her contemporaries were Mrs.
Miller, who wrote " I love to hear the story ",‖ and Albert
Midlane (page 241), among whose Gospel-songs was " There's
a friend for little children ".¶   Godfrey Thring contributed
" All that's good and great and true " ** and William
Canton, who had a specially light touch with children,
" Through the night thine angels kept watch beside me
while I slept ".††

F. T. Palgrave and Bishop How have also made distinguished contributions that are still to be found in our
hymn-books.   Matilda Betham-Edwards wrote a good
hymn beginning " God, make my life a little light " ‡‡
which would have been a great hymn if the adjective in each
first line had been changed.   " God make my life a little
light, a little flower, a little song, a little staff, a little hymn "
—the pictures are there, but they would have been more
colourful had they been, we will say, " a shining light, a
happy flower, a cheerful song, a sturdy staff, a faithful
hymn."

But my readers, even if they know few hymns, will certainly know some children's hymns, and there is not much

---

* *Hymns Ancient and Modern*, 572/443.   † *Ib.*, 728/437.
‡ *C.P.*, 104.   § *E.H.*, 599.   ‖ *E.H.*, 594.
¶ *E.H.*, 607.   ** *C.P.*, 34.
†† *E.H.*, 609.   ‡‡ *C.P.*, 705.

to be usefully said here about the familiar ones ; the un-familiar ones of the last century are hardly worth resurrecting here.

It is, perhaps, worth quoting some of the best examples of modern hymn-writing for children. In our own time we find a wider and deeper sympathy with children which is more than a by-product of academic " educationism ". This new sympathy shows itself partly in the recognition that children have qualities of their own which are worth rejoicing in and thanking God for, partly in the practice of introducing children in their earliest days to the great and simple hymns of the Universal Church, and partly in the increased attention paid in schools to the religious needs of children, and to their education by means of good hymns. In this movement that brave musician, Martin Shaw, has been a pioneer, and *Songs of Praise* is the hymn-book which, with its derivatives for school use, best gives expression to the new educational techniques.[65]

Incidentally, the more recent growth of interest in older young people, the emergence of youth clubs and youth organizations in the churches, the building up even in some denominations of national youth assemblies, has encouraged the writing of hymns for young people " of riper years ", among which are some excellent experiments. Up to the end of the First World War hymns for people of this sort were the preserve of the Public Schools, and examples of them from the public schools of the nineteenth century, whose religious interest was so keenly kindled by Thomas Arnold of Rugby and later by Nathaniel Woodard,[66] have already been mentioned under hymns by schoolmasters. To these we might here add Kipling's " Land of our birth ", which first appeared in his *Puck of Pook's Hill,* and some of the " secondary-school " hymns to be found in those very inter-esting collections, *School Worship* * and *The Church and School Hymnal.*†

It has been recognized in our generation that the mind

* Independent Press, 1926.　　　　　† S.P.C.K., 1926.

of the child loves a picture and loves a story, and that it likes
both much better than it likes abstract ideas and doctrines.
I myself can remember the great appeal to my ten-year-old
contemporaries of " O Jesus, thou art standing " ; * the
sentimentality of most of its thought—and indeed of Holman
Hunt's picture—was discounted for us by the picture which
its opening lines left in our minds. " Lead, kindly light "
made the same impression. " Our God, our help in ages
past " was no use to us at all, but we were fascinated by a
queer hymn for Saint Matthew that contained the lines

> Give us thy grace to rise above
> The glare of this world's smelting-fires.†

The " watch-fires " of " City of God " and the big words
and images of " O worship the King " continue to attract
children who are unmoved by the might of Charles Wesley.
It was, significantly enough, Mrs. Alexander who wrote of
the smelting-fires. Her more celebrated adult masterpiece,
" I bind unto myself today ", catches the youthful imagination with lines like these :

> I bind unto myself today
>   The virtues of the starlit heaven,
> The glorious sun's life-giving ray,
>   The whiteness of the moon at even.
> The flashing of the lightning free,
>   The whirling winds' tempestuous shocks,
> The stable earth, the deep salt sea,
>   Around the old eternal rocks,

and she makes theology picturesque in such as these :

> His bursting from the spicèd tomb,
> His riding up the heavenly way.‡

---

* *Hymns Ancient and Modern*, 198/355.

† *Hymns Ancient and Modern*, (standard edn.), 420. The school was,
as a matter of fact, not far from the Sussex hammer-ponds, which may
have had something to do with our interest in the " smelting ".

‡ *E.H.*, 212, verses 2 and 3.

The grand old tune to these words turns out in experience to be a rather advanced adult taste. But there was no doubt at all at school, thanks partly to Dr. Dykes's help, about the appeal of " Fierce raged the tempest ".*

Modern hymn-writers for children have made great use of the pictorial technique, and in order to vary the subject matter from created nature they have tended to draw now and then on the language and images of medieval chivalry. Jan Struther's " When a knight won his spurs " does this rather agreeably. Its third and last verse is :

> Let faith be my shield and let joy be my steed
> 'Gainst the dragons of anger, the ogres of greed ;
> And let me set free, with the sword of my youth,
> From the castle of darkness the power of the truth.†

Jan Struther is also a practitioner of the new informality of language that addresses our Lord as " you ", rather than the conventional " thou ".‡ Opinions are divided on the merits of this use ; but it is an attempt to allow the child to express himself in as natural a fashion as possible.

Informal language is perhaps carried to its farthest point in a delightful little poem by Canon J. M. C. Crum. This author has made some charming contributions to children's hymnody, most of which will be found in the *Church and School Hymnal*. One of his better known hymns is " To God, who makes all lovely things ". The second verse of this happy hymn runs thus :

> How plentiful must be the mines
>   From which he gives his gold away ;
> In March he gives us celandines,
>   He gives us buttercups in May.§

It continues in this pleasant fashion to its end ; but as the next quotation will show it is, by Canon Crum's standards,

* E.H., 541.   † C.P., 535, verse 3.
‡ As in " Lord of all hopefulness ", C.P., 534.
§ C.P., 41, verse 2.

conventional.   Is not the following one of the most agreeable
pieces of verse ever put into a child's mouth ?

> O once in a while
> We obey with a smile
> And are ever so modest and prudent,
> But it's not very long
> Before something is wrong,
> And somebody's done what he shouldn't.
>
> In meadow and wood
> The cattle are good
> And the rabbits are thinking no evil ;
> The anemones white
> Are refined and polite
> And all the primroses are civil.
>
> O Saviour, look down
> When we sulk or we frown
> And smooth into kindness our quarrels ;
> Till our heart is as light
> As a little bird's flight
> And our life is as free as a squirrel's ! *

That is about as far as we shall ever get from the threatenings
of the nineteenth-century Puritans ; and it is perhaps the
only example in all the literature of a hymn that intention-
ally uses *humour*.

Perhaps less whimsical than this, more conventional,
but never irrelevant or ponderous, is Canon G. W. Briggs,
of Worcester. A collaborator with Martin Shaw in the
crusade of education through hymnody, Canon Briggs has
in his hymns manifested many of the simple and manly
virtues that had nearly disappeared from English hymnody
in the nineteenth century. He has written many felicitous
hymns, some of them full of theology, but he is greatly to
be honoured for the following lines which he wrote for
children :

* *Church and School Hymnal*, 277.

> I love God's tiny creatures
>   That wander wild and free,
> The coral-coated ladybird,
>   The velvet humming-bee ;
> Shy little flowers in hedge and dyke
>   That hide themselves away ;
> God paints them, though they are so small,
>   God makes them bright and gay.*

Percy Dearmer, another of those who sought to let fresh air
in on hymnody, has left us one of his happiest hymns in
" Remember all the people ", a missionary hymn which
brings to the child's mind a picture of the people he is
praying for, like this—

> Some work in sultry forests
>   Where apes swing to and fro,
> Some fish in mighty rivers,
>   Some hunt across the snow.†

And in case it be thought that while country children
are well cared for, town children can never sing of their
own pleasures, let us quote a new hymn which bravely cele-
brates the pleasures of town life.

Come, let us remember the joys of the town :
Gay vans and bright buses that roar up and down,
Shop windows and playgrounds and swings in the park,
And street-lamps that twinkle in rows after dark.

And let us remember the chorus that swells
From hooters and hammers and whistles and bells,
From fierce-panting engines and clear-striking clocks,
And sirens of vessels afloat in the docks.

And let us remember the life in the street ;
The horses that pass us, the dogs that we meet ;
Grey pigeons, brown sparrows, and gulls from the sea,
And folk who are friendly to you and to me.

* *C.P.*, 687, verse 1.
† *C.P.*, 344, verse 2.

Come, let us now lift up our voices in praise,
And to the Creator a thanksgiving raise,
For towns with their buildings of stone, steel, and wood,
For people who love them and work for their good.

We thank thee, O God, for the numberless things
And friends and adventures which every day brings.
O may we not rest until all that we see
In towns and in cities is pleasing to thee.*

For better or worse, Plymouth and Sheffield are with us, and
it is well occasionally to admit that, however much some of
us may rebel against the Industrial Revolution, we get a lot
of fun in Plymouth and Sheffield.

Another excellent thought is expressed in the following
lines, from a hymn beginning " The wisest and greatest in
work take delight " :

By the toil of how many comes comfort for one ;
I live by the labour that others have done.
At plough, forge, and spindle, in mines and at sea,
There are people toiling whose work is for me.†

And then, here is a happy effort by Lesbia Scott to inter-
pret the Communion of Saints to a child's mind which we
cannot forbear to quote with gratitude :

I sing a song of the saints of God,
    Patient and brave and true,
Who toiled and fought and lived and died
    For the Lord they loved and knew.
And one was a doctor, and one was a queen,
And one was a shepherdess on the green,
They were all of them saints of God, and I mean,
    God helping, to be one too.

They lived not only in ages past,
    There are hundreds of thousands still,
The world is bright with the joyous saints
    Who love to do Jesus' will.

* *Methodist School Hymn Book* (1951), 261. The words are by Miss
Doris Gill.   † *Ib.*, 452, verse 3, by A. Capes Tarbolton.

You can meet them in school, or in lanes, or at sea,
   In church, or in trains, or in shops, or at tea,
For the saints of God are just folk like me,
   And I mean to be one too.*

I suppose that against all these hymns some dogmatic
objection could be raised.   Canon Crum's rabbits are not
quite so white as they are painted, the farmer might say ;
Plymouth and Sheffield appear to some as hives of unrelieved
squalor and perversion ;   the saints are perhaps not just
" ordinary folk ".   But the writers of these hymns have
caught the right note for young minds precisely in using with
boldness that vividness of expression which may make it
necessary to overstate and to over-simplify.   Who ever tried
to stop a child thinking about giants ?   and is it not the
practice of all teachers who know their business to place
knowledge vividly, even if incompletely, before the child
and answer his subsidiary questions and objections when he
asks them ?   Do we begin our Scripture teaching with the
story of Eglon or of Agag ?

In conclusion I want to quote one of the oldest of children's
hymns.   It purports to be, at least, a paraphrase from a
writing of John Tauler, the German mystic and preacher
who lived through the terrible years of the Black Death and
died in 1361.   One hymn-book designed for young people
prints it, and although it is perhaps more of a devotional
poem than a hymn, it deserves to be much better known ;
every line is a picture, and it contains dozens of Sunday-
school lessons within its twenty-five lines.

As the bridegroom to his chosen,
   As the king unto his realm,
As the keep unto the castle,
   As the pilot to his helm,
      So, Lord, art thou to me.

* *Hymnal (1940)*, *U.S.A.*, 243, verses 1 and 3.

As the fountain in the garden,
  As the candle in the dark,
As the treasure in the coffer,
  As the manna in the ark,
    So, Lord, art thou to me.

As the music at the banquet,
  As the stamp unto the seal,
As the medicine to the fainting,
  As the wine-cup at the meal,
    So, Lord, art thou to me.

As the ruby in the setting,
  As the honey in the comb,
As the light within the lantern,
  As the father in the home,
    So, Lord, art thou to me.

As the sunshine in the heavens,
  As the image in the glass,
As the fruit unto the fig-tree,
  As the dew unto the grass,
    So, Lord, art thou to me.*

* *School Worship*, 208.

PART THREE

HYMNS AND ENGLISH LIFE

CHAPTER 19

Our National Anthems

WE come now to the chapter which contains what this whole book was originally designed to contain—some account of what hymns mean to us in our national life. I have explained in the Preface why this subject does not lend itself to Lord Ernle's method of treatment. But I think that there are certain heads under which we can conveniently group what there is to be said. I want to answer the questions, first, what hymns have during the past hundred years meant most to the English people at large? second, what are the hymns that mean most to us at present? and third, how are hymns used in Christian worship.

HYMNS IN THE PAST

If you want to know what hymns have entered into the heart of the nation's life, there are various ways in which you can conduct your preliminary research. You can, of course, to begin with, read all the proceedings of every important national or ecclesiastical concourse. Then you can read every novel that has been written. Then you can read all the newspapers you can lay hands on. You can spend your whole life doing this one piece of research ; and I have first to say why I believe that such enormous labour would be not very fruitful. The reason for this opinion is that I am persuaded that at the end of this great labour you would produce results not far different from those which I am about to produce from a much less assiduous application. They say that if you toss up a halfpenny the chances are precisely even whether it comes down heads or tails ; and that if you toss up a ton of halfpennies you will find that almost precisely half a ton of the resulting heap will show heads and the other half-ton tails.   I believe, by analogy, that if you spent fifty years in research you will still find what I have found (and what the reader could have told me before I tell him), namely, that " Our God, our help in ages past " has been *the* English hymn during the past three generations.   True, he might have asserted that it has been *the* English hymn ever since it was written ; the correction of that error is the kind of modification of the obvious which may be the only interesting thing about this chapter.

I do not think that there is anything very interesting to be said. about the period between the publication of Isaac Watts's hymns (1707) and the year 1861.   What the reader wants to hear, I think, is what hymns *that he knows* have a long history of veneration in England.   This means that we have got to find hymns that were used over and over again and have thus become well seasoned.

Consider the situation between 1707 and the middle of the last century.   It may have been gathered from our foregoing pages, and it may certainly be gathered from the other books on the subject, (*a*) that hymns were not officially part of Anglican worship, that is part of the worship of the National Church, before 1821, and (*b*) that in the Nonconformist and Evangelical-Anglican circles hymn-writing during the eighteenth century proceeded at a great speed ; if you put Watts, the Wesleys, the Olney pair, Montgomery, Kelly, Doddridge, Hart, Medley, and the rest of them together you will have a list of not much less than ten thousand hymns, while if you go down into the area of the Edmestons of this world you will probably double that total.   With ten thousand hymns in circulation it is not surprising if there is not much unanimity in the choice of hymns for special occasions, nor if the recorders of those occasions did not think it worth while to make a note of what hymns were sung at them.   Nor, except for the

National Anthem, which came into use as such shortly after 1745, will you find any use of hymns on occasions of national worship : there were not, in our modern sense, any occasions of national worship.

What you will find is just what Lord Ernle so excellently put before us, that *psalms*, metrical or prose, are used on the great occasions. Hymnody as a national expression of devotion does not come into its own before 1861. If we happen to be able to say (as we can) that " All hail the power of Jesus' name " was sung at the founding of the London Missionary Society (1795), we must regard that as a happy accident.

But why 1861 ? Because that is the most important date in the history of hymnody with the possible exceptions of 1707 and 1821. It was the year in which was published a modest hymn-book of 273 hymns with tunes called *Hymns Ancient and Modern*. Now *Hymns Ancient and Modern* is a national institution ; everybody has heard of it, all the jokes are made about it, and although it has as a matter of fact many competitors, for it never was the official hymn-book of the Church of England (the Church of England never, indeed, had an official hymn-book), it is the one hymn-book whose title I can be sure will not be unfamiliar to our readers. Could Osbert Lancaster's joke recorded on page 83 have been made about the *English Hymnal* or the *Hymnal Companion* ? I do not say that jokes could not be made about those books, but they would necessarily be the stylized and academic jokes of the specialists.

But *Hymns Ancient and Modern* became a national institution for three reasons. The chief was that it was just the book that the Church of England wanted at that time. The second was that it was uncommonly fortunate in its musical editor, W. H. Monk, who produced in its first edition a highly successful new tune to " Abide with me " that drove the two existing ones off the field for good, and in the discovery of a capable musician in the cloisters of Durham Cathedral called Dykes who wrote an equally successful, equally new, and equally victorious tune to Heber's " Holy, Holy, Holy ". The third was that it adopted what was then a novel, though not at that date unexampled, practice of giving each hymn its own tune ; this has many advantages over the much more common practice of having a book of psalms and hymns from one publishing house and a separate book of tunes from another, the collocation of tune and words being substantially the responsibility of the local vicar or precentor.

For these and other less cogent reasons, *Hymns Ancient and Modern* was a quite astonishingly successful book. The years between 1840 and 1880 were the " peak period " for the publication of new hymn-books of every conceivable shape, size, colour, and dogmatic disposition. But *Hymns Ancient and Modern*, published in the middle of that period, achieved a success that made its own editors gasp. That success is what made it a national institution. For now we have a collection of hymns—quickly expanded and frequently re-vised, of course, but basically a single collection—which a large number of people were aware of, and which made its way straight to the great centres of Anglicanism. And that collection not only contained " Our God, our help in ages past " but set it to the tune St. Anne. Pause on that for a moment : it is substantially true to say that people did not think of singing those words to that tune before 1861. The tune was written for " As pants the hart " away back in 1708 ; it was set in that very edition of *Hymns Ancient and Modern* to another hymn as well. For another generation hymn-books set something else to " Our God, our help ". Congregationalists, for example, did not officially recommend St. Anne for that hymn before 1917. But *Hymns Ancient and Modern* began the collocation, *Hymns Ancient and Modern* was the hymn-book of a large number of Anglicans, and therefore by derivation, " Our God, our help " to St. Anne became a national institution.

On a smaller scale the same is true of " Holy, Holy, Holy ", " The King of love ", and " Praise to the Holiest ", all of which were set in *Hymns Ancient and Modern* to brand-new tunes which " stuck ". And when new hymns came out, *Hymns Ancient and Modern* showed an uncanny gift for selecting those that would stay the course ; they gathered up " Now thank we all our God " in this way (it was written in 1863, and is in the 1868 *Ancient and Modern*). Mrs. Gurney's " O perfect love " was written in 1883, and *Ancient and Modern* picked it up in its 1889 revision ; and so on. The editors backed a number of losers, of course, but it is remarkable how few winners they missed. There is not much nineteenth-century writing in the Church of England worth preserving that *Ancient and Modern* missed—the most conspicuous example of such a miscalculation being, of course, that book's omission of " Come down, O Love Divine " (1867) until 1916.

All this is intended to convey that *Hymns Ancient and Modern* had the effect of focusing the attention of the English people on a few great hymns where before it had been dispersed over a large number of hymns ; the major denominations outside the Church of England were soon obliged to fall into line with *Hymns Ancient and Modern* in its chief choices, and it has not been until 1950 that *Hymns Ancient and Modern* has found it necessary to return the compliment by including for the first time a number of hymns that have become national institutions through their introduction by Free Church denominations.*

HYMNS IN THE PRESENT AGE

I propose now to give quite briefly the conclusions of certain investigations I made recently with a view to finding

* Examples of such hymns, appearing for the first time in *Ancient and Modern* in its 1950 edition, are " The Lord will come and not be slow ", " Immortal, invisible ", " City of God ", " Thy kingdom come ! on bended knee ", and " Immortal love, for ever full ", all but the first of which owe their introduction to the Congregationalist editor, Dr. Garrett Horder.

out which are the hymns that have become part of our national life in the present generation. The processes on which these conclusions are based are these :

First, an examination of certain documents at Westminster Abbey, namely,

   (*a*) the service-lists for the years 1913 and 1914,
   (*b*) the service-lists for the years 1931 and 1932,
   (*c*) the bound volumes of distinguished wedding and funeral and memorial services between 1886 and 1936 ;

Secondly, the collation of all advertisements in the *Radio Times* for the first six months of 1950 containing references to hymns sung at broadcast services and hymn-singings ;

Thirdly, a tour of fourteen churches in Oxford to make a record of the hymns used in them on the first Sunday after Trinity, 1951.

The Westminster Abbey service-lists provide two distinct points of interest. In the first place, they show what hymns were used in a normal cathedral foundation in which hymns were regarded as a minor adjunct to the sung services ; and secondly, they show the movement of taste between 1914 and 1931 in a striking way. I chose the Sundays after Trinity because choice of hymns on those Sundays is not predetermined by the traditional festivals of the church's year. What we want in this chapter is evidence of the hymns that commend themselves to Christians in England on the most general grounds, and therefore I leave out of account even in the selected list those associated with special saints' days and with the Holy Communion. On the other hand, it will be interesting to see where we go for our hymns on the great occasions, weddings, funerals, and national occasions of various kinds ; and for these Westminster Abbey is, of course, an excellent source.

A review of broadcast hymns needs no explanation or justification. The religious broadcast is now an integral part of our national life, thanks to the entirely admirable and often courageous work of the Religious Broadcasting Department of the B.B.C.

My tour of the Oxford churches was conducted on the Saturday afternoon preceding the first Sunday after Trinity, 1951. Here again, I chose a day that was not a Great Festival because I knew that if, for example, I had visited the churches on the previous Saturday I should have found " Holy, Holy, Holy " on every service list. I confined myself to the Anglican churches for reasons which will appear later. In most cases the next day's hymns were already displayed on the hymn-board or at the door. Here and there I could find no evidence that hymns were to be sung on the morrow—not even on the organ-bench ; and two of the parish churches were impenetrably locked. But I did include in my travels the Cathedral and the chapels of New College, Magdalen, the Queen's College, and St. Peter's Hall.

First of all, then, let us see which hymns have the most regular showing in these lists. What would be the reader's guess ? " Our God, our help " ? No ; that hymn is always to be heard on our great national occasions, but not especially often in the ordinary services of the church. We will come back to it. The " winner " is " Praise, my soul ". Look at its record : six times in the 1913–14 lists, seven times in the 1931–32 lists, seven weddings, including those of King George VI, the Princess Royal, the Duchess of Kent, and the present Queen ; two funerals ; three great national occasions, including Armistice Day, 1918, at the Abbey and the Jubilee of King George V at St. Paul's ; it comes seven times in the broadcast lists and was sung at least once in Oxford on the day of my record. " Praise, my soul " combines the dignities of being, nowadays, *the* Royal wedding hymn with being our national hymn of thanksgiving.

Next in order of faithful service comes Tate and Brady's 34th Psalm, " Through all the changing scenes of life ". It is the second most popular hymn in the 1913–14 list, appearing

H.H.L.

T

five times, and the most popular in 1931–2, appearing nine times. I do not find it in the wedding lists, but it was sung at five distinguished funeral and memorial services, and has four appearances in the broadcast lists and one on my Oxford list.

Only two others deserve this kind of general notice. " Now thank we all our God " happens not to be in the earlier service lists, but it has four appearances in the 1931–2 lists, three at weddings, one at a memorial, and was sung in two Oxford churches on the day of the record, one of which was New College Chapel. " The King of love " also had two Oxford appearances, three on the earlier service lists, one on the later, and two at weddings.

Now let us take the divisions separately.

The Abbey Services

In the 1913–14 lists we find on the fifty-one Sundays an average of five hymns sung per Sunday, with a repertory for those 254 occasions of 108 hymns. The most popular were " As pants the hart ", " Praise, my soul " and " Jesus, where'er thy people meet ", which appeared six times each ; the following appeared five times :

> Glory to thee, my God, this night
> Saviour, again to thy dear Name we raise
> Sweet Saviour, bless us ere we go
> Abide with me
> Lead us, heavenly Father, lead us
> Through all the changing scenes of life.

Among those which appear three or four times are

> Sun of my soul
> Jesu, lover of my soul
> ★ Thy kingdom come, O God
> ★ Hark, hark, my soul
> ★ Nearer, my God, to thee
> The King of love

    ★ For ever with the Lord
    ★ Pleasant are thy courts above
      Lead, kindly Light
    ★ The day thou gavest
      The Lord my pasture shall prepare.

Those which I have marked with a star do not appear at
all in the 1931–2 lists. An indication of the change of
taste in the later generation will be found if we look for a
moment at the favourite hymns in them. We have here,
because of the addition of a periodic Choral Eucharist and a
popular 6.30 evening service, the increased total of 407
occasions of singing ; but increased occasions of singing do
not imply an increased congregational repertory, and the
advance of the repertory from 108 to 149 hymns is not
discreditable. We have said that " Through all the changing scenes of life " comes nine times in this list. Eight
times we have " The God of love my Shepherd is " and
" Rejoice, O land, in God thy might ". Seven times :

    ★ Light's abode, celestial Salem
    ★ Pray that Jerusalem may have
    ★ The Church of God a kingdom is
      Praise, my soul

and six times :

    ★ All people that on earth do dwell
      As pants the hart
    ★ City of God
    ★ Immortal, Invisible
      Jerusalem the golden
      Lead us, heavenly Father
      Soldiers of Christ, arise
    ★ Praise to the Lord, the Almighty.

The starred hymns do not appear in the earlier lists.

I do not want to weary the reader with long lists of this
kind ; he will probably prefer to receive my conclusions
undocumented. But the change of taste at the Abbey
services, which shows itself all the way through the lists,

is due in general to the substitution of the *English Hymnal*
for *Hymns Ancient and Modern* and the *Westminster Abbey
Hymn Book* as the main hymn-book of the Abbey, and in
particular to the presence in the later years of Canon Percy
Dearmer in the Abbey Precincts.   Hymns popular in the
previous generation that held their own under his critical
eye can be assumed to be made of sturdy material, and
these hymns turn out to be

> As pants the hart
> Praise, my soul
> Jesus, where'er thy people meet
> Glory to thee, my God, this night
> Lead us, heavenly Father, lead us
> Through all the changing scenes of life
> Sun of my soul
> Jesu, lover of my soul
> Oft in danger, oft in woe
> Let saints on earth in concert sing
> Soldiers of Christ, arise
> The Son of God goes forth to war
> Glorious things of thee are spoken
> The Lord my pasture shall prepare.

In general it can be said that the Abbey selections in the
two periods show a progress from the more intimate hymns
to the more outward-looking, credal and social hymns, and
this can be supported from other evidence.   " Judge eternal,
throned in splendour " and " City of God " are hymns
which can almost be counted on in our cathedral services at
the present time ; you are extremely unlikely to hear " Hark,
hark, my soul " or " For ever with the Lord " on such
occasions.

It is worth observing, finally, a sidelight that is thrown
on the Abbey practice of 1913-14 by the fact that the
declaration of war in August, 1914, had scarcely any effect
on the choice of hymns.   The appearance of " God moves
in a mysterious way " and " Holy Father, in thy mercy "
on Sunday, 30 August, neither of which comes in the

1913 lists, may be an indication of a sense of crisis ; on November 22nd we find " God the all-terrible " for the first time. But even in the darker years of 1916–17 the hymn-lists tend to continue on their serene way ; occasionally, though not usually, whole sets of hymns are carried over from one year to the next on corresponding Sundays.

But in general we may say that the most frequently used hymns at the Abbey in 1913–14 were the particular legacies of the *Hymns Ancient and Modern* era, while those most frequently in the later lists are equally the importations of the *English Hymnal*. There are only a few exceptions to this generalization, and all these we have already noted.

SPECIAL AND PRIVATE OCCASIONS

Now let us turn to the weddings. The " winner " here is obvious, of course—" O perfect love " It was sung at thirteen of the thirty-one weddings recorded in the column under review, the most distinguished of which was that of Princess Patricia to Commander the Hon. A. R. M. Ramsay, 27 February, 1919. It was first sung to Barnby's famous tune, by the way, at the marriage of H.R.H. Princess Louise with the Duke of Fife in July 1889, and it was this occasion, with the introduction of the tune, which made the hymn so fashionable. We have mentioned " Praise, my soul ". It was a felicitous accident that its use at the marriage of the present Queen, then Princess Elizabeth, to the Duke of Edinburgh in November, 1947, fell a hundred years to the month after its author's death.

Its partner at the weddings of King George VI and of the Princess Royal was " Lead us, heavenly Father ", and at that of the Duchess of Kent, " Gracious Spirit, Holy Ghost." The Royal wedding of 1947 broke new ground in associating it with " The Lord's my Shepherd ", which has become a favourite wedding hymn of late years, and was on this occasion, a happy tribute to the Scottish family from which our Queen-Mother comes.

Wedding hymns, considered more generally, fall obviously into three groups—hymns traditionally associated with weddings or written for that occasion specially ; hymns of praise and thanksgiving, and " our favourite hymn ". The following are the hymns, apart from those mentioned, which appear in the Abbey wedding records. They are an interesting selection and they are given in the order of their appearance :

> Our God, our help in ages past (3)
> Now thank we all our God (3)
> Love Divine, all loves excelling (3)
> Holy, Holy, Holy (2)
> ★ O thou, who gavest power to love (2) (*E.H.*, 347)
> The God of love my Shepherd is (2)
> The Lord is King (2)
> Our Blest Redeemer
> ★ The voice that breathed o'er Eden
> O worship the King
> Thine for ever !
> O God of Bethel (2)
> The King of love my Shepherd is (2)
> Ye holy angels bright
> Take my life, and let it be
> Praise the Lord, ye heavens adore him
> Come, gracious Spirit, heavenly Dove
> Praise to the Holiest
> Lord, enthroned in heavenly splendour
> I bind unto myself today
> " Jerusalem "
> All people that on earth do dwell
> Glorious things of thee are spoken
> Let all the world in every corner sing
> Who would true valour see. [67]

It will be noticed how a traditional and even sentimental choice near the beginning gives place to adventurousness and a note even of social earnestness towards the end (in such things as " Jerusalem " and the " Pilgrim Song "). It will also be observed how poor a showing the hymns specially set aside for weddings in the hymn-books (here marked with a star) make in this list. On this it ought to be said, however, that in less exalted circles the " wedding hymns " are in much greater use, and " The voice that breathed o'er Eden " can still be heard. When the wedding hymns are the choice of the clergy and not the bride and bridegroom, as happens more usually in the ordinary parish churches than it would at the Abbey, the official wedding hymns have their way. I should, however, be prepared to add to the foregoing list from my own experience the following :

> Lord of all hopefulness (*C.P.*, 534)
> Praise to the Lord, the Almighty
> Come down, O Love Divine
> King of glory
> Come, Holy Ghost, our souls inspire
> Love of the Father, love of God the Son (*E.H.*, 438)
> Jesus, Lord, we look to thee (*C.P.*, 240)

The choosing of favourite, rather than appropriate, hymns at weddings leads away from the beaten track, as we saw in the first list ; sometimes it takes the couple into unexpectedly rough country. Everybody makes the joke about " Fight the good fight " at weddings—which for all I know has really been chosen at a wedding, and a very good hymn it is too ; but there is real historic warrant for the appearance at a wedding service of Clifford Bax's " Turn back, O man ".

Wedding hymns, however, give some indication which hymns among those in normal use make an impression on people, and those hymns which have become traditionally or by temporary adoption wedding hymns have for that reason a special place in our English life.

In a manner little different from this we can make a few inferences from the hymns used at distinguished funeral and memorial services in the Abbey. In the documents there preserved 114 such services are recorded, in which we find 65 different hymns. Like wedding hymns, funeral hymns are sometimes conventional ; but not infrequently they represent a tribute paid to the personality of the departed by his relations or the church authorities.

There is one funeral hymn which is even more traditional than " O perfect love " for weddings ; it is, of course, " Our God, our help ", which appears in thirty of these records. Its appropriateness needs no explanation. Four other hymns are outstandingly in vogue—" Abide with me " (15 times), " For all the saints " (11), " Now the labourer's task is o'er " (11) and " Lead, kindly Light " (10). These are the only hymns that appear more than five times, and the only one that has five showings is " Through all the changing scenes of life "—which we have before mentioned as having a high place in popular estimation.

The personal nature of funeral and memorial services makes it interesting, perhaps, to recall some of these occasions.

At the funeral of H.M. Queen Victoria, 2 February, 1901, two hymns were sung, " Our God, our help " and a poem by Mrs. Browning beginning " What would we give to our belov'd ? " ; the same two had been used at Robert Browning's own funeral on 31 December, 1889. The three used at Mr. Gladstone's funeral, 19 May, 1898, were " Praise to the Holiest ", " Our God, our help ", and " Rock of ages ", the last being printed alongside Gladstone's own Latin translation. " Praise to the Holiest " was also the only hymn at the funeral of Sir Henry Irving, 20 October, 1905. Tennyson's funeral included one hymn only, " Holy, Holy, Holy ", which he had himself commended as one of the best he knew.

" Our God, our help " appears as the only hymn at the funerals of Sir Henry Campbell-Bannerman (27 April, 1908), George Meredith (22 May, 1909), H.M. King Edward VII (20 May, 1910), and John Galsworthy (Memorial Service, 9 February, 1933). It appears also with " Before Jehovah's awful throne " at the funeral of Field-Marshal the Earl of

Ypres (26 May, 1925), and with " Abide with me " and
" Jesus lives ! " at the memorial service for H.M. King
George V (28 January, 1936).

Hymns of the Resurrection such as "Jesus lives ! "
appear occasionally in the later records. " On the Resurrection morning " was sung, with " Now the labourer's
task ", at the funeral of H.M. Queen Alexandra (27 November, 1925), and " The strife is o'er " at that of Bonar
Law (5 November, 1923). " Abide with me " is, of course,
a hymn of the personal Resurrection, and its brave words
were heard at the memorial service to Edith Cavell (15 May,
1919), and at the funeral of Field-Marshal Earl Haig
(3 February, 1928), where it was associated with " Onward,
Christian soldiers ".

The quieter devotion of " Lead, kindly Light " was heard
at the funeral of Thomas Hardy (16 January, 1928) and at
the memorial service to the fourth Earl Grey, Governor-
General of Canada from 1904 to 1911 (1 September, 1917).

And here are some examples of memorial hymns re-
flecting the lives and personalities of their subjects.   When
a memorial window was dedicated to the memory of Lord
Strathcona, the pioneer of the Canadian Pacific Railway,
on 1 July, 1919, "Thou, whose almighty word " was
sung, with its brave refrain, " Let there be light ! "   Distinguished Americans are usually honoured with " Mine
eyes have seen the glory of the coming of the Lord " ;
among these was Walter Hines Page, U.S. Ambassador to
Great Britain (dedication of memorial window, 3 July,
1923) ; and with this event we may associate the great
memorial service, held in St. Paul's Cathedral on July 4th,
1951, in commemoration of the Americans who died in
the Second Great War ; this was attended by members
of our Royal Family and by General Eisenhower, and
the marching American hymn was sung again there, to
its American tune, " John Brown ".   At the memorial
for Dame Millicent Fawcett, the great supporter of
women's rights and opponent of the militant suffragettes

(19 November, 1929), they sang Blake's "Jerusalem" and George Herbert's "The God of love ".⁶⁸ " The God of love " seems to have been favoured by theologians, having been sung at the funerals of Archdeacon R. H. Charles (4 February, 1931) and of Archbishop William Temple at Canterbury (31 October, 1944). Lord Grey of Fallodon's memorial (11 September, 1933) contained " Our God, our help ", " I vow to thee, my country ", and the modern hymn-anthem that stands last in *Songs of Praise*, " Zeal of the Lord ". " I vow to thee " was heard again at Lord Allenby's funeral, 19 May, 1936. Rudyard Kipling's funeral service (23 January, 1936) contained " Abide with me " and his own " God of our fathers " ; the " Recessional " had been heard already at the memorials for W. F. Massey, Prime Minister of New Zealand (14 May, 1925), and for Lord Milner (18 May, 1925).

The note of thanksgiving was sounded at the funeral of Archbishop Lord Davidson (29 May, 1930) with " Praise, my soul ", and even more at Canon Percy Dearmer's funeral (3 June, 1936) in his own two hymns, " A brighter dawn is breaking ",* " Jesu, good above all other ",† and Heber's hymn of spring, " When spring unlocks the flowers ".‡ The liberal and generous mind of Bishop Gore was well celebrated at his funeral (21 January, 1932) in the singing of " City of God ".

We find a more adventurous selection of hymns in the later records than in the earlier : this corresponds with the enlarged repertoire which we noted in the Abbey service lists of the later period. Two distinguished musicians, Sir Frederick Bridge and Sir Charles Stanford, were honoured by the singing of hymns to their own tunes ; at the dedication of the memorial window to Bridge, who was organist at the Abbey, " The sower went forth sowing " was sung to his famous tune, and at Stanford's funeral and memorial services " Now the labourer's task ", " Love divine, all loves excelling " and " Blessed city " were sung, all to tunes

* *E.H.*, 126.   † *E.H.*, 598.   ‡ *E.H.*, 299.

of his own.   When the bust of the Australian poet, Adam
Lindsay Gordon, was unveiled in Poets' Corner on 11 May,
1934, a hymn by Stopford Brooke, poet and critic, " Let
the whole creation cry ",* was not inappropriately sung.

The other hymns mentioned in these records are " Nearer,
my God, to thee " (President McKinley's memorial service, 14 September, 1901), " At the Lamb's high feast we
sing ", " Just as I am " (both at the memorial to the Duchess
of Northumberland, 10 July, 1913), " O God of Bethel ",
" Sun of my soul ", " Peace, perfect peace ", " Through the
night of doubt and sorrow ", " Let saints on earth in concert
sing ", " Hark, hark, my soul ", and " A safe stronghold
our God is still ".

It seems proper, both in duty to our late Sovereign and
in order to complete the story, that I should add a short
account of the hymns that were associated with the greatly
lamented death of King George VI, on the 6 February
1952.   The note sounded upon all sides was that of Christian
victory and gratitude for his life.   On Monday, 11 February,
before the coffin was carried out of Sandringham church,
" The King of love my Shepherd is " and " Abide with
me " were sung.   At the funeral service in St. George's
Chapel, Windsor, on Friday, 15 February, the hymn was
" The strife is o'er ".   The memorial service broadcast on
the evening of Sunday the 10th contained Paraphrase 61,
" Blest be the everlasting God ", and the hymn " Jesus
lives ".   At the memorial service at St. Paul's on the same
day one of the hymns was " Immortal, Invisible ", which
had been chosen by the King and Queen for their silver
wedding thanksgiving service in April 1948.   It was further
recorded by the Rev. John Lamb, Parish Minister at Crathie
(British Weekly, 14 February), that among the late King's
favourite hymns were " The Lord's my Shepherd ", " Now
Israel may say ", and the Paraphrase " Father of peace
and God of love ".   The memorial service held at the time
of the Funeral in the parish churches of the country included

* Songs of Praise, 558.

" Jesus lives ", " Our God, our help in ages past ", and, with singular and moving appropriateness, " I vow to thee, my country ".*

NATIONAL OCCASIONS

It is proper to consider next a few of the great national occasions of the last sixty years or so. At the thanksgiving service for the Golden Jubilee of Queen Victoria's Accession (1887), no hymn was prescribed in the order of service. A record remains of the thanksgiving for the Sovereign's Accession offered in 1894, which contains the hymns " Praise the Lord, ye heavens, adore him " and an adaptation by Dean Stanley of " Let us with a gladsome mind ".

At the Diamond Jubilee things were done more comprehensively. The reticence of 1887 is replaced here by a booklet of specially written hymns, some of them with specially written tunes. The almost hysterical note of adulation in the hymns and the grievous sentimentality of the tunes makes us feel that it is kinder to quote neither. The contributors to this booklet were S. J. Stone, H. D. Rawnsley, Godfrey Thring, Henry Twells, Jackson Mason, and W. C. Dix, all of whom have received notice in our earlier pages. A separate Jubilee hymn was also composed by Bishop How and was published with Sullivan's tune BISHOPSGARTH—but here again we had better hurry on.

The Queen's eightieth birthday was celebrated on 24 May, 1899, with " All people that on earth do dwell ". Of her funeral we have already written.

The records contain nothing that concerns King Edward VII ; the first occasion in which King George V is involved, apart from his own coronation, was a thanksgiving for his safe return from India, at which " Rejoice again with one accord " † and " Now thank we all our God " were appropriately sung. Much later in his reign, a great service was held to celebrate his recovery from a dangerous

* See additional note, p. 327. † *E.H.*, 537.

illness in 1928–9. On this occasion, the hymns were " I vow to thee, my country ", " All people that on earth do dwell ", " Our God, our help in ages past ", " Praise, my soul ", and Blake's " Jerusalem ". His Silver Jubilee in 1935 was celebrated in St. Paul's by singing " All people ", " I vow to thee, my country ", and " O God of Bethel ".

The other great national occasion which these records hold in remembrance is the Armistice of 1918, when a service was held containing no fewer than six hymns :

> Praise, my soul
> All people that on earth do dwell
> And now, O Father, mindful of the love
> Through all the changing scenes of life
> God of our fathers
> Before Jehovah's awful throne.

The exuberance of popular joy made it necessary on this occasion, as the reader will not fail to notice, to sing the Hundredth Psalm twice over.

More recent great national occasions include the Armistice of 1945, when the M.P.s went to church at St. Margaret's, Westminster, on May 8th and sang the 124th Psalm, " Now Israel may say, and that truly " ; the Royal Wedding of November, 1947, to which we have already made reference ; and the opening of the Festival of Britain, May 3rd, 1951, at which the hymns were " Rejoice, the Lord is King " (because it was Ascension Day), " Worship, honour, glory, blessing ",* " Lord, while for all mankind we pray ",† and Blake's " Jerusalem ". Nor should we omit to mention the funeral service of the late William Temple, Archbishop of Canterbury (31 October, 1944), at which the hymns " The God of love my Shepherd is " and " My soul, there is a country " were sung.

The most spectacular ecclesiastical occasion during the past century must be the union of the divided Church of Scotland in 1929, which is thus described by Dr. Millar Patrick :

* *E.H.*, 535, part II.　　　　　　† *E.H.*, 561.

When the two great branches of the divided Church of Scotland were united in October, 1929, as the two processions marched, one upwards from the Mound, the other downwards by the Lawnmarket, to meet and coalesce at the top of Bank Street, on their way to St. Giles', the watching crowds who lined the streets spontaneously broke into singing, chiefly of Psalm cxxxiii, " Behold, how good a thing it is ", and of Psalm cxxiv.

The incident belongs to Lord Ernle's province rather than to mine, but it happens not to be mentioned in his book. A similar gesture of union between divided denominations was the covenant Communion Service of the Presbyterian Church of England and the Congregational Union, held in Westminster Chapel, London, in May, 1951. On this occasion the second Scottish Paraphrase, " O God of Bethel ", and " In the cross of Christ I glory " were sung.*

Hymns and Broadcasting

It would be graceless as well as bad history to miss the opportunity this chapter gives of paying tribute to the work done by the Religious Broadcasting Department of the B.B.C. " Listener-research " indicates that not a large proportion of listeners take advantage of the various forms of religious service provided in broadcasting ; but, for what it may be worth as evidence, it does indicate that broadcasts of hymns are the most popular programmes that the Corporation makes available.

Virtually all broadcast services contain hymns ; these services are those broadcast at 9.30 a.m. and 7.45 p.m. in the Home Service and 11 a.m. in the Light Programme on Sundays, the daily devotions on weekdays at 10.15, the Schools Service, broadcast at 9.35 on Fridays and repeated on Tuesdays, and the Sunday Epilogue. Beyond these there are " Sunday Half-Hour " and " Think on These Things ", devoted exclusively to hymns, on Sundays. The

* See additional note, p. 328.

Choral Evensong on Tuesday afternoons does not normally include hymns.*

One of the impressive aspects of these broadcasts, from the point of view of our own subject, is the great wealth and variety of hymns which may be heard in them. Taking as our source-book the *Radio Times* for the first twenty-five weeks of 1950, we find that on 707 occasions of singing there recorded, no fewer than 404 different hymns (including metrical Psalms and Paraphrases) were to be heard. Since the *Radio Times* does not publish the hymns sung at the " People's Service " in the Light Programme, and occasionally does not publish those in the Home Service broadcasts, the total of occasions for singing probably rises towards 800 and the number of different hymns may well be increased to, say, 420.

The secret of this is, of course, that all orthodox denominations have a hearing in the B.B.C. programmes, and that many different hymn-books appear as sources. The period under review contains, also, the credal half of the church's year. Tables and comparative statistics would here be too long to sustain the reader's interest ; but it is worth observing that the two hymns that appear most frequently in these programmes are " Come down, O Love divine " and "Rejoice, the Lord is King " ; both of these appear eight times, partly because Ascension Day and Whit-Sunday fall within the period. " Come down ", for example, appears five times in the week of Whit-Sunday. Seven times we see " When I survey " (the most popular in " Sunday Half-Hour "), " Ye choirs of new Jerusalem " (for Easter, of course) and " Praise, my soul ". " Christ whose glory fills the skies " comes six times, and the following come five times :

> Hail to the Lord's Anointed (Epiphany)
> There is a green hill (Passiontide)
> Our Blest Redeemer (Whitsuntide)
> I bind unto myself today

* Some modifications have been made in the Light Programme since this was written.

Blest are the pure in heart
Guide me, O thou great Redeemer
Judge eternal
O for a thousand tongues
Through the night of doubt and sorrow
Let us with a gladsome mind
Ride on, ride on in majesty (Palm Sunday)
Awake, our souls, away, our fears
Ye servants of God
Father of peace and God of love (Paraphrase 60)
My song is love unknown.

It is interesting to observe that among the hymns that do not appear at all are " O worship the King ", " Abide with me ", and " Ye holy angels bright ". Evening hymns are somewhat at a discount because of the preponderance of morning services.

These lists do not tell us much about the hymns that are not included in them ; but since about half the hymns in them are chosen by the Religious Broadcasting Department and half by the local churches, they give some indication of the popularity of those which do appear, and of the diet of worship which the B.B.C. provides. Neither the Department nor the broadcasting churches or preachers broadcast hymns which they do not think people will want to hear ; but the Department in its daily services gives a simple but complete system of praise which is entirely to be commended.

A Local Survey

In conclusion it might be worth while mentioning the results of a survey of the parish churches of the city, Oxford, in which I happened at the time to live. The following list shows the hymns that were sung in these churches in the course of the first Sunday after Trinity 1951. I have omitted the Communion hymns from this list as falling outside my terms of reference ; I shall explain this in a moment.

Abide with me   *E.H.*, 363
All hail the power of Jesus' name   364

At thy feet, O Christ, we lay	256
†Be thou my guardian and my guide	369
Christ is our corner-stone (2)	A. & M., 239/243
For the beauty of the earth	E.H., 309
God moves in a mysterious way	394
God, who madest earth and heaven	268
Gracious Spirit, Holy Ghost	396
Hail, gladdening Light	A. & M., 18
Jesu, Lover of my soul	414
Jesu, my Lord, my God, my All	417
Jesus shall reign	420
Lead, kindly Light	425
Let all the world in every corner sing	427
*Light's abode, celestial Salem (2)	431
†Now thank we all our God (2)	533
O praise ye the Lord	A. & M., 308/376
‡O thou not made with hands	E.H., 464
O thou who camest from above	343
Onward, Christian soldiers	643
Our God, our help in ages past	450
Praise, my soul	470
Soldiers of Christ, arise	479
The duteous day now closeth	278
The King of love my Shepherd is (2)	E.H. 490
‡There is a book, who runs may read	497
There is a land of pure delight	498
Three in one, and One in three	501
*Through all the changing scenes	502
We love the place, O God	508
*‡Ye holy angels bright (4)	517
Ye servants of the Lord	518

This list does not tell us very much by itself, but as a cross section of the Oxford churches, from the residential, industrial, and university areas of the town, it may be put in as

* The Cathedral.   † New College.   ‡ Magdalen College.

Note.—In nine churches the *English Hymnal* was in use, in the others it was replaced by one or more of the following : *Hymns Ancient and Modern* (standard), 2, (revised) 1 ; *The English Catholic Hymn Book*, 1 ; *Songs of Praise*, 1.

U

H.H.L.

evidence for the impression which will have emerged from the preceding chapter or two ; and the accumulated evidence, as I contended at the beginning of the present chapter, leads in a direction that is not likely to be substantially altered by more extensive investigations. There seems to be a " canon " of hymns which the average churchgoing Englishman, fitful or regular, knows, and which he may reasonably expect to hear sung in any parish church ; to these he turns naturally in those moments when he is most moved to praise or prayer. Opinions on the precise limits of this " canon " will vary ; but I think there is no doubt that the following hymns, at any rate, are hymns which the ordinary Englishman knows, whose tunes he can immediately place, and which have a place in his common life more assured perhaps than any other religious literature, the Bible not excluded.

	E.H.	*C.P.*
Abide with me	363	622
All hail the power of Jesus' name	364	163
All people that on earth do dwell	365	1
As pants the hart	367	390
At even, when the sun was set	266	632
Awake, my soul, and with the sun	257	590
City of God	375	253
Christ whose glory fills the skies	258	594
Come, ye thankful people, come	289	645
Eternal Father, strong to save	540	680
Fierce raged the tempest	541	108
Fight the good fight	389	512
For all the saints	641	363
Glorious things of thee are spoken	393	243
Glory to thee, my God, this night	267	617
God moves in a mysterious way	394	56
Hark, my soul, it is the Lord	400	374
He who would valiant be	402	
How sweet the name of Jesus sounds	405	182
Holy, Holy, Holy, Lord God Almighty	162	223
Jerusalem the golden	412	352
Jesu, Lover of my soul	414	473

Jesus shall reign	420	158
Just as I am	316	385
Lead, kindly Light	425	509
Lead us, heavenly Father	426	507
Love Divine, all loves excelling	437	179
Nearer, my God, to thee	444	480
New every morning is the love	260	596
Now thank we all our God	533	42
O for a thousand tongues to sing	446	180
O God of Bethel	447	55
Once in royal David's city	605	89
Onward, Christian soldiers	643	527
Our God, our help in ages past	450	52
O worship the King	466	17
Praise, my soul, the King of heaven	470	18
Praise the Lord, ye heavens, adore him	535	13
Praise to the Holiest	471	71
Praise to the Lord, the Almighty	536	45
Rock of ages	477	477
Saviour, again to thy dear name	273	635
Soldiers of Christ, arise	479	497
The day thou gavest	277	626
The King of love	490	61
There is a green hill	106	136
Through all the changing scenes	502	46
Through the night of doubt	503	504
Thy kingdom come, O God	554	584
We plough the fields and scatter	293	646
When I survey the wondrous cross	107	131
Who would true valour see		486
Ye holy angels bright	517	5

These fifty-two hymns are those which from the foregoing investigations, only partially recorded here, I have concluded to be " our national anthems ". My last task is to show the limitations of this " basic canon ".

If I had thoroughly examined the hymn-lists of the Nonconformist churches of Oxford I should have been able to present a much longer list than that which I gathered from the Oxford parish churches and college chapels. This would have included many hymns that the reader might not know. There are not many in the reported list that he will not know ; but he might well have to turn to a reference book for " I love thy kingdom, Lord ", for example, and " Give me the faith that can remove ", which happened to be sung in two of our Nonconformist churches on that day. But although we must concede that in the Nonconformist churches the visitor might have heard greater hymns than those in the list, I do not think he would have heard many that would add to my " basic canon ".

Now the reason why I left out the Nonconformists is that whereas the tradition in the Church of England is that the incumbent shall choose what the people can sing without (on the first Sunday after Trinity, anyhow) yielding to any pressure other than that exerted by the repertory of his congregation and his knowledge or what will do them most good, the tradition in most Nonconformist churches is for the hymns to be carefully chosen as part of the liturgy of the service. The Nonconformist minister, therefore, has to meet the additional demands of a creative and constantly renewed liturgy which is the pride of Nonconformity. Very broadly speaking, on the first Sunday after Trinity, 1951, the Anglican vicar choosing his hymns for Eucharist, Mattins, and Evensong, is in the position of having twenty hymns or so to choose from for any particular point in the service ; the Nonconformist minister usually finds that for his liturgy at any given point there are only two or three that will serve his purpose. Not infrequently there is only one.

To illustrate this, let me refer the reader to the instructions given in *Songs of Praise* * about choosing hymns. I quote the instructions for the Communion :

    1st Hymn : *On ordinary Sundays for the Gospel*
    Offertory : *The longest*
    Communion : (*A second hymn from Part III, 259–81, or elsewhere may sometimes be needed*)
    Last Hymn : *Short hymn of Praise ;*

              * Edition of 1931, page 853.

and for the Evening service :

  1st Hymn : *Key note*
  2nd Hymn : (*In the place of the Anthem*)
  Before Sermon : *For one of the Lessons*
  Last Hymn : *The longest and the most popular in character.*

With this compare the famous footnote in an essay by the
late Bernard Manning :

The two village services which I attended on Easter Day
perfectly illustrate this contrast between the Anglicans and ourselves. In the Parish Church there was appropriate liturgical
celebration of the Resurrection ; the Proper Preface in the
Communion, the Easter Collect, and in place of the *Venite*
commonly sung at Matins the special anthem, " Christ our
Passover . . ." But the hymns were a gamble. One could
not be sure what the Vicar would choose. I feared the worst
and I was right. But in the evening at the Chapel, though I
was uncertain about the prayers, there was no gamble about the
hymns. I knew we should have Charles Wesley's Easter hymn,
" Christ the Lord is risen today " and we did have it. . . .
Our hymns are our liturgy, an excellent liturgy. . . .*

  It may seem unfair to compare the rubrics of *Songs of Praise*
with the polemic of Bernard Manning—but the difference is
the very point I want here to make. Hymns, about which
most Anglicans are fairly, and designedly, casual, are a
matter of deep thought to the Dissenters. The whole
approach to hymnody in Nonconformist churches—and here
the Wesleyans partake very much of the dissenting tradition
—is different from that in the Church of England ; and if it
is in Dissent that you will find the highest devotional value
given to hymns, it is in the Church of England that you will
look for the semi-conscious valuing of hymns as " part of the
scenery " which brings out the point this chapter was
designed to make.†

* *The Hymns of Wesley and Watts*, p. 135.
† See additional note, p. 328.

CHAPTER 20

Hymns and Places

IT is possible that a brief chapter on the connections between certain hymns and certain places will not be unwelcome here.

There is nothing to be gained by mentioning any hymn unless we can identify its place of origin with some exactness. Practically every hymn-writer has been tracked down to a place of birth and death, and these places know how to honour their illustrious sons well enough not to need any further urging from me ; and if they do not know the facts, these are given in very easily accessible places.

Nor, of course, must we hope to follow every hymn, or indeed every popular hymn, to its place of origin. Such hymns as are mentioned here will be exceptional rather than normal in having connections with some place or occasion ; but such as there are to be found, we ought to mention.

In a general way we can trust that at Olney, in north Buckinghamshire, the names of Newton and Cowper are suitably revered. Northampton has not forgotten Philip Doddridge, who wrote all his hymns during his ministry there from 1729 to 1751. Sackville College, East Grinstead, Sussex, remains as a memorial to the gentle genius of J. M. Neale, as does the Parish Church of Hursley, Hampshire, which was restored on the proceeds of John Keble's *The Christian Year*. Whether we can be sure that Catherine Winkworth, who translated the German chorales with such felicity, among them " Now thank we all our God ", is sufficiently remembered at Alderley Edge, near Manchester, we must be less certain. Crewe is now, we feel sure, more celebrated for the legacy of George Stephenson than for that of John Ellerton.

But here and there we can perhaps remind a local community of a heritage which has been forgotten in the passing years.

Devonshire has two parishes notable in our story ; Broadhembury (the Rev. Augustus Toplady) and Lower Brixham (the Rev. H. F. Lyte), which account for " Rock of ages " and " Abide with me " respectively ; we can be pretty sure that both hymns were in fact written in those places. Wiltshire's small parish of Bemerton is sacred to George Herbert and therefore has a stake in " Let all the world " and " The God of love my Shepherd is ". Winchester College is the " owner " of Bishop Ken's Morning and Evening hymns, which were written for its scholars, and Southampton will always be associated with Isaac Watts, and especially with " There is a land of pure delight ", which was inspired by the view across Southampton Water to the Isle of Wight. Newport, in the Isle of Wight, can claim Thomas Binney's " Eternal Light " and Mary Fawler Maude's " Thine for ever ". The only certain claims in Sussex are to be found in Brighton, where Charlotte Elliott wrote most of her hymns, and certainly " Just as I am " ; her niece, Emily Elliott, wrote " Thou didst leave thy throne and thy kingly crown " for St. Mark's church in that town. Edwin Paxton Hood, whose best-known hymn is probably " God who hath made the daisies " * was minister of Queen Square Congregational Church there (now Union Church) when he wrote it.

Kent, and in particular Canterbury, has two distinctions. Dean Alford's " Forward ! be our watchword " was written for, and indeed in, Canterbury Cathedral, and the tune MILES LANE for Edward Perronet's " All hail the power " was the work of a nineteen-year-old Canterbury organist, William Shrubsole. Perronet himself hailed from Shoreham, near Sevenoaks, Kent, and was brought up in the old

* C.P., 691.

vicarage there, which is still standing, a hundred yards from the station on the main road from Sevenoaks to Dartford.

Windsor has a claim to " The Church's one foundation " because it was quite certainly written there by the young S. J. Stone. Oxford's claims lie only in the work of its distinguished alumni and professors ; probably the best-known " Oxford " hymn is Edwin Hatch's " Breathe on me, Breath of God ".

Leamington Spa was the home of Frances Ridley Havergal, and most of her hymns, certainly " Take my life ", were written there.

Staffordshire has few associations with hymns, but it was a vicar of Walsall, John Darwall, who gave us the tune DARWALL for " Ye holy angels bright ". Shropshire's most famous association is with Heber, who before he became Bishop of Calcutta was Vicar of Hodnet in that county. That town can claim " Brightest and best " and " Holy, Holy, Holy " ; but " God who madest earth and heaven ", whose first verse is Heber's, was written either at Llangedwyn, near Oswestry, or at his father-in-law's house at Bodryddan, near Rhuddlan, in the same district ; it was in one of those houses that Heber heard the air " All through the night " which inspired the hymn, and to which it was first set when it appeared in the Hodnet church choir-book in 1822. Wrexham parish church itself must have full claim to " From Greenland's icy mountains " for reasons we have already mentioned. Oswestry, not far away, was the Rural Deanery which William Walsham How held at the time when his hymns were published in 1864, and therefore that district is the home of " For all the saints " and " We give thee but thine own ".

Leicestershire cannot do much for us, but it does contain Gopsal House, near Ashby de la Zouch, where Charles Jennens, who wrote the libretto of Handel's *Messiah*, lived, and which gave its name to Handel's famous hymn-tune for " Rejoice, the Lord is King ".

Cheshire is principally to be celebrated here for John Byrom of Stockport, who wrote " Christians, awake " and " My spirit longs for thee ".   The organist of Stockport parish church, John Wainwright, wrote the tune to " Christians, awake " in time for Christmas, 1750, and the choir came and sang it on Christmas Eve outside Byrom's house : the custom of singing this hymn in the small hours of Christmas morning persists in those parts.   The name of this tune, YORKSHIRE, is entirely misleading ; it should more properly be called STOCKPORT.

Sheffield will always be able to claim the hymns of Montgomery, one of its most distinguished citizens.   Not very far away is the village of Horbury Bridge, where Baring-Gould was vicar, and which therefore owns " Onward, Christian soldiers ", " Through the night of doubt and sorrow " and " Now the day is over " ; Dykes's tune to " Nearer, my God, to thee ", called HORBURY, was written at that vicarage.

But Dykes's county was Durham, and the Cathedral there was the birthplace of most of his very famous tunes, for he spent a good part of his ordained life as Precentor at the Cathedral and Vicar of St. Oswald's.   Two centuries and a half before, Bishop Cosin of Durham had written " Come, Holy Ghost ".

Only London is left, and to search all the parish churches of London for hymnological references would be a lifetime's work, and is no part of a study of this kind.   We must mention, however, that Margaret Chapel, now called All Saints', Margaret Street, is the home of the familiar translation of " Adeste Fideles " beginning " O come, all ye faithful " ; Oakeley, the translator, was vicar there at the time, and it was first sung in English there, although Oakeley not long afterwards joined the Roman Catholic Church. St. Luke's, Chelsea, is the home of " Here, Lord, we offer thee all that is fairest ", which was written for a flower-service there.   St. Anne's, Soho, where Croft was organist, is the eponymous home of our most famous hymn-tune,

St. Anne for " Our God, our help in ages past ", and St. James', Piccadilly, Regent Square Presbyterian Church, St. Matthias, Stoke Newington, and St. Bride's, Fleet Street, have all given their names to famous hymn-tunes.

In Scotland there are the manses of Kelso (for Bonar), Innellan (for " O love that wilt not let me go "), Irvine, the birthplace of James Montgomery and Crimond (for the tune Crimond). The great Welsh hymn, " Guide me, O thou great Jehovah " was first published in 1771 in English, and became known from the following year as " A favourite hymn sung by Lady Huntingdon's young Collegians " ; these were the theological students at Trevecca College, South Wales, which is the lineal ancestor of Cheshunt College, Cambridge.

We could make this chapter much longer, but these are the only references which concern popular hymns, and of which we can be sure without venturing into the regions of legend.

CHAPTER 21

The Shame and The Glory of Hymnody

I DO not believe that this book would be complete, nor that I should be giving an honest picture of the relation between hymns and human life, if I did not here offer some judgment on the grounds and the limits of controversy about hymns.

It is tempting, of course, to make this chapter an anthology of eccentric and ludicrous hymns. That would entertain us all ; and it is possible that to have a good laugh at some of our religious eccentricities is not entirely unhealthy. But that is not what I feel it my duty to do here. I had better first try to show in what directions a hymn can offend, and then give a few examples of such offences. But my object all the time is, by contrast with the badness of the bad ones, to throw light for the reader on the goodness of the good ones.

The good hymn is the hymn that passes two tests. One is simple to apply ; as a piece of craftsmanship in literature it must be without blemish. It must not offend against the rules of grammar, syntax, or scansion ; its thought must not be such that if it were a chair or a table it would collapse as soon as any weight was put on it. To judge a hymn on this test is tolerably easy ; either the author has split an infinitive, or left a hanging participle, or written nonsense, or he has not.

The other test is more difficult for the author to pass and for the critic to judge. It is necessary that when written the hymn shall do, precisely and in full, the thing it was designed to do. A hymn is designed to be a congregational act of praise. If therefore it is not the kind of thing a

297

congregation can sing, being more suitable for personal devotion, it fails ; and if it is not praise, that is, addressed to God and dealing with the things of God, it fails. Furthermore, if it distracts the congregation from the act of worship by obscurity, by irrelevance, or by seductive language or music, it fails, and if it offends a particular congregation by making it say what, on that day and at that time, it could not possibly be wanting to say or required to say, it fails.

Now these propositions are subject to a good deal of modification. First, the dividing-line between what is suitable for personal devotion and what is suitable for public praise is hard to draw ; probably as good a rough guide as any is the answer to the question—does this hymn contain sentiments which John Smith and Elizabeth Jones, neither of whom you know personally, will in your view either be familiar with or be well advised to cultivate ? What John and Elizabeth do not now understand is only rightly included in hymns if you are assured that they will not get to heaven without making some effort to understand it. This allows " Come, O thou Traveller " and " Praise to the Holiest ", neither of which is simple, to pass, both being founded in Christian Scripture, whereas it might well relegate some lines of Whittier to the category of dispensable luxuries. It supports, indeed, the excellent rule that language in hymns should be either familiar or Scriptural, since we may require of our congregations education in the Scriptures but not in any other field.

Again, it is properly to be said that some lines not addressed to God fall so easily into the context of public worship that they may be deemed to be addressed to Him. This may perhaps cause us to modify our hasty definition of " praise " into the following more serviceable form : let a hymn say nothing that could not be said in the presence of God. That is to say, let it avoid hatred, contempt, irreverence, and triviality. These, rather than the absence of precise ceremoniousness of diction, are the real enemies of praise ; and this rule will let in " City of God " though it may make us hesitate about Kingsley's " The Day of the Lord ".

Finally, we have to admit that the perfection of a good hymn lies not solely in the hands of its author ; it does not become a good hymn until its work has been done and it has been sung. A certain spiritual neighbourliness and magnanimity in the congregation, without which there can be none of the sweet discipline of communal worship, is part of the perfection of a good hymn, and for lack of it a hymn may fail as a rose-tree will fail for lack of water and sunlight.

A hymn, then, is not really a good hymn until it has been well written, well chosen, and well sung. A hymn which will do for one century may not do for another. A hymn may have a hundred years of life as a good hymn and then be due for placing on the retired list, failure to perform which service for it will render it a bad hymn. What is right for a congregation of down-and-outs in Leeds is possibly wrong for a congregation of solicitors in Littlehampton. All these forces affect the goodness of a hymn. And yet it is still obvious that some hymns are immortal while others are not only ephemeral but strictly non-starters.

Let us have a few examples. Here are lines which, for all I know, Mr. Osbert Lancaster may have had in mind when he wrote what we quoted in an earlier page.

I. FOR A BISHOP

In faithful strife for thy dear name
Thy servant earn'd the saintly fame,
Which pious hearts with praise revere
In constant memory, year by year.

Earth's fleeting joys he counted nought,
Far higher, truer joys he sought,
And now with angels round thy throne
Unfading treasures are his own.*

This will, we suspect, meet criticism on several grounds.   It

* E.H., 189, verses 2 and 3.

appears to disparage the joys of this life and to exalt some
person unnamed to high honour because he would have
nothing to do with them ; it provokes the question, " How
do you know that the old man did not enjoy the flowers
or music or a glass of wine, and why think the worse of him
if he did ? "—and this in casually conventional language
that may strike the reader as bordering on the sycophantic.
Upon the other side it will be urged that we are singing
here not of a mitred unbeliever of the eighteenth century
but of Augustine or Anselm, and that in the Middle Ages
you were likely to have to forgo many tempting and even
harmless pleasures if you were to achieve a saintly life in the
office of bishop. And if this defence does not achieve
acquittal and freedom for the defendant, it might well
cause the sentence to be commuted from public ridicule to
honourable retirement.

> 2.   O oft forsaken, oft denied,
>   Forgive our shame, wash out our sin ;
>   Look on us from thy Father's side,
>   And let that sweet look win.*

Here is another familiar hymn—also for a saint's day,
with a verse that has caused some readers and singers to
pause. Is " sweet " really the adjective to describe what
Peter saw on that occasion when the Lord looked on him ?
Could not this be accused of that same unreality and
remoteness from common thought and truth that has been
laid to the charge of the other ? Possibly—and yet its
author, Mrs. Alexander, was a master of the art of writing
for children ; and although she did not write this for
children she has inevitably painted a child's picture here,
and the simple diction of this hymn has in fact done much
in past days for some upon whom sterner language would
make no impact.

A more serious charge of " unreality " might be laid
against this :

* * E.H.*, 227, verse 5.

3. Once more the solemn season calls
   A holy fast to keep ;
   And now within the temple walls
   Let priest and people weep. . . .

   We smite the breast, we weep in vain,
   In vain for sins we mourn,
   Unless with penitential pain
   The smitten soul be torn.*

Such ecstatic exhibitions of communal grief do not commend
themselves to Anglo-Saxon congregations ; nor, we suspect,
did they do so when the lines were written. And yet the
hymn has something to say ; its message is that the ugliest
vice of a church is impenitence, the refusal to see sin when
it is there, and it is even possible to say that the experience
of a person who honestly faces evil is not altogether im-
properly figured in the language here used.

Here is an example of a type of hymn that has now gone
right out of fashion—the hortatory hymn for children.

4. O boys, be strong in Jesus ; to toil for him is gain,
   And Jesus wrought with Joseph with chisel, saw, and plane ;
   O maidens, live for Jesus, who was a maiden's Son ;
   Be patient, pure, and gentle, and perfect grace begun.†

It is all very badly done ; the second line is a *non sequitur*,
and it is implied that courage and humour and faithfulness
are not feminine virtues. And yet—are we thus entitled to
argue *ex silentio* ? May it not be urged that the characteristic
demerits of the generation of maidens immediately suc-
ceeding that for which this was written were a combination
of impatience, impurity, and discourtesy ? If that is putting
the case too strongly, at least we may be asked to commend the verse for a good intention. But there is a fatal
facility in its diction that suggests to a pensive reader that
the whole matter is being taken too easily ; young people

* *Hymns Ancient and Modern* (standard edn.), 84, verses 1 and 3
(Chandler " and Compilers ").
† *Ib.*, 341, verse 3 (J. J. Daniell, 1875).

are up against problems and anxieties that fall right outside
the little world which speaks this kind of language.

5. Is it reality that is wanted? Then let us look at
this :

> Ill masters good ; good seems to turn
> To ill with greatest ease ;
> And worst of all, the good with good
> Is at cross-purposes.*

That is Father Faber, writing for the Catholics of Birmingham and London in 1849.   The truth of the contention
is incontestable ; but it could be called one of the most
prosaic verses ever committed to print.   We require of
hymns a certain minimum of lyrical elegance to which this
verse does not reach.   And yet Faber may have done
something with this that nobody else was doing better.   For
who else was writing about such problems in hymns in 1849 ?
The Christian Socialists, perhaps, and some admirable
Americans : precious few others.

6. A little less crude, but still rather odd to modern ears,
is this :

> Speak thou the truth ! let others fence
> And trim their words for pay ;
> In pleasant sunshine of pretence
> Let others bask their day.†

This is not, as you might expect, Charles Kingsley or one of
the poets of *Hymns of the Spirit,* but Dean Alford.   It offends
in being addressed by one member of the congregation to
another, and in evincing a sentiment which could not un-
fairly be paraphrased in the words of the Pharisee who
thanked God that he was not as other men.   This is an
example of the kind of hymn which would probably fail
under the test of whether it contained material fit for the
presence of God.   But one could certainly say for it that it
cuts well adrift from the conventionality and remoteness of

* *Worship Song*, 441, verse 3.   † *Ib.*, 781, verse 1.

our first example ; it is, at least, talking about real things that are in real people's minds, even if these things have not sufficiently been purged for worship.

7. For our last example let us venture boldly into the underworld of hymnody.   I am quoting this in full because I doubt if the reader will find, without extensive searching, a hymn that breaks more rules than this one.   Be prepared for illiteracy, for a magnificent split infinitive, and for subject matter which is not commonly dealt with in our hymn-books.   But one thing you will find—there is nothing unreal or insincere or remote here.

> What gives the breath an awful smell,
> And hinders one from feeling well ?
> A single word the tale will tell—
> > Tobacco.

> (*Refrain :*)
> > Tobacco's a curse in the land *
> > I pledge you, my friend,
> > I'll never defend
> > That villainous weed, Tobacco.

> What keeps one spitting all the day
> On fence and wall, till people say
> " I guess he'll spit his life away " ?
> > Tobacco.

> I often ask the doctor why
> So much of suffering have I,
> In one short word he makes reply—
> > " Tobacco."

> No more will I my health abuse,
> Nor chew this weed, nor spit its juice :
> I'll give my pledge to never use
> > Tobacco.

* I have not had access to the musical edition of the source of these words, but I feel sure the first line of the refrain is repeated in performance.

H.H.L.   X

> I tell you, friends, I will be free,
> No more a slave to habit be ;
> And in my mouth no one shall see
> Tobacco.

I call that a hymn because it is included in the *National Temperance Hymnal*.* We will assume that it represents hymnography—at least public and printed hymnography—at its nadir. And yet—exactly why does it move us to protest ? What is wrong with the wretched thing ? If I can persuade the reader that even here he must beware of dismissing it as a sickening freak, I do not think I need continue this discussion further. To that end I should make no attempt to defend the illiteracy of the verses. They are indeed crude—though they lack not only the elegance but also the sensational, Gothic-romantic horror of some of the other pieces in this source. But when we have exhausted ourselves in protesting that tobacco is a curse more to the pocket than to the morals (and I suspect that more of my readers smoke it than chew it), and, more generally, that the cause of Temperance, meaning total abstinence from both alcohol and tobacco, is directed wide of the true mark of evangelism, it remains possible for the defence to call as witness any social historian of our country,† who will tell us precisely and in nauseating detail, if we require him, just what it was that the temperance reformers of the nineteenth century were attacking.

This will, I feel, be enough to show that if we base our judgment of hymns on their contents alone we shall invariably meet argument from the other side. I believe it is true to say that there is no published hymn in existence that has not done some good somewhere. The real shame and vice of hymn-singing is not in the content of the hymns.

For you will meet argument not only when you attack

* The book is undated. The copy I saw was lent to me by the Rev. F. E. Quick, late of Paddington Chapel, to whom I here express my great gratitude. He picked it up in 1924.

† E.g., G. M. Trevelyan's *English Social History*, pp. 341–3 and 570.

hymns you are persuaded are bad hymns, but when you defend your favourites. I hope I may be allowed to record here my judgment that Cowper's " There is a fountain filled with blood " is a magnificent piece of evangelical rhetoric that has done good to many in the six generations since it was written. But that hymn is furiously attacked because of its insistence on the Biblical imagery of the Blood of Christ ; and it gives offence to so many that even those, who feel that a congregation that has grown into an understanding of its deep truth is better off than one to whom the chance of such growth is denied, know that they must choose it with the very greatest care.

Again, great controversy continues about hymns that deal with heaven and the communion of saints, especially those that do so under the Biblical imagery of the resplendent and renewed Jerusalem as it is pictured in the Book of *Revelation.* In some of our hymn-books you find these lines :

> Thy turrets and thy pinnacles
>   With carbuncles do shine ;
> Thy very streets are paved with gold
>   Surpassing clear and fine. . . .
>
> Thy gardens and thy gallant walks
>   Continually are green ;
> There grow such sweet and pleasant flowers
>   As nowhere else are seen.*

The force of these images is that the joys of eternal life are real, solid joys, that a grown and full-blooded man would really *like.* The Englishman who wrote these lines brings in the beauty of his own desire—the English garden—alongside the fervid imagery of the Bible. But both this and Cowper's hymn take us into the main stream of Christian thought by way of the language of the Bible, and this is their defence and their splendour.

But when we have defended the stuffy hymns of *Hymns*

* *E.H.,* 638, verses 8 and 17.

Ancient and Modern and the Sankeys and the songs of Temperance, and have admitted the danger of escapism in some of the classics, are we left with no conclusion at all ? I here contend that the conclusion which will finally lay the ghost that we raised on our first page is this, that the shame of hymn-singing is not ultimately in the hymn but in the singer.

In a word, where hymn-singing is a self-indulgence, it is thereby not a sacrifice ; and where hymn-singing is community singing by a closed company, it is not a means of evangelism. I do not say that the singing of hymns for enjoyment is bad ; I am saying only that if you are singing hymns for fun you need not expect to be thought advanced in Christian virtue for doing so. Nor do I say that the hymns of a closed community, intelligible only to that community, carrying associations only connected with that community (like the camp-fire songs of the Scouts or the merry nonsense sung of an evening by a walking party) are an evil ; I am saying that if you sing hymns in that way you must not blame people outside your community for thinking your noise a nuisance and your behaviour eccentric. There are some hymns that will stand anything : that is perhaps the real definition of our " basic canon "— that it consists of hymns that no amount of battering will force out of shape, that no amount of suffocation by sentimentality will kill. But there are others, and among them some of the most exquisite, which if they are chosen with care and discernment can speak with power, and which if chosen casually will be only sentimental songs.

In this age, which has been called " post-Christian England ", the Church is fighting on several fronts. In England it is living down a not very creditable past, and it is faced by secularism and in places by active atheism. It is the consideration of such facts as these which must determine the Church's use of hymns ; for it is because of the discreditable aspects of the Church's past that non-Christians hate its hymn-singing, and it is because of the temporary victory of secularism that they despise it. In the present situation, then, the glory of our hymnody is in its power for converting unbelief, strengthening faith, and binding together the Christian community in that disciplined charity of which singing together is a symbol. The shame of our hymnody is in unreality, complacency, and spiritual slovenliness. We do wrong, at this time of day, to make the Christian challenge seem falsely easy ; therefore it is wrong for an educated congregation to sing *Sankey*. We do wrong to make the Faith appear less than intellectually respectable ; therefore hymns that discredit Christian doctrines are out of place. We do wrong to reach too low, to identify the Faith with a party or a social programme ; we do wrong to take refuge in hymn-singing from the exactions of the world.

C. S. Lewis recently wrote as follows about hymn-singing :

Is it . . . obvious that the people are edified by being allowed to shout their favourite hymns ? I am well aware that the people like it. They equally like shouting *Auld Lang Syne* in the streets on New Year's Eve or shouting the latest music-hall song in a tap-room. To make a communal, familiar noise is certainly a pleasure to human beings. . . . I have often heard this noise ; I have sometimes contributed to it. I do not yet seem to have found any evidence that the physical and emotional exhilaration which it produces is necessarily, or often, of any religious significance. . . . We must beware of the idea that our music can " please " God as it would please a cultivated human hearer. That is like thinking, under the old Law, that he really needed the blood of bulls and goats. To which the answer came, " Mine are the cattle upon a thousand hills." . . . All our offerings, whether of music or martyrdom, are like the intrinsically worthless present of a child, which a father values indeed, but values only for the intention.[69]

There is the heart of the matter. The shame and the glory are in the *intention*. I have found it difficult to run to earth another hymn containing a split infinitive ; but we can, and often do, sing hymns for the very worst of bad reasons.

But now, in conclusion, let us see how the masters have gone about their business. I am going to rehearse here nine hymns in full.[70]   Only one of them, the last, has become a popular hymn ; but they are all great Christian utterances, and they come from four different centuries. Let them speak for themselves, whether in the exalted language of Charles Wesley, the rugged poetry of Watts, the meditation of the seventeenth-century bishop, the fresh vision of the modern Chinese, or the vigorous grace of our leading contemporary hymn-writer.

The first is a paraphrase of a German original into rich English poetry.

> 70—1.   The duteous day now closeth,
>   Each flower and tree reposeth,
>   Shade creeps o'er wild and wood ;
>   Let us, as night is falling,
>   On God our Maker calling
>   Give thanks to him, the Giver good.
>
> Now all the heavenly splendour
> Breaks forth in starlight tender
>   From myriad worlds unknown ;
> And man, the marvel seeing,
> Forgets his selfish being
>   For joy of beauty not his own.
>
> His care he drowneth yonder,
> Lost in the abyss of wonder ;
>   To heaven his soul doth steal :
> This life he disesteemeth,
> The day it is that dreameth,
>   That doth from truth his vision seal.
>
> Awhile his mortal blindness
> May miss God's lovingkindness,
>   And grope in faithless strife ;

But when life's day is over
Shall death's fair night discover
The fields of everlasting life.
                    ROBERT BRIDGES, 1899, based on
                    PAUL GERHARDT, 1656.

Here is Charles Wesley in his most monolithic style, working in the massive, hard material of theological definition and making of it high poetry.

70—2.   Let earth and heaven combine,
              Angels and men agree,
           To praise in songs divine
              The incarnate Deity ;
           Our God contracted to a span,
           Incomprehensibly made man.

           He laid his glory by,
              He wrapped him in our clay ;
           Unmarked by human eye,
              The latent Godhead lay ;
           Infant of days he here became,
           And bore the mild Immanuel's name.

           Unsearchable the love
              That hath the Saviour brought ;
           The grace is far above
              Or man or angel's thought ;
           Suffice for us that God, we know,
           Our God, is manifest below.

           He deigns in flesh to appear,
              Widest extremes to join ;
           To bring our vileness near,
              And make us all divine ;
           And we the life of God shall know,
           For God is manifest below.

Made perfect first in love,
And sanctified by grace,
We shall from earth remove
And see his glorious face :
Then shall his love be fully showed,
And man shall then be lost in God.

CHARLES WESLEY, 1741.

Out of a rich experience of modern needs of the Gospel
gained partly in the Navy and partly in the industrial
parishes of England, a contemporary poet, Canon Briggs,
wrote thus in 1928 of the human life of Christ :

70—3.   Son of the Lord most high,
Who gave the worlds their birth,
He came to live and die,
The Son of man on earth :
In Bethlehem's stable born was he,
And humbly bred in Galilee.

Born in so low estate,
Schooled in a workman's trade,
Not with the high and great
His home the Highest made ;
But labouring by his brethren's side,
Life's common lot he glorified.

Then when his hour was come,
He heard his Father's call :
And leaving friends and home,
He gave himself for all :
To heal the sick, the lost to find,
To give their eyesight to the blind.

Toiling by night and day,
Himself oft burdened sore,
Where hearts in bondage lay,
Himself their burden bore :
Till, scorned by those he died to save,
Himself in death, as life, he gave.

O lowly Majesty !
Lofty in lowliness !
Blest Saviour, who am I
To share thy blessedness ?
Yet thou hast called me, even me,
Servant divine, to follow thee.

G. W. BRIGGS, 1928.

Now let us hear Isaac Watts singing of the unspeakable mystery of the Passion.

70—4. Nature with open volume stands
To spread her Maker's praise abroad :
And every labour of his hands
Shews something worthy of a God.

But in the Grace that rescued man
His brightest form of glory shines ;
Here on the Cross 'tis fairest drawn
In precious blood, and crimson lines.

Here his whole name appears complete :
Nor wit can guess, nor Reason prove
Which of the letters best is writ,
The Power, the Wisdom, or the Love.

Here I behold his inmost heart,
Where grace and vengeance strangely join
Piercing his Son with sharpest smart
To make the purchas'd pleasures mine.

O ! the sweet wonders of that cross
Where God the Saviour loved and died ;
Her noblest life my spirit draws
From his dear wounds and bleeding side.

I would for ever speak his name
In sounds to mortal ears unknown,
With angels join to praise the Lamb,
And worship at his Father's throne.

ISAAC WATTS, 1707.

A Nonconformist minister of high distinction and saintly
life writes here of the social obligations of the Christian.

70—5.   Brother, who on thy heart didst bear
      The burden of our shame and sin,
And stoopest ever still to share
      The fight without, the fear within ;

Whose patience cannot know defeat,
      Whose pity will not be denied,
Whose loving-kindness is so sweet,
      Whose tender mercies are so wide ;

O brother Man, for this we pray,
      Thou brother Man and sovereign Lord,
That we, thy brethren, day by day
      May follow thee and keep thy word ;

That we may care as thou hast cared
      For sick and lame and maimed and blind,
And freely share as thou hast shared
      In all the woe of all mankind ;

That ours may be the holy task
      To help and bless, to heal and save ;
This is the privilege we ask,
      And this the happiness we crave.

So in thy mercy make us wise,
      And lead us in the ways of love
Until at last our wondering eyes
      Look on thy glorious face above.
          HENRY ARNOLD THOMAS, 1916.

Here is the humble meditation of a seventeenth-century
bishop, Jeremy Taylor. Before he became a bishop in
Ireland, he was twice imprisoned (in 1645 and 1655) by
the victorious Roundheads. These lines were published
during the year of his second imprisonment, and reverently
fashioned into a hymn by an anonymous hand in the nineteenth century.

70—6. Draw nigh to thy Jerusalem, O Lord,
Thy faithful people cry with one accord ;
Ride on in triumph ; Lord, behold, we lay
Our passions, lusts, and proud wills in thy way.

Thy road is ready ; and thy paths, made straight
With longing expectation seem to wait
The consecration of thy beauteous feet,
And silently thy promised advent greet !

Hosanna ! welcome to our hearts ! for here
Thou hast a temple too, as Sion dear ;
Yes, dear as Sion, and as full of sin ;
How long shall thieves and robbers dwell therein ?

Enter and chase them forth, and cleanse the floor ;
O'erthrow them all, that they may never more
Profane with traffic vile that holy place
Where thou hast chosen, Lord, to set thy face.

And then, if our stiff tongues shall faithlessly
Be mute in praises of thy deity,
The very temple stones shall loud repeat
Hosanna ! and thy glorious footsteps greet.

JEREMY TAYLOR, 1655, edited in
the *Sarum Hymnal*, 1868.

The next hymn is a vision of heaven from the indigenous
Church of Christ in China, lately translated by an English
scholar.

70—7. Salem, from heaven descending,
   Home, light, felicity,
Beneath man's sore oppressions
   Our hearts cry out for thee.
The hope of thy pledged coming
   Assuages grief and pain,
Kindles to high emprises,
   The weak makes strong again.

Salem from heaven descending,
  Here milk and honey flow,
Here rules the son of Mary,
  Whose head was cradled low :
Here sorrows shall be ended,
  Nor gold nor power divide,
Nor brethren here be sundered
  By huckster's guile or pride.

Salem from heaven descending,
  Here reigns in joy and peace
The Lamb that bore our sorrows
  That we might find release.
No more the lust of empire
  Nor rift of race-disdain !
Sword shall be turned to ploughshare,
  And slaughter shall be slain.

Salem from heaven descending,
  Where heart and mind are free,
Behold the Word eternal
  Is light and Lord to thee.
Here violence is vanquished,
  Nor bars nor bonds prevail ,
And who now travel darkling
  Shall see without a veil.

Salem from heaven descending,
  Home, light, beatitude,
The hopes of thy pledged coming
  Our grief and pain extrude ;
On earth, as now in heaven
  God's holy will be done ;
May we, from doubt delivered,
  In toil and hope be one.
          Translated from the Chinese of
          TIMOTHY LEW by Nathaniel Micklem,
          D.D., 1937

The Chinese Christian looks for heaven coming down to
earth to swallow up earth's sorrows ; now hear an English-

man of the nineteenth century looking for the gathering up
to heaven of all things in the earth. This, says Montgomery, is what all life is leading to.

70—8. Hark, the song of Jubilee,
Loud as mighty thunders' roar,
Or the fulness of the sea
When it breaks upon the shore.
Hallelujah ! for the Lord
God omnipotent shall reign.
Hallelujah ! let the word
Echo round the earth and main.

Hallelujah ! hark, the sound
From the depths unto the skies,
Wakes above, beneath, around,
All creation's harmonies.
See Jehovah's banner furled.
Sheathed his sword ; he speaks ; 'tis done !
And the kingdoms of this world
Are the kingdoms of his Son.

He shall reign from pole to pole
With illimitable sway ;
He shall reign, when like a scroll
Yonder heavens are passed away.
Then the end ; beneath his rod
Man's last enemy shall fall ;
Hallelujah ! Christ in God,
God in Christ, is all in all.

JAMES MONTGOMERY, 1817.

And lastly, here is what is perhaps the finest of all hymns ;
Thomas Kelly has here comprehended the whole Gospel,
and he tells of the Good News and of the mysterious mercy
by which we may lay hold on it. It forms a fitting conclusion to this story of hymns and human life.

70—9. The head that once was crowned with thorns
Is crowned with glory now ;
A royal diadem adorns
The mighty Victor's brow.

The highest place that heaven affords
    Is his, is his by right ;
The King of kings, and Lord of lords,
    And heaven's eternal light.

The joy of all who dwell above,
    The joy of all below,
To whom he manifests his love,
    And grants his name to know :

To them the Cross, with all its shame,
    With all its grace, is given ;
Their name an everlasting name,
    Their joy the joy of heaven.

They suffer with their Lord below ;
    They reign with him above ;
Their profit and their joy to know
    The mystery of his love.

The Cross he bore is life and health,
    Though shame and death to him ;
His people's hope, his people's wealth
    Their everlasting theme !

THOMAS KELLY, 1820.

NOTES

CHAPTER 2

1. *P. 19.* For a discussion of the extravagances of later medieval music, in the early days of polyphony, see my book, *The Church and Music*, pp. 95 ff., for an allusion, and Stanford and Forsyth, *History of Music*, pp. 138 ff., for an explanation.

2. *P. 22.* The three hymns of Ambrose are *Aeterne Rerum Conditor, Deus Creator Omnium,* and *Iam surgit Hora Tertia* (C. S. Phillips, *Hymnody Past and Present*, pp. 51 f.).

CHAPTER 3

3. *P. 31.* For the story of the " Prose of the Ass ", see *Songs of Praise Discussed*, pp. 99 f.

CHAPTER 4

4. *P. 33.* For an excellent introduction to Luther's work and personality, see Gordon Rupp, *Luther's Progress to the Diet of Worms, 1521* (1951).

5. *P. 37.* For an introduction to John Calvin, see R. Carew Hunt, *Calvin* (1933).

CHAPTER 5

6. *P. 40.* See, for example, the controversy so ably conducted in *The Catholicity of Protestantism* (ed. Flew and Davies, 1950), chh. 3–5, and the article by Bishop Aulen in *Theology* (March, 1949) there referred to, in which it is demonstrated that critics of Luther are really aiming not at Luther but at seventeenth-century pietism.

7. *P. 42.* See *Songs of Praise Discussed,* p. 364 (for *Wachet auf*) and 62 (for *Wie shon leucht'uns der Morgenstern*).

8. *P. 43.* For Rinkart, see *Songs of Praise Discussed*, at Hymn 350.

9. *P. 44.* The quotation is from Catherine Winkworth, part 1, hymn 5 in section " After Easter ".

10. *P.* 45. A version in the original metre (7.6.7.6.D) by Winfred Douglas (1867–1944), the great American hymnologist and translator, will be found in the *Hymnal (1940)* of the Episcopal Church of the U.S.A., no. 446.

11. *P.* 48. Gerhard Tersteegen (1697–1769), author of the hymn translated " Thou hidden love of God " by John Wesley (*Congregational Praise*, 469), though a pastor of the German Reformed Church, shows in his writings a close affinity with the spirit of pietism. Tersteegen's conversion (1724) was marked by a solemn covenant with God which he wrote and signed with his own blood (*Julian*, p. 417).

12. *P.* 50. It is reported of Gellert that he was so generous that, when Prince Henry of Prussia sought him out, he was found to be living in an empty room without food or fire (*Songs of Praise Discussed*, p. 101).

13. *P.* 51. Another hymn of Spitta's which has had a wide popularity is " How blessed, from the bonds of sin ", which contains the excellent lines :

> Through evil or through good report,
>   Still keeping at thy side,
> And by my life or by my death,
>   Let Christ be magnified !
>   (*Hymns Ancient and Modern*, standard edn., 357.)

CHAPTER 6

14. *P.* 53. The Strasbourg Psalter of 1539, Calvin's first hymn-book, was published in an edition by Sir Richard Terry ; the Introduction to that work, together with an article by G. R. Woodward in *The Proceedings of the Musical Association*, Session 44, there quoted, provide the best sources for the history of this and the Genevan Psalters.

15. *P.* 56. One of Sternhold's psalms from the Old Version is preserved in the hymn " O God, my strength and fortitude ", which is taken from Psalm 18. A version altered by George Rawson appeared in the *Congregational Hymnary* (no. 53) in seven verses ; another, in five, rather nearer to the original but still altered, is in the *Methodist Hymn Book* (no. 24).

16. *P.* 57. George Wither (1588–1667) wrote over 100 books and pamphlets. In the earlier part of his life he was an ardent royalist, serving under Charles I in 1639. But in 1641–2 he

sold his hereditary estates and raised a troop for the Parliament, and subsequently held office as a Justice under the Long Parliament. He was imprisoned at the Restoration for writing democratic pamphlets, and subsequently was committed to the Tower.

17. *P.* 58. John Wesley wrote in the Preface of 1779 to the first book of *Hymns for the People called Methodists* :

Many Gentlemen have done my brother and me (though without naming us) the honour to reprint many of our hymns. Now they are perfectly welcome to do so, provided that they print them just as they are. But I desire they would not attempt to alter them—for they really are not able. None of them is able to mend either the sense or the verse.

His version of George Herbert's " Teach me, my God and King " (see *E.H.*, 485) had this for its third verse :

> All may of thee partake,
> Nothing so mean can be,
> But draws, when acted for thy sake,
> Goodness and worth from thee.

He rearranged John Austin's " Hark, my soul, how everything " in L.M., beginning " Hark, my dull soul, how everything ", and George Herbert's " King of glory " in C.M., beginning " O King of glory ". He was also responsible for the change of the first word in " Our God, our help in ages past ".

18. *P.* 61. For this and some other similar stories, see Dr. Patrick's notes in the *Supplement* to the *Handbook to the Church Hymnary*, pp. 51 ff.

19. *P.* 61. For stories about Psalms 124 and 68, see Lord Ernle's book, or the *Supplement* to the *Handbook to the Church Hymnary*, pp. 83 ff. for Psalm 124. The 68th Psalm, " Let God arise ", with its Genevan tune (*E.H.*, 544) was a battle-song of the Reformation second only to " Ein feste Burg ".

CHAPTER 7

20. *P.* 63. For an excellent biography of Isaac Watts, see *Isaac Watts*, by A. P. Davis (Independent Press, 1948). A paragraph on Benjamin Keach, who anticipates Watts in the use of hymns by a generation, but none of whose work survives, will be found at a later stage, p. 148.

H.H.L.   Y

21. *P.* 66. See *Songs of Praise Discussed*, p. 196.

22. *P.* 68. See Bernard Manning, *The Hymns of Wesley and Watts*, p. 11 and elsewhere.

23. *P.* 68. There are several quotations from Charles Wesley in Howard Spring's *Fame is the Spur*; perhaps this is the place to mention that Mr. Spring in one of his earlier chapters commits a minor " howler " ; he makes his amiable Methodist local preacher look in his hymn-book for " Let all the world combine " (which I quote in full on p. 309), and tells how the preacher knew it so well that he didn't have to look it up in the index : he was sure it was number 133. The scene is in the 'nineties, and that hymn is not no. 133 until the *Methodist Hymn Book* comes out in 1904. Mr. Spring quotes several " Sankeys " in *There is No Armour*.

24. *P.* 68. See chapter II of Adam Bede for the introduction by George Eliot of Wesley's " Thy ceaseless, unexhausted love ".

25. *P.* 73. St. Ignatius to the Romans (about A.D. 110), chapter VII. The phrase may have originally meant " my self-love is crucified ", but it has frequently been interpreted in Wesley's sense as " my beloved is crucified " ; see John Mason's " My Lord, my Love, was crucified " (*C.P.*, 605) and Faber's " O come and mourn with me " (*E.H.*, 111) with its refrain, " Jesus, our love, is crucified ".

CHAPTER 8

26. *P.* 75. Readers who care to explore the eighteenth-century classics of hymnody may wish to consult some extended studies of some of their authors in my book, *I'll praise my Maker* (Independent Press, 1951).

A full-length biography of John Newton has recently been published by Bernard Martin (1951), and is warmly to be recommended.

A study of Philip Doddridge, edited by Geoffrey Nuttall, was published in 1951 by the Independent Press under the title, *Philip Doddridge*.

27. *P.* 76. The Olney Hymns will be found in two sources. Cowper's 68 are to be found in the standard (Oxford) edition of his works. The whole 348 are to be found in the collected works of John Newton (Aberdeen, 1833) at the end of the second volume.

28. *P.* 79.   James Merrick (1720–69) was an ordained clergyman of the Church of England and a Fellow of Trinity, Cambridge. He never held a parochial charge. His psalms were first published in 1765. The only one in common use now is " The festal morn, O God, is here " (*C.P.*, 607), a version of Psalm 122.

29. *P.* 80.   Methodism was established as a separate denomination in 1808.

30. *P.* 80.   " Praise the Lord ! " was first printed in a four-page tract that was pasted into the *Psalms, Hymns and Anthems of the Foundling Hospital* (music edition of 1796 and words edition of 1801). It is there marked " Hymn from Psalm cxlviii. Hayden ". Haydn's tune was written and published in 1797 for a patriotic hymn sung on the birthday of the Austrian Emperor, 12 February in that year. Its first appearance in England was in Miller's *Sacred Music* of 1802 (*Songs of Praise Discussed*, pp. 330 and 264).

31. *P.* 82.   The passage from which the quotation comes is this :

. . . Or if we seek a relief from *Ancient and Modern*, there is the *English Hymnal*, better it is true, but stuffed out with second-rate creaking translations of Greek and Latin hymns, fusty as a second-hand Lewis and Short, more like the meritorious exercises of the classical Sixth than Poetry, the handmaid of Piety. (*The Hymns of Wesley and Watts*, pp. 33–4.)

This amiable dissenting truculence is not without some justification. See the pages immediately following in this book, and below, p. 299.   " Lewis and Short " is the standard Latin dictionary for students.

32. *P.* 82.   The bibliographical history of *Hymns Ancient and Modern* is as follows :

1859.   Trial volume, words only, 138 hymns.
1860.   First edition, words only, 273 hymns.
1861.   First edition with music.
1868.   First edition with appendix, 386 hymns.
1875.   First complete revision, 473 hymns.
1889.   Second edition (1875) with supplement, 638 hymns.
1904.   Third edition, 643 hymns.

1916. " Second Supplement " to 1875 and 1889 editions, beginning at no. 639. 141 hymns.

1922. Second edition with both Supplements reset, 779 hymns.

1939. " Shortened edition ", 286 hymns omitted from 1922 edition but old numbers retained.

1950. Fourth edition, 636 hymns. " Hymns Ancient and Modern Revised."

The only edition which failed to win acceptance was the third of 1904, which was the basis of W. H. Frere's Historical Edition of 1909. The 1875 revision was therefore retained intact, with supplements added, for seventy-five years. In the 1950 edition many of the familiar hymns retained their 1875 numbers.

33. *P*. 84. Some doubt was thrown on this date by *Songs of Praise Discussed,* but it was established with documentary evidence by W. Maxwell Lyte, the grandson of the hymnwriter, in 1947 in the correspondence columns of *The Times* and in the *Bulletin* of the Hymn Society (October, 1947).

34. *P*. 86. The version of this hymn to be found in some books (e.g., the *English Hymnal*) appeared in the hymn-book edited by Montgomery and Cotterill at Sheffield to which we refer below, p. 123 ; the alterations can be ascribed to one or other of those editors (*Julian*, p. 850).

35. *P*. 87. This hymn is based on a famous utterance of the Scottish divine, Samuel Rutherford (1600–61) of Anwoth, which appears in his *Letters and Dying Sayings*. It is taken from a poem of nineteen verses written by Mrs. Cousin, the wife of the Free Church minister at Irvine, Ayrshire, and published in 1857. It was the last hymn given out by Spurgeon at a service in his rooms at Mentone, January 17, 1892, which was the last he ever conducted.

CHAPTER 9

36. *P*. 93. Another hymn of Kingsley's, " Who will say the world is dying ? " will be found at *Worship Song*, no. 801. It contains the lines—

> Fools ! who fancy Christ mistaken ;
> Man a tool to buy and sell ;
> Earth a failure, God-forsaken,
> Anteroom of Hell.

37. *P.* 95. Chesterton is said to have used this metre because he did not know one tune from another, and it occurred to him that AURELIA ("The church's one foundation") was the typical English hymn tune ; an undeniable, if undeserved, compliment to AURELIA.

38. *P.* 104. This is from the Mansfield College manuscript (typescript) collection, written by R. T. Brooks, who is now Assistant Director of Religious Broadcasting in the North Region. This was one of three hymns submitted for the annual Scott Psalmody Prize ; the other contributors were G. B. Caird (now Professor of New Testament Studies at McGill University, Montreal) and W. T. Davies (now Principal-Designate of Memorial College, Brecon, and known in Wales by his bardic name, "Pennar"). Dr. Caird's hymn will be found at *Congregational Praise*, 564. Dr. Davies's has not been published, but has frequently been sung from printed sheets in Wales. It begins :

> Father of all, who didst create
> All things for good, all men for life ;
> Right thou the wrongs of church and state ;
> End thou our folly and our strife.

CHAPTER 10

39. *P.* 106. Works of Toplady (1849 edition), p. 725.
40. *P.* 106. *Ib.* p. 762
           Ib. p. 729
41. *P.* 108. *Ib.* pp. 448–50, where, however, the hymn is not quoted, since it appears in the collection of hymns at the end of the *Works*.
42. *P.* 109. See L. Elliott Binns, *Religion in the Victorian Era*, chapter 5.
43. *P.* 112. See *Songs of Praise Discussed*, p. 192.

CHAPTER 11

44. *P.* 125. "Lift up your heads" was originally written in nineteen verses.

CHAPTER 12

45. *P.* 135. See the *Hymnal (1940) Companion* (U.S.A.), p. 125.

46. *P.* 141. See *English Church Music*, July, 1950. The reviewer is Dr. Micklem, Principal of Mansfield College, Oxford.

47. *P.* 143. See *Songs of Praise Discussed*, p. 278. Mgr. Knox in *Enthusiasm* (1950) appears to have missed this incident. If the date in *S.P.D.* given for Mason's birth (1645) is right, the " old man " referred to in this passage was 49 at the time.

48. *P.* 144. Marriott was a friend of Sir Walter Scott, who dedicated the second canto of *Marmion* to him.

CHAPTER 13

49. *P.* 152. It is interesting to compare with Binney's hymn, considered as a romantic expression of Christian piety, the passage in the Preface to C. S. Lewis's *Pilgrim's Regress* (2nd edn., 1944), in which he deals with the meaning of the word ' romantic '. He writes :

> The experience (sc. to be called ' romantic ') is one of intense longing. It is distinguished from other longings by two things. In the first place, though the sense of want is acute and even painful, yet the mere wanting is felt to be somehow a delight. . . . In the second place, there is a peculiar mystery about the object of this desire.

50. *P.* 165. Examples of horrid lines in Bonar are " The brief, bright hour of fellowship with thee " from " Here, O my Lord, I see thee ", and " Truest of all that's true ", from " O everlasting Light " (*Congregational Hymnary*, 285 and 25).

CHAPTER 14

51. *P.* 176. See *John Ellerton, His Life and Writings on Hymnology* (1896), ed. by Henry Housman, p. 343.

CHAPTER 15

52. *P.* 184. Irenaeus, concerned to vindicate the Faith against speculations of Greek and Oriental origin, evolved the doctrine of " recapitulation " of which no more convenient paraphrase can be given than to say " he became man that we might become as God ". See *Adversus Haereses* (about A.D. 180), book iii.

53. *P.* 185. These quotations are from the " Gender-rhymes " and the preposition-mnemonics in Kennedy's *Revised Latin Primer* (1888).

54. *P.* 189. See *The Psalms in Human Life*, pp. 149 f.

55. *P.* 193. Sir George Gilbert Scott designed, among other public buildings, St. Pancras Station and the Albert Memorial.

56. *P.* 201. The Scottish version of Psalm 121 is ambiguous in sense. Henry Vaughan's (*Songs of Praise*, 686) unequivocally makes the hills the source of help. The Duke of Argyll's hymn is no. 586 in the *Church Hymnal for the Christian Year* and is there dated 1877.

CHAPTER 16

57. *P.* 204. Dom André Wilmart has recently established this hymn as the work of a late 12th century Englishman, probably a Cistercian.

58. *P.* 205. Knox, *Enthusiasm*, pp. 338 f. Mrs. Jellyby is a malicious caricature by Dickens in *Bleak House* of a certain kind of missionary-minded busybody.

59. *P.* 207. César Malan (1787–1864) compiled a hymn-book, *Chants de Sion*, in 1843. One of his hymns, translated " It is not death to die ", is still occasionally to be found in our hymn-books (*Worship Song*, 740).

60. *P.* 219. *Songs of Praise Discussed,* p. 151.

CHAPTER 17

61. *P.* 225. See Latourette, *History of the Expansion of Christianity*, vol. ii, chh. 8–9.

62. *P.* 227. W. Cullen Bryant, like Theodore Monod, appears in Rachel Field's *All this and Heaven Too*, part iii.

63. *P.* 228. Theodore Parker's hymn was originally a sonnet, first published in 1875 (*Julian*, p. 882).

64. *P.* 241. Enquiries substantiating this statement were made in the course of preparing *Congregational Praise*.

CHAPTER 18

65. *P.* 255. A modern children's hymn-book which has carried on in the best tradition is *Children Praising* (ed. H. Wiseman and W. H. Hamilton, Oxford University Press, 1936).

66. *P.* 255. Nathaniel Woodard (1811–91) was the founder of the chain of " Woodard schools " of which Lancing College, Sussex, is the oldest (founded in 1848) and the head.

CHAPTER 19

67. *P.* 276. This list excludes two unidentified hymns which were no doubt private and occasional compositions. The two

occasions on which " The Lord is King " were sung—in both cases to the EASTER ALLELUIA—were separated by a month. Obviously there was some connection.

68. *P.* 280.   Dame Millicent Fawcett (1847–1929) was President (1897) of the National Union of Women's Suffrage Societies, and a strong opponent of the " militant suffragettes ". " And did those feet " was, of course, first sung at a meeting in the Albert Hall to celebrate the achievement of women's suffrage.

CHAPTER 21

69. *P.* 307.   This quotation is from an article by C. S. Lewis in *English Church Music*, vol. xix, no. 2 (April, 1949).   The same author in a more celebrated work, *The Screwtape Letters*, has this memorable description of the sight presented by a hymn-book to the eyes of an unchurched member of the public—" a shabby little book containing corrupt texts of a number of religious lyrics, mostly bad, and in very small print " (p. 16).

70. *P.* 308.   (1) *Nun ruhen alle Wälder*, by Paul Gerhardt, paraphrased by Bridges in the *Yattendon Hymnal* (*E.H.*, 278).

P. 309.   (2) From *Hymns on God's Everlasting Love*, 1741, originally in ten verses.   This selection appears in the *Methodist Hymn Book*, no. 142.

P. 310.   (3) From *Prayers and Hymns for Use in Schools* (1928), no. 56.   Also appeared in *Songs of Faith*, a collection of Mr. Briggs's hymns (1945).   The text has been slightly altered by the author, and it appears as here in *Congregational Praise*, no. 117.

P. 311.   (4) From *Hymns and Spiritual Songs* (1707), book iii, no. 10.   In *Congregational Praise*, no. 129, a verse is omitted and one word is altered.

P. 312.   (5) From the *Congregational Hymnary*, no. 505.

P. 313.   (6) Arranged in the *Sarum Hymnal* (1868) from the following lyric, which first appeared in *The Golden Grove*, (1655) and is reprinted as no. 174 in Roundell Palmer's *Book of Praise* (1862) :

> Lord ! come away !
> Why dost thou stay ?
> Thy road is ready ; and thy paths made straight
> With longing expectation wait

The consecration of thy beauteous feet !
Ride on triumphantly ! Behold, we lay
      Our lusts and proud wills in thy way !
Hosanna ! Welcome to our hearts ! Lord, here
Thou hast a temple too ; and full as dear
As that of Sion, and as full of sin ;
Nothing but thieves and robbers dwell therein ;
Enter, and chase them forth, and cleanse the floor !
Crucify them, that they may never more
            Profane that holy place
      Where thou hast chose to set thy face!
      And then, if our stiff tongues shall be
      Mute in the praises of thy Deity,
      The stones out of the temple wall
            Shall cry aloud, and call
Hosanna ! and thy glorious footsteps greet ! Amen !

The hymn as given here appears in *Congregational Praise*, no. 121, and is the best example known to me of editorial amendment.

P. 313. (7) Unpublished, and printed here by permission. Timothy Lew is a distinguished Chinese Christian who wrote many hymns in Chinese for the hymn-book of the Church of Christ in China. The translation was first printed on a leaflet for the Edinburgh Conference of Churches in 1937.

P. 315. (8) From the *Evangelical Magazine*, 1818, and Montgomery's *Collected Hymns* (1853). Written for the London Missionary Society. *C.P.*, 325.

P. 315. (9) From the 1820 edition of Kelly's *Hymns*, &c. *E.H.*, 147.

ADDITIONAL NOTES

P. 282. At the funeral of Queen Mary in February 1953, the hymns sung at St. George's Windsor were " Abide with me " and " Glorious things of thee are spoken ".

Later in the same year the nation joined in the acts of prayer and praise at the Coronation Service (2 June 1953) of Queen Elizabeth II. The inclusion of a congregational hymn in this service was a departure from tradition. The hymn, sung at the " Offertorium ", was " All people that on earth do dwell ", to a special setting of the OLD HUNDREDTH, arranged by Dr. R. Vaughan Williams. The service was relayed to enormous crowds in London by loudspeaker, and it is possible that the hymn was sung by a million voices. At the end of the service, " God save the Queen " was sung in a new arrangement, of searching and memorable effectiveness, by Dr. Gordon Jacob.

P. 284. At the Reunion of the branches of the Methodist Church in 1932, the hymn of Charles Wesley, " Captain of Israel's host " (*Methodist Hymn Book* 608), was sung with moving effect.

P. 291. I have been told that at this point I have been less than just to the Anglicans. I now think that it would have been better put thus : that there is a large difference between the duty of choosing hymns as adornments of an already sufficient liturgy, and that of choosing them that they may themselves provide a liturgy. Perhaps Bernard Manning makes the word " liturgy " bear too much strain when he says that hymns are the Dissenters' liturgy; and he has recently been criticized for this phrase. But the difference is there, none the less. What it amounts to is that certain errors are probable in Anglican choices, and certain other errors in Dissenting choices. There is no doubt that on both sides the standard has been raised very notably during the past twenty years or so, and an apology is certainly due from me if I left the impression that Dissenters know, and Anglicans do not know, how to choose hymns.

Index

First lines of hymns are printed in italic ; titles of books and sources are further distinguished by inverted commas. Names of hymn tunes are in capitals. A star indicates verbatim quotation including the first line. A dagger indicates quotation not including the first line.

329